THREE MOONS
IN VIETNAM

9   Full Moon in Hoi An   156
10   From Hue to Hell   185
11   Free Bacteria   214
12   Evolution of Peace   233
13   Unexpected Attachments   247
14   Between Two Worlds   281

     Postscript   285
     Historical Notes   287
     Acknowledgements   290

CONTENTS

1	*A Promised Moon*	1
2	*Don't Drink the Ice*	6
3	*Honda Dreams*	25
4	*A Hard Tour*	51
5	*Night Bus to Nha Trang*	81
6	*Under Arrest*	103
7	*A Pair of Da Trang Crabs*	116
8	Qua Roi	138

For Hanh and Tuyen

1

A PROMISED MOON

One summer night in 1980, I sat in a Manchester garden with Hanh, watching the moon rise up into a dark, clear sky. The air smelled of honeysuckle, and was warm enough for us to be wearing light cotton dresses. At the time, I was a teacher at a Reception Centre for Vietnamese refugees. Hanh was one of my students; she had also become my friend. She didn't usually talk much about her experiences, and bore her self-imposed exile with a quiet dignity. But the balmy night seemed to draw her out. In her smattering of English, she told me of how she, her husband Tuyen and their small children had escaped by boat from Vietnam. There were some grisly details: weeks at sea, food and water running out, attacks by pirates, old people dying and their bodies being put overboard. Then she spoke of all the relatives she had left behind in Vietnam, and who she would never see again. We were both silent for a while, gazing at the moon. Hanh began to weep. I held her hand, knowing there was little other comfort to offer her.

'In Vietnam, moon very beautiful,' she said sadly.

'One day,' I told her, 'you'll go back there.'

'No,' she sighed. 'Never go back.'

'Then I'll go,' I joked, in an effort to cheer her, 'and bring back the moon for you.'

We laughed a little, then talked of other things, neither of us dreaming that I would in fact go to Vietnam, and see the moon rise there, fourteen years later.

Time passed. I moved to Canada, married Dag Goering, and began a new career as a writer. Hanh and Tuyen settled in Birmingham. Their lives were changing fast. Each time I visited them, they would have more acquisitions to show me: a television, a video, a car, a Walkman. Their children acquired strong Birmingham accents and began to forget their Vietnamese. But some things remained the same. Dotted around their small council house were shrines where joss sticks burned and offerings were left. Like most Vietnamese, Hanh and Tuyen were Buddhists, whose religion was underpinned by animistic beliefs. They told me about spirits who lived in rivers and the sea, in stones and in trees. One watched over things in their kitchen, another guarded the entire house. If placated with offerings, these spirits brought them good fortune; if not, they could wreak havoc in their lives. Hanh and Tuyen also worshipped their ancestors. In their front room was a shrine dedicated to the spirit of Tuyen's mother, where money and tidbits of her favourite food were left, so that she would be as comfortable in death as she had been in life. It is the men of Vietnamese families who tend to their ancestors, and Tuyen expressed concern to me that his Westernized sons might not look after him so well when he was in the afterlife. If they disregarded their duties, he explained, he would become a lost spirit, wandering around and causing trouble. In Vietnam, special altars and temples were built to appease these wandering spirits; in Birmingham, however, no such provisions were made, and his spirit would be destined unhappily to roam forever.

In September 1993, Dag began an eight-month locum with a vet's practice in North Wales. Our temporary move to Britain allowed me to see more of Hanh and Tuyen. During a visit late in the year I noticed in their front room a statue of a woman in flowing white robes. They told me this was *Quan The Am Bo That*, the Goddess of Mercy, who was revered in their fishing village in Vietnam.

'Even now?' I asked. 'After eighteen years of Communism?'

Oh yes, they said. Their relatives also worshipped The Whale God, called *Ca Ong* or *Ong Nam Hai*, and *Thien Hau*, The Goddess of the Sea and Protector of Fishermen. They pulled out a map of Vietnam and pointed to their village. I stared at the map; it was the first time I'd looked beyond the lines and colours to what they represented: a narrow slip of land, clinging to the edge of South East Asia, dominated by a huge coastline. I did a quick calculation: one and a half thousand miles of coast, stretching in a dramatic S-shaped curve between the two great deltas of the Mekong River in the south and the Red River in the north. A little spark went off in my head.

'Do you remember in Manchester, when I said I'd go to Vietnam for you?' I asked Hanh.

'You were joking,' she said.

'I'm not joking now. I'd like to go there, and travel up the coast.'

Hanh and Tuyen looked at me blankly.

'Perhaps I'll visit your village,' I continued.

Their faces clouded over, then closed. 'Dangerous,' they said. 'Police.'

'Even now?' I asked.

'Same same,' insisted Hanh.

As our plans unfolded over the coming months, she grew ever more fearful for me and for Dag. And, despite many hints on my part, she never gave me the addresses of any of her relatives in Vietnam. I knew better than to push her on this; for all her gentleness, Hanh was tough and strong minded. Whether her reticence was based on fear or embarrassment or maybe a mixture of both was something I never discovered.

In Vietnam, changes were afoot. Years of war and economic isolation had pushed the country to the brink of bankruptcy, forcing the government to instigate some changes. In 1986 the Sixth Party Congress had introduced *doi moi*, 'renovation', which was a move away from centralized planning and towards free-market principles. Over the next few years, people were allowed to set up private businesses and, despite the US trade embargo, some foreign companies established offices in Vietnam. But the door to outsiders had only opened a crack; tourists were regarded with suspicion and distrust and were required to have special travel permits stating their exact route through the country and where they intended to stay each night.

Then, in early 1994, that door suddenly swung wide open. The US finally lifted its embargo and the Vietnamese government scrapped the travel permit requirement. Foreign investment flooded in. Within days, Miss Vietnam was advertising Pepsi on state television. Flights into Vietnam began filling up. Predictions abounded that Vietnam was soon to become the fastest-growing economy in South East Asia and the 'next' destination for tourists. The time to go there, I decided, was now, before it became unrecognizable as the country Hanh and Tuyen had told me so much about.

Dag was easily persuaded into a trip across the deltas and up the coast of Vietnam. The magic word was *boats*. To get to know local people, I told him, it was necessary to take local transport. And local transport along the coast meant, I presumed, boats. Dag loves boats, especially of the sailing kind, and he immediately started reading up on junks and sampans. Unfortunately, his passion wasn't shared by the official I talked to in the Vietnamese Embassy in London.

'*Boats?*' he repeated.

I rambled on about wanting to travel and live like local people, about wanting fully to experience the rhythms of daily life along the coast. He was far from impressed.

'In Vietnam, tourists travel only by plane, train or car,' he firmly told me. 'I can give you the phone numbers of agencies who will help you to arrange your holiday.'

I knew it was hopeless trying to explain to him that we didn't want a travel agency to arrange our holiday, that what we wanted to do was meander up the coast, led by fortune and chance encounters. I also held back from telling him that I intended to write about our journey. Foreign writers, journalists and broadcasters in Vietnam were supposed to arrange their visits through the International Press Communications Cooperation Centre in Hanoi. I had learned from the writers, journalists and broadcasters I spoke to that this process was not only expensive but highly restrictive. Working through IPCCC would mean having a set itinerary, and guides and interpreters chosen for us. But I'd also learned that without official guides and interpreters, we might not get very far. The coast of Vietnam was still a very sensitive area. We'd need to communicate not only with fishermen but with the local police who tightly controlled the movements of their boats. If we didn't pay IPCCC for their services, we'd probably have to pay off local policemen. For weeks, we mulled over the problem. In the end, we decided that meandering, albeit without official permission, was what suited us best and would be worth the risks. We applied for two tourist visas. We read everything we could get our hands on about life along the coast. We purchased some US Tactical Pilotage Charts of Vietnam. Then we emptied our bank account and set off.

2

DON'T DRINK THE ICE

I locked the door, turned off the ceiling fan and spread the
money over the bed. From all the advice we'd received about
our trip along the coast of Vietnam, one consistent fact had
emerged: our money had to be in cash US dollars. Credit
cards were of no use, received wisdom informed us, and trav-
ellers cheques were little better. We took the advice to heart.
And, because we had no idea of what awaited us, we took all
the dollars we could muster: several thousand of them, in five,
ten and twenty dollar bills. It looked like a fortune. By
Vietnamese standards, it *was* a fortune. We certainly weren't
used to travelling with so much money, and it made us feel vulnerable and uncomfortable. When we arrived in Ho Chi Minh
City, or Saigon as almost everyone except travel agents still call
it, I set about concealing our loot. For half an hour, I shuffled
it about on the bed, trying to make five neat bundles. One was
destined for the lining of Dag's hat, two for the inside of our
bags, and the remaining two for our money belts.

The room was like an oven. After half an hour, sweat was
dripping from my forehead, my hands were slick, and the

money was damp. I was staring at the five bundles and considering what it would feel like to be robbed of them, when
there was a tap on the door.

'It's me,' said Dag.

He'd been to find a bank and change some money into
Vietnamese dong.

Getting up carefully, so as not to disturb my handiwork, I
padded across the room and let him in.

'Great exchange rate,' he said sardonically, waving around
two huge wads of bank notes. 'For a hundred bucks I got one
million ninety thousand dong, all in five-thousand dong bills.'

I stared at him, speechless. There were dark patches of
sweat on his shirt, and strands of hair were plastered against
his forehead.

'It's hotter in here than it is outside,' he said, flicking on the
fan switch to its highest setting.

'*Don't!*'

I twirled towards the bed, my hands outstretched and ready
to clamp down on the painstakingly arranged bundles of
money. Then there was another knock on the door.

'Hello, come in?' called Madame Vo, the owner of Guest
House 72.

'*NO!*' I cried, twirling back towards the door.

But she was already standing in the doorway holding a tray
of tea, and several thousand dollars were fluttering about the
room like pieces of large, green confetti. I saw her gazing
around, open mouthed, then her hands went limp, the tray
tipped forwards and a teapot crashed to the floor.

We'd been in Vietnam for less than a day; as Dag turned off
the fan, the money wafted down and Madame Vo picked up
pieces of china, I wondered what was to come in the next
three months.

That night I dreamed a damp cloth was wrapped around my
face, and that when I tried to breathe it was drawn up my
nostrils and into my mouth, choking me. I woke in a panic,
taking great gulps of moist air. For a few seconds, I couldn't
remember where I was. Then the heat reminded me, and the
noise. Even at five thirty in the morning, along a small city

street, there were already poorly tuned scooter engines puttering by, plastic sandals slapping on the pavement, radios crackling, roosters crowing, horns beeping, bicycle bells trilling and someone crooning karaoke. My nightmare had disturbed Dag; the heat and the noise meant there was no chance of either of us regaining sleep. We dressed and descended several flights of stairs to the front room of Guest House 72, where a young woman lay stretched out on a mat.

'You go out?' said Lan, sitting bolt upright.

The previous afternoon, a taxi driver had deposited us outside the Guest House, and we'd looked in puzzlement at its front window, filled with bales of luridly printed polyesters and a legless mannequin garbed in a frilly blouse, thinking we'd been brought to the wrong place. Then Lan had rushed to greet us.

'You want room? We have nice room, please come in!'

Like all the other buildings tightly packed along Bui Vien Street, Guest House 72 was one room wide, three rooms deep and four storeys high. As well as being home to a family it was a private hotel, a dressmaker's and a hire shop for bikes and scooters. All over Saigon, private enterprise was booming, and such establishments were popping up like mushrooms.

'Okay, I open door for you,' said Lan, fumbling about for a key.

She was dressed in the same pyjama trousers and loose blouse that she'd worn the day before, but now her long black hair was wound into large spongy curlers.

I felt guilty about disturbing her, for she seemed to spend all her waking hours at work: washing sheets by hand, cleaning out the bathrooms, swabbing down the stairs, enticing tourists into the guest house and even, at ten o'clock at night, massaging the back of her boss, Madame Vo.

'Sorry! Sorry!' we whispered, as she sleepily padded over to the iron gates across the doorway, wrestled with the padlock, and let us out.

Bui Vien Street was bathed in a dusty, golden light. Men stretched out fast asleep in their cyclos, the large scale tricycles with a passenger seat between the front wheels that they pedalled round all day in search of custom. Children lay in doorways with their arms covering their eyes, a ginger cat snoozed on the lap of an old gentleman who sat in the front of his tailor's shop drinking coffee. Two women pushed a wooden box cart past us. They were shrouded in conical hats, scarves tied bandit-style over their faces, long-sleeved shirts and pants and thick gloves, leaving only their eyes and their brown feet exposed. They swept up and shovelled into the cart all the rubbish that lay in the gutters: fruit and vegetable peelings, fish and chicken bones, coconut husks, egg shells, discarded cigarette packets. Outside each house they paused and rang a bell, then waited for the occupants to run out with something or fling it through a window. As they passed, the cyclo drivers stretched and yawned, and the children stirred and rubbed their eyes. Up and down the street, metal shutters were pulled up from doorways to reveal businesses run from the front rooms of houses: chemists and grocery stores, bike repair shops and barber shops. Glass-topped concession stands offering cigarettes, aspirins and newspapers were wheeled out onto the pavement. The food stalls were already in business, serving noodle soup, rice, baguettes, coffee. Within half an hour the city was wide awake. Smartly dressed men buzzed along on scooters with brief cases tied to the handlebars; poorer men went by on bicycles. Women on their way to office jobs looked elegant in their traditional *ao dais*, the silky trousers worn under filmy tunics slit to the midriff. Other women in more prosaic pyjama suits, and heading to the markets, managed to walk gracefully despite the heavily laden baskets they carried on shoulder poles. A girl close to us got off a bike, set a basket of bananas on the pavement and hunkered next to it, waiting for customers. Everyone appeared to be hurrying to work, eager to make some money, as if cashing in on the freedoms of this fledgling market economy before they were snatched away.

We had breakfast at one of the busy food stalls along Pham Ngu Lao Street, around the corner from our guest house. Its tiny wooden stools and low tables reminded me of infant school furniture, and the other customers looked up from their noodle soup to observe Dag's efforts to find somewhere to put his large hairy legs. In the doorway behind us, several large pots sat over charcoal burners, and cooked noodles lay curled in baskets like skeins of wool. The smell of baking bread drifted from the back of the room, where a wood fire glowed in a large brick oven.

'*Pho?*' asked the owner of the food stall, a cheerful woman with protuberant, betel-stained teeth.

We nodded; it was, after all, the only item on the menu, and the traditional Vietnamese breakfast. She put handfuls of noodles into a couple of bowls, then lifted the lid of one of the pots. Inside, some large bones bobbed about in the simmering liquid. Pushing these aside with a ladle, she scooped up broth and poured it over the noodles. Next came handfuls of bean sprouts, slivers of raw beef and an array of garnishes: finely chopped green onions, chilli paste, black bean paste, green, leafy herbs, squeezes of lime. The soup was salty and spicy; the sprouts crunchy, the noodles soft and comforting. I worked my way around the slivers of meat, which had turned a pale grey colour. They didn't go to waste; a scruffy child had sidled up to watch me eat, and when I'd finished he grabbed the bowl and gobbled up my left-overs.

The beggars and the street children knew that in this part of the city tourists weren't usually found at local food stalls but at a place called Kim's Café. It was easy to spot by the striped umbrellas and white plastic tables and chairs squeezed tightly together along a stretch of pavement, and the young tourists packed around them like sheep in a pen. Kim's Café was a success story in the making. After a humble beginning as a cheap eating place for the sudden influx of tourists, it had quickly expanded into the ground floor of the next door house, and now included a burgeoning tour company. Madame Vo and Lan had insisted that at Kim's Café we could find all the information we needed about getting a local boat across the Mekong Delta. But when Kim, a genial-looking man with a cellular phone in his shorts pocket, brought us a menu that offered croissants, noodles, jam, boiled eggs and Lipton tea with milk, I began to have my doubts.

*

I felt rather conspicuous among the Kim's Café crowd. I didn't insist on calling myself a traveller. My nose wasn't pierced and I wasn't avidly poring over my copy of the *Lonely Planet Guidebook*.

'In Nha Trang there's a place called Second Best that serves awesome banana splits,' an American man to my left told the woman with him.

'Second Best? Is that in The Book?' she asked.

'Not yet. But just ask any traveller, and they'll tell you where it is.'

'Madam, you buy postcards?' said a whining voice in my ear.

I turned my head and saw, at eye level, a small boy with a scar from one ear to his chin. Each stitch mark stood out in a weal, and the whole effect was like a fake scar, the sort that North American kids stick on their faces for Halloween parties.

'Madam, you buy map of Vietnam? You buy book?' In his arms was a tray, with all his wares carefully displayed. 'You buy gum, madam, you buy cigarettes, you get high, madam, you tell me, I get you Buddha cigarette, madam.'

Although he looked about seven, he insisted he was thirteen, and was one of several teenagers working the tables with well-practised repartees. Some sold T-shirts with pictures of Ho Chi Minh on the front, others were doing a brisk trade in old Zippo lighters they claimed had been plundered from the bodies of dead Marines.

'Madam, look,' said one, pushing a lighter at me.

I read out its rough inscription to Dag: 'Let me win your heart and win your mind or I'll burn your hut down, Cam Ranh '68–'69.'

'Excuse me, can I see that?' asked the banana-split man, and seconds later the boy had a sale.

Hovering around the edges of the café area were shoe-shine boys, who were getting little work from the tourists in their fashionable nylon and rubber sandals, and women clutching plastic shopping baskets filled with tiny bottles of bright nail polish, offering manicures and pedicures. Out in the street, taking their chances with the traffic, were the beggars. These were pitiful creatures – one man standing on knee stumps, holding out his palm; another lying on a wheeled tray, his legs completely bent up onto his back, pulling himself along with his hands; a leper with ravaged limbs and face. There were old women as thin as wafers leaning on staffs, and young mothers holding up their scabby babies for the tourists to see. But the tourists feigned renewed interest in their guide books and it was Kim, agitated about his customers being disturbed, who pressed 500-dong notes into the beggars' hands, and shooed them away.

A young Frenchman sat down opposite us. One of his eyes was inflamed and weepy.

'It is the towels,' he advised, pointing to the cool, damp face cloths that were served up with the food. 'They don't wash them in hot water, and everyone gets this red eye. I've just come back from the delta and there it is *very* bad.'

We asked him how he had got to the Mekong Delta.

'Like this,' he said, pointing to the white minibus parked outside the café.

Minutes before, he and nine brightly dressed backpackers had spilled out of it and settled like butterflies around the white plastic tables. 'It is a good trip, and very cheap. You drive to Cantho, you stay in a hotel and the next day you take a boat trip for a few hours, and then come back to Saigon.'

Silently, Dag and I digested this information.

'Tomorrow I go to Nha Trang, Danang and Hue in this bus,' he continued.

'I hear there's a terrific place for ice cream in Nha Trang,' I told him.

'Oh yes? Tell me, I'll write it down,' he said, as he pulled out a pen and his copy of The Book.

The Mekong River is known to the Vietnamese as Song Cuu Long, or River of the Nine Dragons. It originates in Tibet, separates Burma from Laos and flows through Cambodia, where it splits into the Hau Giang, or Lower River, and Tien

Giang, or Upper River. In Vietnam these two branches sub-
divide and spread out like a web, depositing silt to form the
Mekong Delta, the most fertile and intensely farmed area of
Vietnam. These river branches, along with innumerable manmade channels, also make up a complex system of
communication, plied by thousands of local boats. This much
The Book could tell us; what we couldn't glean from it was
how to get ourselves on to one of these boats.

On the wall of Kim's Café Tourist Office was a large board
with information about minibus trips, and spaces for people to
sign up for them. A couple dressed identically in hiking boots
and harem pants were carefully scanning 'Mekong Delta,
Three Days' and 'Nha Trang, Danang, Hue, Eight Days'.

'The problem with travelling by local boat is security,' Nhut,
one of the Kim's Café guides, was telling us. 'The boat drivers
will think you are rich, and when you are in an isolated place
they will rob you.'

'We need an interpreter who can tell them we are not rich,'
said Dag. 'Perhaps one of your guides could help us?'

Nhut fiddled with his pen. 'The trouble is the police. If the
police see you in a minibus with a Vietnamese driver, they
will be happy. But local boats have no security, and the police
will be worried.'

He glanced over at the couple. The girl was writing 'Two
Germans' under the sign-up list for the Nha Trang, Danang,
Hue tour.

'Do you know where we might get information about boats?'
asked Dag.

Nhut sighed; we'd been sitting at his desk for fifteen minutes
and he was visibly fed up with us.

'You cannot travel by boat,' he said testily. 'There is *no
safety*.'

There certainly wasn't much safety in the cyclos that transported us around the city for the rest of the day. Our drivers
were wily, likeable characters with a smattering of English they
claimed to have learned when 'working for the Americans'
during the Vietnam War. They also had the ability to be totally

at ease in the midst of the city's madcap traffic. Moments after climbing into a cyclo, I found myself being propelled feet first into a torrent of oncoming vehicles. Cars, scooters, bikes and other cyclos loomed up and veered away at the last second. It got worse when we joined a roundabout, where no one gave way and every driver, including mine, simply set his course, dodging and weaving about to avoid collisions. I cowered in my seat, legs pulled up, hands in a white-knuckled grip on the arm rests, watching the near-death experiences being enacted around me. A scooter zipped past, the pillion passenger holding a wide pane of glass that barely missed decapitating a woman cyclist and her bug-eyed baby. A cyclo heading straight for me was piled so high with baskets that I couldn't see the driver and he certainly couldn't see where he was going. A taxi blasted right down the centre of the road, giving way to nothing, as if the man behind the wheel was playing a giant video game and trying to zap everything in his way. And six white geese strapped to a set of bicycle handlebars were having a terrible time of it, their yellow beaks bumping and grazing along the ground as their owner threaded through the traffic. There was a terrible racket of honking horns and shrilling bells, and clouds of exhaust smoke hung around at nose level.

Despite the chaos, almost everyone except Dag and I appeared to be relaxed. Our drivers chatted companionably to each other, as if they were heading down a country lane. Long-haired, straight-backed school girls in white *ao dais* cycled sedately through the mayhem. Poised young women wearing elbow-length gloves and holding sun umbrellas sped through on scooters. Pedestrians crossed the road like sleepwalkers, and I saw a pretty girl with a missing foot confidently swinging her way through the traffic on crutches.

I was just beginning to think that this might be safer than it looked when, right ahead of me, a scooter zipped out of a side road and hit a cyclist side on. There were screeching, crunching, splintering sounds, and bicycle and bicyclist crumpled under the impact. The traffic slowed and knotted up as people gathered around the scene of the accident, but there was no shouting or excitement, just a sense of resigned curiosity. The cyclist was sprawled on the road, his leg grotesquely twisted to one side, with a pool of blood forming beneath it.

'Poor bugger!' Dag called to me. 'Looks like one hell of a fracture.'

As we were pedalled off, two men grabbed the cyclist under the armpits and hoisted him into a cyclo. He began to scream, and his leg flopped about as if attached to him by nothing but skin.

Our route took us along wide boulevards, past ritzy hotels and imposing neoclassical buildings and down to a narrow strip of dusty park land. On scrubby grass, beneath the shade of large trees, old men in cotton shorts did their morning callisthenics, slowly stretching and bending. Behind them was the Saigon River – wide, khaki brown and with large clumps of water hyacinths drifting along on its slow currents. Moored to the bank were tourist boats, offering rides along the city riverfront and advertising Heineken beer on signs tacked to their cabin roofs. Beyond these, women stood in the backs of sampans, rowing them with long oars. Along the opposite shore, a shanty town huddled beneath huge billboards advertising Sanyo, Panasonic, Milo and Coca Cola.

'Hello, sir, madam!' A tiny woman in silky purple pyjamas raced across the grass towards us. 'My name Muoi,' she said, taking off her conical hat and fanning me with it. 'I have five children, no husband, very nice boat!'

She pulled us towards a jetty where motorized sampans were tied up three and four deep, waiting for customers who needed ferrying across the river.

'The best,' said Muoi, pointing to a boat that was identical to the others. It was about twenty feet long by four feet wide, built of rough planking with a low wooden canopy over one end. Not wanting to disappoint her, we agreed to a short ride. She insisted we sit under the canopy, and checked to make sure no part of me was sticking out of it and catching the rays of the sun. Pulling up the sleeve of her shirt, she held her brown arm against my pasty white one.

'You beautiful!' she cried, referring to my pale skin, and it suddenly occurred to me that those smartly dressed girls on the Honda scooters wore long gloves not for fashion, but to prevent a tan.

After pulling a string to start the engine, which looked and sounded as if it belonged in a lawn mower, Muoi steered us out into the river, working the tiller with her foot. Her toes were splayed like fingers, and the nails were immaculately manicured and painted with pink and silver-flecked polish. We'd not gone far when the engine cut out. The propeller was on the end of an eight-feet-long shaft, which Muoi swung around so that it came alongside the boat. Nimbly as a cat, she stepped along the gunwale and disentangled from the propeller a collection of river debris: hyacinth roots, grasses, bits of sacking and plastic bags filled with evil-looking slime. All the way back to the jetty, she fixed me with a dazzling smile. I had taken an instant liking to this spirited woman, and was sorry that she didn't have a bigger boat to transport us right across the Delta. Her eyes filled with tears as we said goodbye – but then she spied another couple of Westerners clambering down from their cyclos, and without another word she raced away and began fluttering around the two elderly and bewildered Americans.

Later that night, we bumped into Muoi on Pham Ngu Lao Street. Her hair was curled and her face made up. Bubbling with excitement at the sight of us, she latched onto my arm, gazing up at me with a huge smile. We were close to Kim's Café, and as it came into view Muoi's footsteps slowed. She tugged me towards the white plastic tables. One of the waiters greeted us uncertainly, his eyes skittering over Muoi.

He placed us at the edge of the crowd, under a tree hung with fairy lights and a sign saying 'Night Club'.

'You pay?' asked Muoi nervously, scanning the all-English menu.

As part of *doi moi*, and in an effort to draw in much-needed dollars, the government had introduced a dual pricing system. Foreigners were required to pay twice as much as locals to travel by air and rail, to stay in government-run hotels and to get into museums and historical sites. As the market economy spread, fledgling entrepreneurs picked up on this pricing system. Our cyclo drivers that day had charged us over twice the local rate, and going across the river with Muoi cost us four times what a Vietnamese commuter would pay. In Kim's Café, everything was 'foreigner price', and far beyond the means of someone like Muoi.

More customers kept arriving, extra tables and chairs were carried out and soon people were seated right up to the edge of the pavement. There was a lot of noisy chatter – some Germans were clunking beer glasses together, and a twenty-first birthday was being celebrated. At the foot of the tree a woman squatted on her haunches, surrounded by four children. Each child clutched a flat basket, and the woman was preparing her small sales force for the night's work, sharing out Cellophane packets filled with monkey nuts and individual sticks of chewing gum. Close by, cyclo drivers lounged in their vehicles waiting for custom, and a woman leaned on a glass-topped concession stand filled with tourist fare: bottles of water, aerogramme letters, rolls of toilet paper. She looked bored and rather tired. Suddenly one of the cyclo drivers sprang to his feet and peered down the road. The woman wheeled away her concession stand, the children fled with their baskets. Kim began squeezing his way between the tables, talking into his cellular phone, calling to the waiters and asking people seated next to the kerb if they could move inside. Amid a confused scene of tables being hoisted over heads, chairs falling backwards and people bumping into each other, a police jeep arrived. Five men in green uniforms jumped out. One ripped down the Night Club sign. Two more began grabbing vacated chairs and tables and throwing them into the jeep. Muoi clutched my hand and I turned to see her sliding down in her seat, as if hoping she could somehow shrink away out of sight. The fourth policeman disappeared inside the restaurant with Kim while the people who had lost their tables stood in the doorway, clutching glasses and plates as if at a cocktail party, and giggling rather nervously. Five minutes later the police were gone, taking the Night Club sign, three tables, eight chairs and whatever extra Kim had deemed to give them.

'It happens most Saturday nights,' said a Englishman at the

table next to ours. 'But this is the first time they've nicked the sign.'

He was short and stocky, with thick glasses and brush-cut hair. He told us he'd been in Saigon for nine months, and was teaching English and learning Vietnamese.

'Really, you can speak Vietnamese?' I said admiringly.

'Well, a bit. Here, I'll try some on your mate.'

Muoi looked blankly at him as he spoke.

'I just can't get the tones,' he said sadly. 'It's much easier if you can sing. There's a fella from Swindon living here, he's got a great voice, and when he sings in Vietnamese all the locals know exactly what he's on about. But when he talks it, they can't understand a bleeding word he's saying.'

This made me feel a little better about my struggle to master even the simplest phrases in Vietnamese. Then it occurred to me that after nine months in Saigon, this man might have some advice for us on the trip we were about to take. But when I told him of our travel plans he looked puzzled.

'I've never heard of anyone doing that. You're bound to run into trouble with the police.'

When I asked why, he shrugged. 'You just will. That's the way it goes here.'

Our bill came. We left five dollars, and Muoi looked wide-eyed at what, for her, was the equivalent of a week's wage.

For two days, we wandered around the city, trying to organize a boat trip across the Mekong Delta. All the travel agents we talked to reacted like Nhut, telling us our plan was impossible. We went back to the river, found some small wooden cargo boats loaded with bananas and coconuts, and asked their owners where they were going and if we could travel with them. Most of them barely understood our few words of Vietnamese; those that did couldn't understand why we should be requesting such a thing. What we needed, we quickly realized, was an interpreter. But finding one who was prepared to travel on rustic boats instead of in air-conditioned cars seemed impossible.

'No safety,' the guides we met repeated, as if this was their mantra. 'Problem with police.'

We began to despair. And then, when we weren't looking, a guide found us.

Loud rock music blared from Café Dao. Its low-slung, red plastic garden chairs had been arranged in rows, all facing out to the street. Exhausted by the sticky heat of the city and the frustrations of our search, we sank into a couple of them. The waitress served Dag with a bottle of BGI beer and, for me, a coffee which was dripping from a small aluminium filter into a glass filled with chunks of ice. I'd not yet seen a refrigerator in Saigon, and had wondered where the ice always served with drinks came from. I found out when a huge block of it was delivered to Café Dao on a cyclo cart. The driver heaved the steaming, dripping block onto the pavement and shoved it across the ground and into the back of a café. There, one of the waitresses began hacking at it with a cleaver, scooping up the lumps from the floor and throwing them into a cooler box.

'Your coffee's ready,' said Dag sardonically.

The hot liquid had already melted most of the ice. I peered at the remains of one of the lumps, which seemed to have some bits of grit frozen into it, then cautiously sipped the coffee.

'I think it better if the foreigner don't drink the ice,' said a voice.

A man had sat down next to Dag. He had a narrow face and large, stained teeth. On his neck, a few inches below his chin, a long, curly hair grew from a mole. As he talked, I found it hard to take my eyes off this hair.

'You have holiday?' he asked.

'Sort of,' Dag replied.

'My name Binh. I help all my friend make holiday in Vietnam. In the war I work for the Americans, so now I cannot be government guide. I don't care. The government charge the tourist twenty-five dollar a day for guide, give the guide two dollar. I am free guide, I get all the money the tourist give.'

From a plastic attaché case he pulled out a bundle of business cards and handed them to Dag. 'These the card of my foreigner friend. A friend mine, he camera man from Holland,

I organize for him trip to Mekong Delta. Every day he have phone call back to Holland and all this I arrange.'

Dag and I exchanged a look.

'We want to travel by boat across the Mekong Delta,' I told Binh.

He lit a cigarette, and regarded me through a cloud of blue smoke. 'I can help you. My homeland in the delta. It easy for me.'

'What about police?' asked Dag. 'And safety?'

'You know, the central government they like the tourist, they say no problem. But the local government have different policy. In the small village, maybe you get big problem from the policemen, because they want get money from the people. But I can help you, I am free guide.'

He passed us a school exercise book in which his former clients had written their comments. The praise was glowing. Mr Binh was commended as being an excellent pool player, a good drinking companion, a first-class guide and very knowledgeable about his country.

'My friends from Germany, we take adventure tour to Mekong Delta. We take boat along Cambodia border. When police come I tell my friends hide on the bottom of the boat. My friends pay me seven dollar a day. After, my friends they give me tip – but not a big one.'

This time, Dag and I exchanged a very meaningful look. We warned Binh that we'd need him for at least two weeks, and that it wouldn't be a comfortable journey. We told him of my plans to write a book. We also offered to pay him a third more than his usual rate.

'Yeah, OK, how much you like,' he said nonchalantly, but I caught the gleam in his eye.

'You have guide?' he asked me.

'Well,' I said, confused by the question, 'I thought we had just agreed that you—'

'Guide *book*,' he cried, rather irritably. 'You have?'

I passed it over to him, and he took out a pair of reading glasses from a case attached to the wide leather belt holding up his trousers. Setting the glasses halfway down his nose, he quickly leafed through the book.

'On our trip, you take this, throw away,' he said disparagingly. He tapped his head. 'I have information for Vietnam here.'

After we struck a deal with Binh, he suggested we go immediately to Cholon to look for a boat. Three cyclos took us across Saigon to this old Chinese quarter of the city. Along dank alleys and back streets, crumbling, once elegant houses leaned towards each other, connected by tangles of electric wiring, and people peered out of doorways. The atmosphere was even less friendly along the dock area of the Kinh Tau Hu Channel, one of the maze of waterways leading off the Saigon River. The air reeked of the dried fish that was heaped up for sale on wooden stalls. Gap-toothed, shifty-eyed men hunkered around these stalls, playing cards. Moored along the dock were wooden cargo boats with deep, windowless holds. Men, bent under the weight of drums of oil and sacks of rice, staggered up to them along narrow planks.

'Be careful your money,' warned Binh, as he went from boat to boat, talking to the owners.

Trailing behind him, I began to feel increasingly wretched. The day had grown overcast and horribly muggy. Even the slightest movement caused me to break out in sweat. My hair was stuck to my face, my dress was plastered to my back. And my guts were rumbling and complaining. Gazing at the boats, I vaguely wondered about the toilet arrangements on them.

'Sit here, wait,' instructed Binh, pointing to a drinks stand.

Gratefully, I sank onto a low stool in the shade of an umbrella and accepted a bottle of the only drink on sale, a bright green cordial that tasted like toothpaste. The woman running the stall called over a couple of friends, and they clustered around me, admiring my white skin. After half an hour Binh returned, looking triumphant.

'A family take us Long Xuyen, in middle of delta. Cost five dollar each, I go free. They leave tomorrow. I think this okay. I think they good people.'

'Can we go aboard and have a look at the boat?' I asked, my mind still on toilet arrangements.

Binh frowned. 'Only quick. The people they worry for police.'

After gingerly making our way up a narrow plank, we were introduced to Nguyen Van Kiep, his wife Khue, their two young daughters, Chi and Em, his brother Di and his teenage cousin Sang. They were an attractive group, limber and strong, with wide faces and sharply defined cheekbones. All of them lived aboard the forty feet by ten feet wooden boat. It was a very basic craft, with no lights, and no navigation or safety equipment except for the pair of sleek eyes painted onto the prow, which, according to tradition, can see where the boat is going and scare away evil spirits. On the aft end of the top deck was a low wooden canopy, from where the tiller could be steered. The family's living area was in the aft hold, which opened onto a tiny lower deck. This held a large brown ceramic urn, emblazoned with a dragon and filled with water. The back of the deck stuck out over the river, and a hole was cut into one corner of it. Before I could ponder over this hole, Binh started urging us to leave.

'We come back tomorrow very early, first light, while police sleep.'

On the way back to the guest house we passed a temple to Thien Hau, Goddess of Fishermen. I insisted that we stop off and pay our respects. Incense spirals, each about eight feet high, hung from the wooden ceiling of the temple. Below them were large brass urns filled with sand and bristling with incense sticks. Thien Hau sat on an altar that was dripping with gilt and heaped with offerings of coconuts, pineapples and irises. She was a portly creature, with a round gold-plated face, and most unsuitably dressed for any seagoing activities. Her red robes were decorated with gold braid and sparkling sequins, and her headdress was a complicated arrangement of tinsel, sequins, peacock feathers and red rosettes. I bought a few incense sticks from the custodian of the temple, a bad-tempered, toothless old man who chain-smoked and watched my every move with great suspicion. Copying some people worshipping at the altar, I lit the sticks from a candle, held them between my palms and bowed several times to Thien Hau, then placed them in one of the brass urns. The custodian had positioned himself right next to an offertory box. When I pushed some notes into it he banged on a gong, then shuffled off to light up another cigarette.

Binh was standing at one side of the altar with a brown-robed monk, looking into a pen where several land turtles lay around the edges of an ornamental pool.

'What are the turtles for?' I asked.

'For *lucky*,' he answered irritably, as if I should have known all along. 'Maria, for you, I ask this man about gondess temple. You ready, make notes, okay? This man say the gondess born in China, long time ago, in fishing village home. In that area lot of typhoon come, so she help the people. And after she die, she is a gond. When the typhoon come she appear on a cloud and make safety for the boat. The people, they poor, they believe she good gondess.'

Two small boys had sidled up to us during Binh's monologue. One held a chameleon, a beautiful creature with an iridescent pale blue body and a yellow throat. Binh put on his glasses to have a look at it.

'In my homeland we have the gecko like this, about the half metre,' he said. 'The people can eat it, tastes good. Some of them, they put it in the poddle—'

'In the what?' I asked.

'In the *poddle*. And after they put the rice wine in the poddle and they leave for three or four months and they drink it.'

The children were teasing the chameleon, pulling its tail and poking it mercilessly with a stick. It turned a deep, angry blue. The young monk in brown robes looked on disapprovingly, but did nothing to stop the boys' cruelty.

'Tell them to treat it more kindly,' I implored Binh.

He laughed.

'It okay. This one not big enough for the poddle.'

We made it back to Guest House 72 just before a storm hit. The traffic along Bui Vien Street changed colour as drivers donned bright blue, yellow and red rain capes that completely covered them save for their skinny legs. This was the very beginning of the rainy season, and bare-backed children dashed excitedly into the street, frolicking in puddles and splashing each other with water. In the guest house, Lan was sitting on the floor with Madame Vo, applying green oil to her neck. She was using a metal spatula and rubbing so hard that four-inch-wide angry red weals were appearing on Madame Vo's skin.

'She has cold,' said Lan when I asked her why she was doing this. 'It is problem when the rains come.'

We told her we were leaving the next day for the delta, and asked if we could store a bag of books and papers in the guest house.

'You go with Kim Café bus?' she asked. 'Come back three days?'

No, we told her, we go local boat, come back two weeks.

Her mouth dropped open. 'You *crazy*!' she squealed.

3
HONDA DREAMS

It took over an hour to get through the early morning traffic jam along Cholon's congested waterways. Small sampans jostled for space against narrow cargo boats like ours and transporter boats as big as arks, with rudders the size of barn doors. The air was filled with the noise of hundreds of outboard engines and the smells of exhaust fumes and raw sewage. All along the Kinh Tau Hu Channel, communal outhouses stood on stilts over oily black water, and people squatted in them, chatting companionably. Behind them was a city of shacks, built from corrugated iron, bamboo, chicken wire and palm leaves, crowded together, stacked one on top of another and bristling with television aerials.

Finally leaving the traffic behind, Kiem turned the boat onto a narrow, plumb-straight canal. And it was like going through a looking glass. The water became a rich olive green. The banks were cloaked in lush, tropical vegetation. Against a soft grey sky, the leaves of mango, papaya, palm, bread fruit and betel nut trees were intensely green. On the verandas of thatch houses nestling in the trees, pots and baskets were filled with yellow and red flowers, trailing roses, herbs and chilli pepper plants. A monkey gazed at us from a branch, a woman waded in the shallows scrubbing a pig, girls poled sampans heaped with fruit prettily arranged on large banana leaves. We passed a house boat, moored to a stake in the mud, where a baby slept in a hammock beneath a thatch canopy while its mother watered the flower boxes on deck. It was hard to imagine there had ever been a war here. From 1954 on, much of the Delta had been a stronghold of Communism, and during the Vietnam War, known locally as the American War, whole areas were bombed, napalmed and defoliated. But the vegetation, fed by some of the richest soil on earth, had claimed back the land and covered up many of the old wounds. Now, the peacefulness of this canal was broken only by the puttering of outboard engines.

Sometimes the vegetation made way for waterfront villages. As the canal took the place of a road, all the buildings faced onto it. Grocery stores displayed their wares on verandas, sampans were hitched to the stilts of little cafés where their owners sat on low stools, drinking coffee. There was a coffin workshop with a ramp for loading its products onto boats. The houses had wide doorways and as we chugged along at five miles an hour we caught glimpses into people's lives: a baby being nursed, a woman chopping up vegetables and throwing the peelings into the water, a man repairing an outboard engine on his living room floor.

We'd been travelling for a couple of hours when Khue carried several burning joss sticks and four bananas to the boat's stubby prow. She wedged the incense sticks between a couple of planks, and flung the fruit overboard. Such offerings, I'd read, were made to the spirit of the boat and to *Ba Thuy*, the goddess of water, in request for their protection during the journey. I decided to check this with Binh, who was lying in a hammock he'd strung diagonally across the wooden canopy and reading our guide book.

'Oh, *this*,' he said, when I asked him about Khue's offering. 'The family – they take a look at the lunar calendar and it say today is unlucky day for journey. They ask we wait one more day. I say no, I am Catholic, I do not believe this thing. The family, they want business, they say okay, but they pray to the god for lucky.'

'Which god?' I asked.

'The lucky god,' he said, and went back to the guide book.

As the sun burned off the clouds, Khue went below deck with her daughters and everyone else retreated beneath the canopy on the top deck. It was open at either end, and three feet high. Binh's hammock took up a disproportionate amount of its room, but this didn't seem to bother the family, who, like many Vietnamese, were adept at neatly folding up their bodies and fitting them into a small space. Dag and I lacked this skill, and we seemed to be all knees and elbows as we awkwardly tried to make ourselves comfortable. Sang spent all morning glued to Dag's side. He draped his arms around him, gazed admiringly at his nose and his beard, and stroked his hairy legs as if they were pet animals.

'What I don't need in this heat,' groaned Dag after a couple of hours, 'is a pair of sticky hands all over me.'

Next to him, Binh was peacefully sleeping with his reading glasses on his forehead and our guide book spread open on his chest. To divert Sang's attention, Dag pointed to Binh's chin, which sported a good crop of blackheads. In Saigon, we'd noticed, squeezing friends' blackheads in public was a popular pastime. Sang was easily tempted. Leaning over the hammock, he set to work on Binh. After the first squeeze, Binh jerked and sat up.

'Where the beautiful girls?' he asked groggily. 'Your guide book say the most beautiful girls in Vietnam are here. I take a look.'

For the next twenty minutes he carefully scrutinized the boats going by. They were loaded with wood, bananas and pineapples, and often had entire families on board.

'So, what's the verdict?' asked Dag.

'The women they have soft skin,' pronounced Binh. 'Better than Saigon girls – they have the hard skin, with many boils. It is because of smoke.'

'*An com*?' asked Khue, around one o'clock. 'Eat rice?'

This is a generic term, used to offer food of any description. She was passing around bowls of instant noodles, baguettes

and slices of *thanh long*, a fruit with stubby green leaves, bright
pink skin and a dense mass of white flesh speckled with tiny
black seeds. I only picked at the lunch. My guts were feeling
delicate, and I realized that soon I'd have to face something I'd
been avoiding all morning – the toilet. The hole in the corner
of the tiny aft deck was boxed off with planks about two feet
high. It was simple enough to use: I stepped into the box,
placed my feet on either side of the hole, and squatted. But it
was akin to going to the toilet in the middle of a football sta-
dium. There was a grandstand view into the box from the
canopy, although the family all kindly looked in the opposite
direction. Sadly, there was no such discretion among the occupants of passing boats. Heads turned, necks craned and faces
broke into wide smiles as I crouched down. I barely fitted into
the box, which was built for Vietnamese-sized people. Briefly,
I wondered how Dag would manage when it came time for
him to use it, but this was only a brief distraction during an
excruciatingly embarrassing few minutes. Staring straight
ahead, trying not to catch anyone's eye and smiling wanly, I
did what had to be done as fast as possible.

The sun slipped away. At the far end of the canal the sky
turned shades of purple, pink and gold, and along the banks
the trees rapidly darkened into shadow. We sat on deck with
the family, sharing an alfresco dinner of fried fish, rice and
more instant noodles. Again, I had little appetite, a result of
the heat and the increasingly fragile state of my stomach.
When Kiep produced a bottle of rice wine, I retreated to the
prow. Leaning against the small wooden doors of the front
hold, I watched the moon climb into the sky. Chi and Em
joined me and sat close by, chattering and laughing softly,
playing some sort of a rhyming word game. The dark hulks of
unlit boats loomed up. Villages slid by, some of them pricked
by electric lights. Fire flies hovered in the trees, and the air
smelled of blossom.

Khue jumped down from the top deck, landing lightly next
to me. In her hand were three burning joss sticks, and sparks
blew back from them as she placed them in the prow. Turning,
she pointed to the hold. Earlier in the day, Kiep had put our

bags in there, and had made room for us to sleep, pushing aside his consignment of household goods and laying down one of the twenty-four brand new, plastic wrapped mattresses he was delivering to Long Xuyen. 'He say this your bed,' Binh had told us. 'He hear foreigners need the soft mats.' Khue opened the doors and held her hands against her cheek, miming sleep. Then she rounded up her daughters, and was gone.

I crawled into the hold. It was pitch black, airless and stiflingly hot. Something ran over my hand; jumping back in horror, I frantically scrabbled to find my flashlight. Its beam found cockroaches, huge, brown and shiny, all over the wooden walls. Quickly, I unpacked our sheet sleeping bag and Therm-a-Rest air mattress and climbed back on the deck.

The bottle of rice wine was still going round. Kiep and Di were laughing uncontrollably and heartily slapping Dag's legs and belly. Binh, who had been brought back to life by the alcohol, was cracking jokes.

'Okay, Dag, you know in our country we have the black buffalo and the red buffalo.'

'*Red* buffalo?'

'Yeah, the black buffalo eat the straw, the red buffalo eat the gasoline!'

I settled down on the far end of the deck, feeling cool for the first time that day. Above me, the stars slipped steadily by. The engine thrummed, water swished against the bow, the men chortled, and I slipped away into a deep, dreamless and contented sleep.

An unfamiliar quiet woke me. There were no puttering outboard engines to be heard, only the whirring of cicadas, the crowing of a rooster, and Dag's steady breathing. The air felt hot, still and damp against my face. Lightning flashed in the distance, tiny bats flitted around my head. Gradually, as my eyes grew accustomed to the dark, I saw we were tied up to a post sticking out of the mud between two float houses. A tiny oil lamp had been left burning in one of the houses, and through the open weave lattice walls I could make out several figures stretched out on mats. I crept to the aft deck, anxious to wash and use the toilet under cover of night. By the time I was cleaning my teeth, dawn was breaking. Someone in the nearest float house woke and gazed in astonishment at the foreigner leaning over the side of a boat, spitting toothpaste into the water.

At six a.m., after several mattresses had been delivered to the village, we were on our way again. Kiep used a long bamboo pole to push the boat from the muddy shore, while Di pulled on a rope to get the engine started. We were now on a main river channel. Men cast nets from sampans, and there were duck farms all along the banks. The fat white birds emerged from their small houses of bamboo and thatch, and waddled over grey mud to swim on the olive-green water. Sometimes, pink ducks emerged: painted by their owners to distinguish them from other flocks, they looked from a distance like short-legged flamingos.

Thirty hours and a hundred and twenty miles after leaving Saigon, we arrived in Long Xuyen, the capital of An Giang Province and a town with a hundred thousand inhabitants. A plank went down from the boat to a rubbish-strewn bank next to a busy road. The men of the family began off-loading the goods. First the mattresses, balanced on their heads, then big bundles of aluminium pots and kettles, folded-up garden lounger chairs and an astonishing array of plastic goods: stools, cups, balls, cooler boxes, drying-up racks, bottles and even bright red and blue spotted toy buckets and spades.

'Where's all this stuff going?' I asked Binh.

He didn't answer; he was staring worriedly at the road. A crowd of curious people had gathered there to look at me and Dag. Among them were two men in green uniforms.

'Police', said Binh. 'Give me passports.'

While he set off down the plank, Dag and I sat under the canopy, trying to look as inconspicuous as possible. We were joined by little Em, who nervously twisted her necklace, a string that had been blessed at the pagoda for her safe keeping. The policemen began paging through our passports.

'Have some five-dollar bills handy,' said Dag.

Binh was talking and flapping his hands about. He didn't appear to be making much of an impression on the policemen, who were now standing with their arms crossed, staring intently at us.

'And maybe one ten-dollar bill,' Dag added.

But minutes later Binh was back, looking tremendously relieved and extremely proud of himself.

'Is twelve miles from Cambodia border, so they worry for your safety,' he said. 'I give them cigarettes. I lie, I say I government guide. They say it is okay.'

Our plans had changed; Kiep and his family had invited us to go with them to their home village of Tanoa, promising to take us the following day to Cantho, from where we could get another boat. Tanoa was an hour away from Long Xuyen, and had only five thousand inhabitants. On the river bank, close to where Kiep docked the boat, a man was feeding his ducks with handfuls of boiled rice. Pot-bellied pigs wandered about the village's sandy streets, and in its centre was a cluster of shops in open-fronted shacks. A pharmacist showed us pictures of his son's luxurious home in Toronto. A woman getting a perm in a hairdresser's shop screamed and leapt out of her chair when Dag hove into view. One shack had a large stock of veterinary supplies, and Dag stopped to chat to the owner for half an hour, while Binh translated. Since *doi moi*, the man told him, there had been no more government immunization programmes for livestock, and infectious diseases were becoming increasingly common. As there was no vet for many miles, farmers had to treat their animals themselves and the only advice they got came from this shop owner.

I took no part in the conversation, and sat feeling hot and utterly wretched. Children were crowding around me, pinching the skin on my arms and tugging at the straps on my sandals. Behind them, the woman from the hairdresser's had arrived, her head covered in curlers. She bent down until her face was close to mine, and began chattering to me.

'She say she look because she see only the foreigner on the television,' said Binh.

He was visibly uncomfortable with the situation, and as he

translated he nervously lit one cigarette after another. 'Since the war, only one foreigner come here, a few month ago,' he called to me over the children's heads. 'He American, he fight here, he want see the place again. He have no travel permit, no guide. The police they take him away.'

In front of each village house was a wooden pedestal, rather like a bird table, set with offerings to the spirits of the wind and sky. Well-fed pigs were tethered below verandas; wide door-ways opened onto thatch-walled rooms. Khue's parents' front room was stuffed with heavy, carved wooden furniture: bed bases, wardrobes, sideboards, chairs and tables. Pinned to the walls were large calendar shots of a pretty Vietnamese girl with long red fingernails and an ample bosom. Dag and Binh sat drinking beer with the men of the family around a low glass-topped table displaying pictures of Asian film stars. I sat on the bed base, drinking green tea with Khue, her mother-in-law and an assortment of female relatives. One of the women, whose name sounded something like 'Sissy', hunkered right next to me, fanning me with her hat and looking in concern at my sweat-stained blouse. Helped by a phrase book, I managed to convey to her my suddenly rather urgent need to find a toi-let. Without further ado, she led me out of the house and along the path to a low bridge over a pond. Around the far edges of the pond, tiny outhouses stood on stilts over the water. These were little more than floors with holes in them, surrounded on four sides by walls about two feet high. Women crouched in them, their faces turned down and hidden by straw conical hats, reminiscent of hens in nesting boxes. The outhouses were connected to the bridge by long pieces of bam-boo resting on Y-shaped branches stuck into the mud. Alongside each of these perilous walkways was a wobbly hand rail made of pieces of wood lashed together with vine. Sissy halted by one leading to an unoccupied outhouse. I looked helplessly at her. She took one of my hands and attached it to the handrail.

'Go,' she said.

Very carefully, clinging to the rail which Sissy steadied for me, I put one foot in front of the next and inched along the bamboo. Three feet below me, faeces floated on green slimy water that was bubbling with fish. After what seemed like a lifetime, I stepped into the box. Crouching and undressing in this tiny space was challenging, particularly as my clothes were practically glued by sweat to my body. Awkwardly, I began to peel off my underwear, and once nearly lost my balance. The prospect of pitching head first into the pond was so appalling it was comical, and it had not been missed by the crowd of women standing next to Sissy. Stealing sidelong glances towards my squirming form, they began to laugh, making a sound like twittering birds. The noise alerted the women in other outhouses; seven conical hats lifted, and seven faces gazed steadily in my direction.

I returned to the house feeling hot and embarrassed, only to find Binh in an agitated state.

'On the street, I hear the people, they ask about your travel permits,' he was telling Dag. 'The police they give you no security and this the big problem. If anything happen, no one can help you. If you want to stay I have to go to police.'

'Would you mind?' asked Dag. 'You dealt so well with them in Long Xuyen.'

Binh brooded for a minute. Going to the police station was obviously the last thing he felt like doing.

'Okay, but you no leave the house!' he barked.

When Binh had gone, Sissy lead me to a place where I could wash and change. At the back of the house a kitchen stood on stilts over a green pond. Khue was in there, plucking the chicken which Dag had bought for dinner, while her mother crouched over a charcoal burner, stirring a large pot of soup. In one corner, a doorway opened onto a small veranda. Two large brown urns of water stood there, and tacked to the wall was a mirror and a shelf with a jumble of toothbrushes, toothpaste, soap and combs. Sissy motioned me to sit down on the veranda. I slipped out of my blouse and trousers and she doused me with water and scrubbed me with her hands. Refreshed, dripping and wearing clean clothes, I returned to the main room. It was empty save for Dag, who was stretched out on the hard wooden bed. All morning rain had been threatening; suddenly it began hammering down. People scurried past the house, their plastic sandals slapping through muddy puddles that had formed in seconds.

'I'm so glad it's raining,' Dag murmured, when I lay down next to him. 'I could hardly breathe before.'

A child ran by, holding by the tail a dead rat the size of a small dog.

'I wonder when Binh will get back,' I mused.

'I wonder *if* he'll get back,' said Dag, yawning. 'I think he's beginning to realize what he's let himself in for.'

I thought for a while.

'So am I,' I said, but Dag was drifting into sleep, and didn't hear me.

Binh did return, an hour later, eager to tell us his story.

'I rent the motorbike, go to police station, three mile. The policeman he sleeping. He put on the trouser, ask me for which company I work. I tell him I am free guide, the foreigner they hire me to take a look at the people. So the police want to know exactly why the foreigner come. I tell a lie.'

He paused dramatically, and took his time in lighting a cigarette. The rain had stopped, and the ground outside was steaming.

'I tell him, one foreigner is doctor for the animals, one lady a teacher. They want take a look the poor people here, help them. The policeman tell me about the Cambodia border, he say he have responsibility for the foreigner. He take a look the passports, write everything about you. And he tell me you stay one night, no more, tomorrow you leave early, and I take care for your safety.'

He leaned back, and drank deeply from his beer glass.

'Well done, Binh!' cried Dag.

'This tour very hard,' he said ruefully. 'I never have tour like this before.'

Khue and Sissy served up a hefty meal. The first course was a soup made of coconut milk, green beans and rice. For the main course we had the chicken, which was undercooked and tough as rubber, and cabbage delicately flavoured with caraway. Dessert was fried bananas, of which Sissy insisted I eat three. After this feast it was decided that a walk around the village was in order. Dag and the other men wandered off towards the river bank, while Sissy and I set off, holding hands, in the other direction. We had not gone far when a scooter puttered up behind us.

'Nzan!' Sissy greeted its driver, a plump fair-skinned young woman heavily adorned with gold jewellery.

Before I knew it I was on the passenger seat, clutching Nzan around her amply padded waist and shooting down the lane.

We sped through the centre of the village, swerving around puddles, then skidded to a halt outside a large brick house. Its airy front room was dominated by a huge altar where a gold Buddha sat framed by strings of fairy lights. Everywhere I looked, there were incongruous knick-knacks – a lamp with long filigrees, a murky fish tank, photos of film stars framed in gilt, a grandfather clock, a set of pottery flying ducks. Nzan's husband, a small and skinny man wearing several knuckle-duster rings, ushered me to a sofa which was upholstered in something resembling gold lamé and covered with thick, clear plastic. He sent out for iced coffee from a nearby café, and with it came a crowd of onlookers. I didn't have a dictionary with me and no one in the room spoke a word of English, so we all smiled and nodded and said incomprehensible things to each other. Nzan's husband disappeared for a few minutes, and I heard a generator rumbling into action. Soon, the fairy lights around the Buddha were winking, the filigree lamp was glowing pink, green and yellow, pop music was blaring from a radio and a large standing fan was blasting me with air.

Presently, the crowd around us parted as people stood back to make way for a frail old man. He was dressed all in black, like a mandarin. His long grey hair was scraped into a bun and a goatee beard fell to his chest. The scholarly effect was rather spoiled by the flattened, damp cigarette butt stuck to his bottom lip. Leaning on a staff, he stared at me through watery eyes. Unsure of what to do in the presence of a mandarin, I played safe, got to my feet and bowed. His eyes twinkled and his mouth stretched into a gummy smile. We were still smiling and nodding to each other when Dag arrived. His appearance caused instant consternation.

'Wah! Wah!' cried the men in the crowd, while the women squealed and fled through the back door. The old man leaned heavily on his stick, his mouth open wide, his bottom lip and its cigarette trembling. Binh who was behind Dag, was equally astonished by the house.

'So rich!' he cried, gazing around him. 'I cannot believe!'

He and Dag sat either side of me on the sofa. More iced coffee was brought, and a plate of bean cake cut into cubes and skewered on tooth picks. A camera was produced, and we had to pose for a dozen photographs. Nzan and her husband bombarded Binh with questions about us – our ages, our jobs, what our house looked like, whether we had mosquitoes in Canada. Between his interpretations, he made snide comments to us.

'Look all gold they wear! They have only three hectare rice paddy – so how they rich like this? I think they are the criminal.'

Darkness was quickly falling, and I was getting very tired, but Binh had no intention of leaving yet.

'You sing karaoke?' he asked. 'Come on!'

Set up on the red-tiled floor of one of the back rooms of the house was a TV with video and karaoke attachments.

'I sing karaoke very good,' boasted Binh.

To prove his point, he commandeered the microphone and crooned three songs in a row. The videos had been made in Hong Kong, smuggled into the country and sold on the black market. Their story lines concerned young men in Western suits who gambled, drank whisky and drove glamorous women around the city in sports cars, while back in their villages their innocent girl friends waited sadly for them to return. Binh seemed deeply affected by the songs, and by his own rendition of them. When he'd finished, he held out the microphone to Dag.

'You sing,' he said.

But Dag was busy slapping his legs, trying to fend off the mosquitoes that had suddenly descended upon us. It was time to go. We made our goodbyes, and walked home.

'That man, he smuggle the drugs,' confided Binh, as soon as

we were out of earshot of the house. 'Now he quit. His partner stay in jail for twenty year.'

There was a festive atmosphere in the centre of the village. Scooters zipped about, food sizzled in pans at street stalls lit by oil lamps, and a couple of Kung Fu videos were being shown in cafés. Back at the house, however, all was quiet. Kiep and his family had returned to their boat, and Binh would follow them. Khue's mother sat out on the veranda, fanning herself. Several battery-powered lights were on, including one that shone down on the bed, now draped in a mosquito net.

'You sleep here,' said Binh, pointing towards the bed. 'I see you tomorrow.'

We stretched out on the bed, fully clothed. In the rafters above us, a gecko chirped. The old lady got up from the veranda, walked into the room and switched on both the radio and a television that stood on a sideboard at the foot of the bed. I groaned, but Dag propped himself up on one elbow and peered through the mosquito net.

'It's a programme about fish farming,' he said cheerfully.

Three men came in, sat around the coffee table and began a noisy card game. I lay in the clammy heat, silently willing them to go away. Which they finally did, leaving on the lights, TV and radio. Khue's father then shuffled out of the back bedroom and began pulling shutters across the wide doorway. There were no windows in the room, and I imagined slowly suffocating to death under the glare of lights and to the jarring sounds of Vietnamese TV and radio. We made various pleading noises, to no avail, so Dag got up and with mime and the help of a dictionary persuaded the old man to leave the shutters half open and to douse the electricity. After a restless sleep I awoke around four thirty and made a precarious crossing to the outhouse and back. When I returned to the house the lights were on again and Dag was dismantling the mosquito net while the old couple stood and solemnly watched him. We left some money in thanks for their hospitality, which seemed to greatly cheer them. They stood on the veranda, next to the soundly sleeping pig, waving to us until we were out of sight.

*

The morning was cloudy, with a cooling breeze, and we spent a pleasant six hours chugging along wide channels past miles of banana trees and paddy fields. Over a breakfast of rice and instant noodles, I asked Binh why the old man had wanted to close the shutters.

'He worry your safety. You know, a policeman guard the house, he stand all night with a gun.'

'I got up really early,' I told him. 'I didn't see a policeman.'

But Binh was obviously in no mood for a discussion. The closer we got to Cantho, the more glum he became.

'Before, I have girlfriend in Cantho,' he confided. 'When I come here with the foreigner, she stay with me in hotel. She very beautiful, only twenty-eight year old, she was Miss Cantho. She love me too much.'

I looked carefully at Binh, trying to imagine what a twenty-eight year old beauty queen might see in him.

'She wait five year for me. But you know, she always have Honda dreams.'

'Honda dreams?'

'Yeah, she dream that a rich man marry her and buy her the new Honda. So last month she get marry. She phone to my office to tell me. She cry. This first time I come here since then. Five year she wait. Now I see her no more. I can't believe it.'

'Did your wife know about this girl?' I asked.

Binh's eyes widened in alarm. 'My wife! If she find out, she cut off my head!'

'*You* should have married this girl,' teased Dag. 'Then you could have a number one wife in Saigon and a number two wife in Cantho.'

'I not playboy!' Binh cried angrily. 'I have two children, I good husband!' Then he sighed deeply, and slipped back into a gloomy silence.

Cantho is the geographical heart of the Mekong Delta and the hub of its transportation network. As we approached the city, duck farms and paddy fields gave way to warehouses, cranes dredging the river bank and fish-sauce factories belching out rancid smoke. The river was busy with sampans carrying people and bicycles to and from Hung Phu Island, and delivering produce and animals to the market. Along the bustling water-front there were flowering trees, swaying palms, a six-storey hotel and a massive statue of Ho Chi Minh, sprayed with silver paint and emblazoned with the slogan: Hero and Leader, Still Alive in Our Hearts. Standing beneath this statue, we waved to Kiep and his family until their boat merged with the traffic and we could no longer pick it out.

Binh led us to the hotel where, he told us sadly, he used to stay with his girlfriend. Our room opened onto a balcony looking down over the harbour. We sat there on a stone bench with the receptionist who had showed us to the room. 'Five year ago I escape by boat to Malaysia,' he told us. ' My girlfriend leave on different boat. The sea robber attack and she dead.'

We all sat quietly for a while. Three storeys below us, scooter horns honked and bicycle bells shrilled.

'I stay in Malaysia camp for four year, learn English. I apply to Canada, Australia, America. Then last year there is a trial. They say I am economic refugee, they send me back to Vietnam. Now I not allowed to have good job, only job in small hotel.'

I shook my head. I couldn't think of a single thing to say.

'Excuse me,' said the young man. 'I go back to work.'

Binh took us along an alleyway to a gold shop, where we could change dollars. Despite this being a black-market transaction, no subterfuge was involved. Under a glass-topped counter by the doorway were gold nuggets, a jumble of rings, and tangles of chains and bracelets. Beyond the counter was a table stacked high with bundles of dong, like building bricks. The woman counting this money came over to serve us. Critically, she examined my wedding ring.

'*Xau!*' she said, fingering the pale, 14 carat gold. 'Bad!'

'The rate for dollar is good today,' Binh advised us. 'And the price for gold is cheap too.'

Most Vietnamese people, he explained, preferred to save in gold, and it was estimated that the equivalent of three billion dollars worth of it was hidden away in houses and gardens throughout the country.

'When Vietnamese travel they wear many gold ring, when they need the money they sell the ring,' said Binh.

'Let's change all our money into gold,' Dag suggested, 'then it'll be much easier to carry around.'

I demurred, unable to quite bring myself to believe in gold as real money – an attitude that was the flip side of the general Vietnamese feeling towards local bank notes. Dag insisted on at least buying a ring, and the woman's son made one for him from two old gold bands. In a work station at the back of the room he trained a blow torch onto them until they melted and fused into one blob. This he hammered into a sausage shape, fed through a wringer, blow-torched, then hammered again. Finally he welded together the two ends to make a circle. It was crude, fast work. Ten minutes later Dag sported on his wedding finger a wide band of deep yellow, twenty-four-carat gold, the equivalent of one hundred and fifty US dollars.

That night we ate at one of the many street stalls along the harbour. It was set up against a wall which had a sign painted on it in large letters. When I asked Binh to translate the sign, he gave me an embarrassed smile.

'It tell the men not to urinate here. This big problem in Vietnam.'

A woman was hunkered by a charcoal grill, turning pieces of meat with chop sticks. I bent down to see what she had on offer. Dimly lit by an oil lamp were slices of what looked like pork. There were also several tiny carcasses, ripped open along the belly, and spread-eagled on the grill.

'What are those?' I asked Binh.

'Rats,' he said. 'You want one?'

Needless to say, I didn't. Dag, of course, did.

'You've got to try all these delicacies,' he chided me, as I ordered plain rice and pork.

I watched him removing slivers of flesh with his teeth and spitting out tiny bones. In the gutter, a live rat nosed about among the rubbish.

'Dag eat the rice field rat,' said Binh, who had also opted for pork. 'Rice field rat very clean.'

'How do they taste?' I asked Dag.

'Horrible,' he said, finishing off his third. 'Exactly as you'd imagine rats to taste.'

'Mekong Delta have many special food,' Binh told us. 'You know coconut frog? The farmer make hole in the young coconut and put inside the baby frog. For three month the frog drink the coconut juice and eat the meat. Then the farmer break the coconut. The frog come out very fat and very white – delicious to eat.'

'Really?' said Dag. 'Where could I get one?'

At five a.m., we were woken by the noise from the waterfront: piped music, the revving of boat and scooter engines, the calls of street sellers, the tattoo made by *pho* delivery boys knocking sticks together. We headed straight for the market, which was only a short walk away, and covered several cobbled streets. Narrow passageways ran between lines of stalls offering produce that was a testimony to the fertility of the great delta surrounding us. There was a herb section where large, flat baskets were arranged with fragrant, leafy plants, and a flower section where women bought offerings for the temple. In the fruit section, vendors were busily peeling and sectioning pineapples and green papayas, and arranging piles of rambutan, mango, lychees, bread fruit, avocados, guavas, passion fruit, bush limes and custard apples. Next to the dried beans and rice were stalls of fresh noodles and bean curd. A line of *pho* stalls stood side by side, accompanied by glass cases full of freshly baked baguettes. And there were eggs: quail eggs, chicken eggs, duck eggs and preserved eggs covered in a sooty mixture of ashes, lime and salt. Around them, baskets were crammed with tiny, fluffy chicks and ducklings, cheeping and wriggling and clambering over one another. By now we were reeling with smells and sights, but more was to come. The indoor market was a large shed with a corrugated-iron roof, where fresh fish and meat were for sale. The fish wriggled and flopped in shallow metal trays. Lobsters with royal blue tentacles and iridescent purple carapaces lay in heaps. White geese with yellow beaks sat tethered next to black geese with red beaks. There were song birds for sale, alive and fluttering inside bamboo cages, or dead and arranged in bunches of five. In the meat section, clouds of flies rose up as customers browsed through the lumps of flesh. I saw something that looked suspiciously like a skinned terrier. For a while I watched a man who was hunkered by a pile of pigs' ears, painstakingly shaving each one and rinsing it in a large bowl of water. He looked up, and graciously presented me with a bald, wet ear.

In a waterfront café, we met Binh for breakfast. He seemed to be in a far more perky mood than the day before.

'If you marry Vietnamese girl,' he told Dag, 'take one from Mekong Delta. Saigon girls are lazy and can't cook. The girls here do everything for the man, they always smile.'

He pointed to the jetty, where a group of women waited for customers who needed ferrying by sampan over to Hung Phu island.

'You see the girl in yellow? I talk to her. She tell me about a boat that go across the delta. She take us to the captain.'

The girl, whose name was Lin, rowed the skinny boat by standing on its stern and taking two neat steps forward, putting her full weight behind the long oars, then taking two steps back. We were a light cargo – many of the other sampans were packed with up to ten people and their bikes. As Lin smiled shyly beneath her conical hat, Binh told us that she had been rowing for seven years, and that she was just starting a twenty-four-hour shift.

'And is she married?' I asked.

'I ask her this already,' said Binh. 'Her husband work Saigon. I make date with her tomorrow.'

Lin took us out to the middle of the river channel, where a large cargo boat, *Tan Nguyen*, was moored. Over a hundred feet long, very wide in the beam and built of rough planking, its resemblance to a convict ship was tempered only by its trim of yellow paint and the large bunch of irises and roses tied onto its forepeak. Binh clambered aboard it, leaving us with Lin who worked the oars to keep her sampan in place against the current of the river.

'We go Sunday,' he told us when he returned. 'Seven dollar

each. The boat go Rach Gia, then Phu Quoc Island. This okay?'

It couldn't be better – a single passage right across to the west side of the Mekong Delta, then a trip over the Gulf of Thailand to an island nestled against the border with Cambodia.

On the way back to shore, Binh flirted outrageously with Lin. But their budding romance came to an abrupt halt when, on reaching the jetty, she charged us 50,000 dong, the equivalent of five US dollars.

'She cheating!' Binh fumed. 'She charge me foreigner price, she think I am Vietnamese overseas!'

He had a deep resentment against these *Viet Kieu*, the people who fled the country after 1975, and were now free to return for holidays.

'They act like big men,' he had often told us. 'They wear too much gold. They hire the car and drive around and buy prostitutes. They think we are stupid!'

Now, he was venting his wrath on Lin.

'I tell her, I not one of these men who act so big! She cannot cheat me like this!'

But Lin had transformed from a shy, simpering girl to a scowling and insistent business woman, who finally and with bad grace accepted 30,000 dong.

Over dinner, Binh continued to rant about 'Vietnamese overseas'.

'I no speak to them. They spend all the money showing off. They forget everything – their homeland, their culture, their ancestors. I say to them, where your father's tomb? And they don't know!'

I told him about my friends in Britain, Hanh and Tuyen, who regularly tended their ancestral shrines, and who had told us much about Vietnamese culture. Binh listened dubiously.

'Really? I never meet Vietnamese overseas like this.'

I explained that Hanh and Tuyen weren't rich, and that life in the West wasn't always easy for them.

'I know this,' he said thoughtfully. 'The West not heaven. I live one year in America, in 1972. The US Navy send me to study. Sometime I work putting the gas in the car.'

This was a part of Binh's life he'd not told us of before, and we plied him with questions about it. But he only wanted to speak of his girlfriend there.

'She black American. She loved me too much. I have long hair then, you know. All the time she comb it. She want me to stay, get married. But every day I think of my homeland. When I come back to Saigon, I put on the tie and go out to the bar—'

'Like a Vietnamese overseas!' Dag and I chorused.

Binh took the teasing with equanimity.

'Yeah,' he said, lighting another cigarette. 'Maybe.'

His dashed hopes for a new romance brought an improvement in our travel plans. 'The boat leave Sunday, okay? So tomorrow we go to see my brother near Soc Trang. He have farm, he is big Communist, he have no trouble with police, we sleep in his house.'

'Binh,' I told him, 'you are wonderful.'

But he had slipped back into lugubriousness, and my praise did nothing to cheer him.

'I want to leave Cantho,' he said. 'Too many memory here.'

We spent seven hours next day in a water taxi, cruising along narrow, picturesque canals. It was a peaceful trip, filled with scenes of children splashing in the water, of ducks and pigs being fed, of women walking through orange groves, of pretty girls with their hats tilted back waving from sampans. Towards mid afternoon our canal flowed into a watery crossroad. Suddenly we were on a river that was a busy highway. There were boats going this way and that, being poled, rowed and pushed by engines, sometimes narrowly missing each other, sometimes getting caught up in jams. This highway led to a floating town. Rafted up along the banks were house boats, fishing boats, passenger boats, trading boats piled high with produce for sale and boats selling petrol in plastic bottles. Behind them, dilapidated buildings crawled up the river bank and water streamed from an ice-making factory that looked like the back of a giant refrigerator. Rumbling across a bridge spanning the river were buses and trucks belching out smoke and exhaust fumes. We had arrived, rather reluctantly, in My Tu.

Clouds like Zeppelins were hanging in the sky, and rain hit just as we disembarked. Quickly, we clambered up the steep bank and into a restaurant that overlooked the river. On a counter top by the doorway was a demi-john filled with a clear liquid and several fat snakes curled up like lengths of rope.

'First we drink the snake wine,' announced Binh casually. 'Then we eat the snake.'

The owner of the restaurant appeared from the kitchen. He wore only a pair of loose cotton shorts and a grimy towel around his neck. He filled four small glasses from the demi-john and brought them over to us, staggering a little and grinning broadly to display his one and only fang-like tooth. While we sipped the snake wine, which tasted like home brewed vodka, he explained the origin of his name, which was *Chin*, or nine. He was the youngest of eight children. As was traditional in Vietnam, his parents had named his eldest sibling *Hai*, or Two, to fool the evil spirits that are said to snatch away first-born children. Then the second born in his family was named *Ba*, or Three, the third born *Bon*, Four, and so on until they got to *Chin*. The telling of this involved another round of snake wine. By now my head was beginning to spin.

'I have to eat soon,' I told Binh.

'Chin want to know which snake you like to eat,' he said.

'Cobra's her favourite,' joked Dag.

This was duly conveyed to Chin, who disappeared into the kitchen. Minutes later he was back. Instead of a towel around his neck, he had a snake. About three feet long, it had a brown back and a cream and black striped belly. Chin placed it on the table, holding onto its tail. It slithered across the Formica towards me, its tongue flickering in and out.

'He say it no poisonous,' said Binh, who had pushed his chair to a safe distance away from the table.

Chin picked up the writhing snake and placed it on Dag's knees.

'For God sake, don't let it go up your shorts!' I cried.

Coolly, Dag picked it up by the base of its head.

'He say price of snake is 35,000 dong,' called Binh, who was now halfway across the room. 'He cook it with the vegetable and spice and hot chilli.'

'Good deal,' said Dag, carefully examining the snake. 'We'll take it.'

While Dag and Binh had another glass of wine, I followed Chin and the snake into the kitchen. It was a gloomy room with only one small window. Two other men were in there, chopping vegetables on a stone counter, while Chin's wife squatted next to a large wok of water heating up over a charcoal burner.

'Hi hi!' shouted the men when they saw me. 'How old you? You have babysan?'

Perhaps sensing what was to come, the snake had wrapped itself tightly around Chin's arm. After carefully unravelling it, he dropped it into the steaming water. The snake didn't take too kindly to this; arching its back, it threw itself out of the wok and began wriggling towards a dark corner. The two men leapt about, whooping loudly, Chin's wife screamed and ducked behind me, while Chin lunged after the snake. Grabbing it by the tail, he flipped it back into the water, which was now vigorously boiling, and held it in there with the end of a wooden spoon while it writhed around in what looked like agonizing death throes.

'How long does it take a snake to die?' I asked Dag, who had heard the commotion and come running into the kitchen.

'It's already dead, those movements are just reflexes,' he said, in his best veterinarian's voice.

At last the snake was still, its jaws wide open as if it had expired screaming.

'I've always liked snakes,' said Dag, ten minutes later.

This was just as well, because he was about to eat one. The creature had been chopped into chunks, fried, and doused in a thick sauce.

'You try, very delicious,' said Binh, who had pulled his chair back to the table.

I used the end of my chop sticks to investigate the sauce,

which had a strong curry flavour. Dag was using his to pick up a piece of snake.

'I'm forever amazed by what you'll put in there,' I commented, as the chunk of flesh disappeared into his mouth.

Half a minute later, some rather surprising things came out. First a sizable piece of bone, then some skin that he'd sucked clean of sauce to reveal cream and black markings and some nicely defined scales. Catching Chin's eye, I ordered an omelette.

It was a long drive by scooter cyclo to Binh's brother's house, near Soc Trang, past endless vistas of misty, rain-soaked paddy fields and down a series of bumpy red dirt roads.

'My brother Hien, he Communist, so we not talk the politics,' Binh warned us, as we clambered down from the cyclo.

Hien was fifty-eight years old. Until his recent retirement he had worked for the government, in the Ministry of Communications. He was a tall man by Vietnamese standards, with greying hair. Thao, his wife, was rotund and cheerful, and spoke a few words of English. They welcomed us warmly into their brick house. In one of its four sparsely furnished rooms we sat on stools, watching state television. A programme about grafting fruit trees was followed by a Russian news bulletin. Clinging to the wall above the television set was a gecko, over a foot long, its white skin delicately speckled with pale green. For minutes it would be utterly still, then it would rush at a passing insect, and trap it with a flicker of its tongue.

'I hate these gecko,' said Binh. 'I like them only when they are in the poddle.'

A silky hen and its chicks wandered in and out of the house, and a puppy capered about our feet, pouncing on Dag's toes. Although the night was relatively cool, Hien carried a standing fan into the room, turned it on to high and trained it straight at Dag and me. Shivering under its blast, we ate rice and meat from bowls balanced on our laps, watching excerpts from Disney's *Snow White and the Seven Dwarfs* dubbed in Vietnamese. Bugs began whining around our ears, and Thao hurried outside to pull a mosquito net over the pig pen, which was on the outside wall of the kitchen. I followed her to watch this procedure, and she proudly shone a flashlight onto a large, pink and astonishingly clean sow.

'I wash pig,' she explained. 'Three time every day.'

We slept on the mud floor of a room which we shared with a huge basket, five feet high and filled to the brim with rice grains. The mosquito net hanging from the ceiling was in far worse shape than the one the pig slept beneath, and had several large rips in it. We doused ourselves with insect repellent, and lay in the dark, listening to the symphony being performed in the fields surrounding the house. Cicadas provided a soothing background melody, other insects chimed in with squeaks and trills, a couple of local dogs did duets of barks and howls, but the star performers were the frogs, gigantic frogs by the sound of them, with their deep resonating bellows. I drifted in and out of sleep, waking up from time to time to find myself scratching mosquito bites. The darkness began to seep away. A cockerel crowed close to the window of our room, and a scooter puttered along the lane. Someone stirred in the house, there were footsteps, the sound of a clanking pail and then a loud chorus of quacking ducks.

I padded through the house and past the sleeping pig, to watch Hien opening up the duck house. More than a hundred birds waddled out and followed him to a pond where he scattered their breakfast of prawn heads and rice. The ducks, Binh later told me, produced at least seventy eggs each day. Forty of these Hien sold in the market, getting six hundred dong a piece, and the rest he traded for food. His one hectare farm was run according to traditional methods, which he'd learned by consulting old farmers and by watching educational programmes on state television. He allowed the ducks to wander the farm, where they fertilized his rice fields and the papaya, mango and coconut trees. In the duck pond, he raised fish that fed on algae, faeces from the family's outhouse standing over it and the pig's droppings. Each baby fish, Binh told us over breakfast, cost him 900 dong. After a year, the fish would be two kilos in weight and would fetch 18,000 dong in the market.

*

While we tucked into baguettes filled with fried pork, the breeding sow woke up and started snuffling about. This animal was the source of most of the farm's profit, and Hien's pride and joy. As soon as it stirred he hurried over to its pen, removed the mosquito net and gave it a friendly slap on its fat rump.

'Can your brother make a good living from this farm?' I asked Binh.

'You know, the bank clerk earn forty dollar a month,' he said evasively, 'and the policeman twenty dollar. But they get much money the other way – you know what I mean? In the office they poor, but at home they rich.'

I was becoming adept at interpreting Binh's tangential answers to my questions.

'So was your brother richer when he worked for the Communist party?'

He paused before answering. 'You know, one Communist leader have wedding for the daughter. He invite many foreigner, he spend ten thousand dollar on this wedding. Someone write about it in the newspaper and the police ask him, where the money from? He say he make money from raising the dogs – the dogs like a sausage – and the police they believe him.'

'So,' I said patiently, 'your brother is poorer since he retired?'

'Yeah, my brother very poor,' said Binh. Because of Binh's ban on discussing politics, I didn't ask about recent reports that only twenty per cent of farmers were prospering as a result of the economic reforms. Nor did I ask if it was true that the corruption associated with the privatisation of co-op lands had created a new class of rich peasants – many of them Party cadres.

On the way back through Soc Trang, Binh took us to what he called the Bat Pagoda. Hanging from the trees surrounding the gaudily painted temples were hundreds of fruit bats. Binh clapped his hands, setting off a cacophony of squealing and flapping as the bats rose from the trees, lazily circled above them, then settled down again on the branches. A dark-haired young foreigner appeared in the doorway of a temple to watch this, then came over to chat. His name was Phil Worthington, and he was from Manchester. After graduating from university, he had started travelling in South East Asia, and had fetched up in Saigon, where he found himself a teaching job. Now he had five days holiday, and was touring around the delta by motor scooter. He was intrigued to hear how we had been travelling, and by our plan to head up the coast by boat.

'Look me up when you're in Saigon,' said Phil, before he zipped away on his scooter. 'I know a couple of people who may have some ideas for you.'

The monks, who were from Cambodia, invited us to have tea with them. We sat on a woven mat, close to an altar with a disconcertingly realistic statue of their founder. It was dressed in the same orange robes as the monks, with a pair of spectacles balanced on its nose. While we drank green tea from tiny glasses, Binh passed around cigarettes. All but one monk lit up. He told us that, after several unsuccessful attempts, he had finally beaten the habit.

'We had long celebration, for six hours I pray in the temple, and all the time I think of cigarettes. Then I decide to stop the smoking. It was hard, it took a lot of meditation to do it.'

The monks also had a pig they were inordinately proud of. It lay sprawled across the doorway of the low stone building where they cooked and ate. Enormously fat, it must have weighed over five hundred pounds and could barely move. They reverently pointed out the fact that each trotter had five, not four toes. Like all animal monstrosities in Vietnam, this one was considered highly auspicious.

'It live all the time in this room,' said Binh. 'When it born the farmer bring it to the pagoda for lucky.'

I thought about the monks, their smoking, their bats and their pig, all the way back to Cantho.

4

A HARD TOUR

Next morning, a distraught Binh barged into our room without knocking. 'I just phone the sister of my girlfriend and she tell me the marriage is over! My girlfriend marry this man because her mother owe him money.'

To avoid disturbing Dag, who was still asleep, I led him out to the balcony.

'She love me too much,' he said, using the cigarette he was smoking to light up another. 'Sometimes I tell her, I old man, not handsome, I have wife, two children, why you love me?'

'What did she say?' I asked curiously.

'She say nothing . . . she cry a little.'

We sat in silence for a while, nursing our own thoughts. I was worried about Dag, who during the night had developed a fever, aching muscles and diarrhoea. Each time he'd stumbled back to bed from the bathroom, he'd insisted that his illness wouldn't stop us leaving on the *Tan Nguyen* next day.

'Last night I go dancing in the International Hotel disco,' said Binh suddenly. 'It very cheap – eight thousand dong to go in, seven thousand dong for big Tiger beer, twenty thousand dong for a girl.'

'A girl?' said Dag, who had appeared in the doorway, rubbing
his eyes. 'What for?'

'For dancing.'

'*Only* dancing?'

'Sure. She beautiful girl, very good dancer. She want come
back here but I tell her, no, I work today. And I tell her I have
no money. Dag, can you pay me? My money is gone.'

'How much would she have cost?' asked Dag.

'Ten dollar.'

'Thank goodness we didn't pay you last night!' I said.

Binh scowled at me. 'I tell her exactly, I have wife and two
children, I not playboy!'

At noon, we boarded the *Tan Nguyen*. Clustered around it
were scores of sampans delivering its cargo. A chain of people
passed up baskets of apples, stalks of bananas, crates of beer,
sacks of rice and individual yams and gourds which they piled
up inside the cavernous holds as meticulously as if they were
building stone walls. For two hours this loading continued,
until the bottom holds were full and most of the floor area of
the inside top deck was covered. The work was supervised by
the skipper, Fan, a glamorous woman in her mid forties with
carefully coiffed hair, pearl earrings and a voice like a megaphone. While she worked, Binh and I sat with her husband,
Thuan, who was elegantly dressed in white pyjamas. He told us
that he had been a commander in the South Vietnamese Army,
and after 1975 had spent thirteen years in a re-education camp.
Fan had taken over the family business, skippering cargo boats
as well as raising their four children, two of whom now worked
with them on the *Tan Nguyen*. When I asked him what happened in the camps he spoke at length, his expression very
calm and unchanging.

'For the first years he look for the land mine,' Binh translated. 'Twenty men, they stand in the line eight hour a day.
Each man have long bamboo stick, and poke in the ground.
Then they take a step. If they find a mine they take it out.
Sometimes they make a mistake and blow up. He say this was
very bad. For the next years he break rocks for the roads. This
was better.'

'Did you go to re-education camp?' I asked Binh.

'No, my job was not important.'

Binh had worked on debris control boats around Cantho and as a fire fighter on destroyers.

'I know this place well. From here to Phu Quoc it take seventeen hours. And in the sea we have the third-class wave. For me, no problem. But you better take the medication.'

If anyone needed medication, it was Dag. During the morning his condition had deteriorated, but nothing I said would convince him to cancel this trip. He was lying in the wheelhouse, on the lid of a large storage box. Jutting from the wall next to him was a shelf with an altar to *Quan The Am Bo That*, the Goddess of Mercy. A pot of joss sticks was tied to the shelf with string, and flies crawled over a plate of offertory grapes. The wheelhouse was disconcertingly spartan. Sticking through its floorboards were a couple of metal levers for the throttle and transmission. There was no glass in the windows, and navigational aids were limited to a search light and siren, which were connected to an anarchic jumble of electric wiring. Looking at this lot, and my feverish husband, I was tempted to make an offering to *Quan The Am Bo That* myself.

'See if you can get some ice,' croaked Dag. 'I need to bring my temperature down.'

At the back of the top deck was a kitchen area, where a couple of women were boiling rice and frying meat. They had large coolers packed with ice for the drinks on sale, and cheerfully wrapped up some of this in a grimy towel. It melted fast as I rubbed it over Dag's back, which was soon covered with little rivulets of water. Binh hovered about anxiously, watching me work.

'Maria, you try like this,' he said, handing me a metal spatula and a pot of something resembling Tiger Balm. 'It make him hot and better.'

He showed me how to rub the balm hard against Dag's skin, creating long red weals down his back.

Neither method seemed to work particularly well, and for several hours, while the boat was loaded, I sat next to Dag, watching him drift in and out of a delirious sleep. The air was still, muggy and unbearably hot, and at times I was tempted to jump into the murky water of Cantho harbour to cool off. Finally, in mid afternoon, the engine started up, Thuan took the wheel and his sons worked the levers with their feet.

As we chugged downstream a cooling breeze flowed through the wheelhouse, and my clammy skin began to dry. But it was a short-lived respite. Soon we stopped at a floating petrol station to refuel. The petrol was poured by hand from plastic containers into the tank, a process which took over an hour. Then the engine refused to start. Another hour or so of Fan yelling down a hatch into the engine room seemed to solve the problem.

We set off again along a canal, one of a system that would lead us right across the delta to the Cai Loa River, which empties into the Gulf of Thailand. As darkness fell, Fan flicked on the search light from time to time, checking for other boats, and sounding the boat's loud wailing siren if they were in the way. By nine, most people on the *Tan Nguyen* were lying in hammocks strung along the side decks and on the top deck, or stretched out on rice sacks. I settled down in the wheelhouse next to Dag, but he was tossing and turning and radiating heat.

Around midnight I went out to the fore deck, and sat against a pile of thick rope. Along the banks of the canal I could make out the dark shapes of trees against the star-studded sky. I thought how strange it was, after all the planning and dreaming, actually to be here, travelling across the Mekong Delta in the deep of night. One of the crew came out and placed burning joss sticks in the prow. They glowed brightly, and golden sparks flew from them. It was a sight that had already become comfortingly familiar. Leaning my head against the rope, I closed my eyes. When I opened them, the joss sticks had burned down, and a pale light was spreading across the surface of the Cai Loa River.

Pale green water, flat as glass, stretched away on either side of us, then merged into sand flats. The air smelled of salt; we were in the mouth of the river, and the ocean was not far away. As I stood up and stretched someone tapped me on the shoulder. I turned to see an old man. He was tall and spindly, and his large ears were so thin they were almost transparent. He presented me with a jug of water, indicating that I should use it to wash. I took it to one of the two large outhouses at the back of the boat which, mercifully, were completely enclosed. When I returned with the empty jug the man was sitting with Binh in the wheelhouse, next to Dag's sleeping form. Binh introduced him as Chu Sau, or 'Uncle Six'.

'Maria, how you sleep?' asked Binh. He looked rumpled and drawn.

'Okay.'

His face folded into a deep frown. 'I have bad night,' he said pointedly, 'I cannot sleep, I worry too much for Dag.'

Uncle Six suddenly patted my hand and pointed towards a long wood and bamboo dock we were approaching. At its far end was a small hut.

'Police,' said Binh. 'The old man say you hide.'

As Thuan set off along the dock, clutching the papers of the boat, Uncle Six motioned for me to lie next to Dag. He lightly rested a hand on my shoulder until we were safely out of sight of the post and I could sit up.

By eight we were on a section of river so shallow that reeds peeked in clumps above the surface. Not surprisingly, we ran aground. Fan screeched at crew members, who scurried from one end of the boat to the other, lowering long bamboo poles over the sides to check the water levels.

It soon became obvious that the tide was dropping, and no amount of Fan's yelling could do anything to stop it. Hours of sitting out in the middle of the river mouth stretched ahead. As the heat of the day began to build, a lethargy fell over the boat. Dag, Binh, Uncle Six and most other people on board snoozed away the morning. For a while I sat in the wheelhouse, staring out at the water, doing some mental calculations. This trip was supposed to have taken eighteen hours. We'd now been underway over twenty hours and had covered about seventy-five miles. We still had ahead of us at least a hundred miles and a ten-hour ride across the Gulf of Thailand. The effort of these calculations, and their results, left me feeling limp. I searched around for an empty hammock and, like everyone else on board, rocked myself to sleep.

'I am afraid of sea robber,' said Binh, when we were afloat once more, heading out of the river mouth and towards the open ocean, 'but on this ship they have four AK-47 gun.'

By now Dag was well on the way to recovery. His fever had subsided and his stomach had settled – which was just as well, because soon we were into the swells of the Gulf of Thailand, and the boat began to pitch and roll through steadily building waves.

Binh, however, was looking far from well. 'Maria, you okay?' he asked. 'This difficult tour, very hard for woman. My wife could not do this.'

Fan arrived with bowls of rice and meat. Binh took one look at the food, his face drained of colour, and he retreated to his hammock, where he nursed his sea sickness for the rest of the journey.

Dawn brought the welcome sight of Phu Quoc Island, stretching for nineteen miles along the horizon. As its mountains, forests and beaches grew steadily closer, the boat buzzed with the activity of people packing and getting ready to disembark. We steamed past some steep islets covered with grass and windblown trees.

'We're a bit too close to those for comfort,' commented Dag once, peering through a window. 'I hope there are no reefs about.'

Unfortunately, there were. Half a mile from Phu Quoc Island, we ran aground on one. Fan strode from one end of the boat to the other, screaming at everyone in sight. But there was nothing to be done: once again we were well and truly stuck, with no option but to wait for the tide to rise. Thuan seemed unperturbed, and sat with us in the wheel house, cleaning his ears with the end of a burned-down joss stick. Fan meanwhile was venting her wrath into the engine room. Suddenly a man appeared from it with a bucket filled to the brim with black oil, which he handed to Fan as if in appeasement. Striding onto the deck she chucked the lot, including the bucket, overboard.

*

At long last, after a fifty-hour journey and a distance of a hundred and eighty miles, we motored into Cay Dua harbour. The wooden fishing boats packed into it were painted blue and red and had round wicker tenders like huge baskets pulled up on their decks. From a hundred yards offshore, we could smell rancid fish, evidence of the island's *nuoc mam* industry. According to Binh, Phu Quoc's fish sauce was famous all over the world, and had made the island rich. As Thuan manoeuvred the boat to the dock, Fan appeared by my side and squeezed my arm hard.

'She invite us to stay one more night,' said Binh. 'I tell her okay.'

He seemed unhappy about the thought of us leaving the boat, suggesting that our presence ashore could cause some problems. Phu Quoc, he told us, was a politically sensitive area. At its northern end, it was only nine miles from the border with Cambodia, which claimed the island as its own. And after 1975, Phu Quoc had been the point of flight for many Vietnamese, including forty per cent of the island's population, who took half of its fishing fleet with them. For these reasons, he said, the police were more than usually suspicious, and might not take kindly to the sight of two foreigners wandering around. But, after being cooped up for so long, we were anxious to stretch our legs. I nervously negotiated the narrow, wobbly plank leading from the boat, conscious of the long drop down to greasy water below. On the wooden dock, red, brown, grey and silver fish were flattened and spread out to dry. Close by, two policemen sat in a small open-fronted café. They looked curiously at us as we wandered past, but continued eating their *pho*, seemingly unconcerned by our presence in the town.

Along Cay Dua's dank side roads we found heaps of rotting rubbish, raw sewage flowing in open drains and houses that had collapsed in on themselves, like packs of cards. A cart piled high with rice sacks got stuck in some deep muddy ruts, and two men pushed at its back end while a third tethered himself with ropes to the front and heaved like a pack animal. A young couple wrestled with a fully grown pig, trying to stuff it into a long, conical basket. Although its feet were trussed and the woman held it firmly by the tail, it managed to thrash furiously in the mud while the basket was manoeuvred over its head. As we passed the couple they hoisted up the basket on a long shoulder pole and carted away the squealing pig.

Following our noses we discovered the fish sauce industry, a lane of gloomy warehouses stuffed with enormous wooden vats. Millions of tiny fish had been mixed with salt and left to rot and ferment in these vats for several months. A tap was open on the bottom of one of the vats, and a reddish-brown liquid was trickling out into a barrel. One of the workers caught some of this liquid in a glass, held it up to the light so that we could admire its clarity, then insisted on Dag tasting it. I began edging towards the door.

'Actually, it's not bad,' said Dag, after a couple of sips. 'Come on, Maria, try some.'

But I was already outside, and in search of a place to buy something more palatable to drink.

In the Do Ray Me Café we sipped cool coconut juice from the shell, feeling uncomfortable about the attention we were drawing. Passers-by gave us suspicious sidelong glances. A crowd of young men stopped to stare at us, sniggering derisively. When Binh arrived, we were relieved to see his friendly face.

'In two days a boat take us from here to Ha Tien,' he said.

'Perfect,' said Dag. 'And from Ha Tien we go to Rach Gia, from Rach Gia to Vung Tau, from Vung Tau to Nha Trang, all by boat, stopping at every village on the way.'

Binh looked away, inhaling deeply on his cigarette.

'Only kidding!' Dag cried, slapping him reassuringly on the thigh.

But Binh's face didn't lift. 'This very hard tour,' he said despondently.

Cargo was still being off loaded from the *Tan Nguyen*, and trading was going on inside it. As we arrived, a scuffle broke out between two women who were arguing over the price of yams. Fan waded into the fray and ordered both women off the boat, then she turned to us with a smile and invited us for dinner. Thuan was at his most charming, and constantly placed tidbits of the choicest food into my bowl of rice: tender green beans, prawns and fried fish doused in Phu Quoc *nuoc mam*. The fish sauce I'd tasted elsewhere in Vietnam had had a powerful, rancid taste, but this one was far more delicate. It was the best *nuoc mam* in the country, claimed Thuan, and his secret recipe was to mix it with lemon juice, a little water and slices of chilli pepper.

Our third night on the *Tan Nguyen* was far from comfortable. The air was oppressively hot, the smell of rotten fish and raw sewage was overpowering, and the noise from the dock was relentless; revving engines, blaring radios, honking horns, ringing bells, shouts, laughter and barking. Some of Cay Dua's rats had come aboard and were nosing around in the wheelhouse. We slept fitfully. Once we woke to see a long tail hanging from the altar, a couple of feet from our faces, where a rat was feasting on the offerings of bananas and apples. Later in the night, I was disturbed again. For a few seconds I thought it was another rat, but then I heard a creak, and a low cough. Turning my head, I could just make out the outline of a figure creeping past me, barely a foot away.

'Hey, you!' I yelled, sitting up and flailing my hands. In seconds the shadowy figure was gone, scrambling over the gunwales of the *Tan Nguyen* and along the dock.

With a flashlight we checked our bags and camera equipment. Nothing had been disturbed. Dag easily escaped back into sleep, but I lay wide awake, wondering what it was that possessed me to embark on such journeys as this. Ruefully, I remembered being interviewed by CBC radio the day we left Canada for Vietnam.

'Maria Coffey and Dag Goering are off on another adventure,' the interviewer had concluded, 'leading lives the rest of us can only dream about.'

Next morning a boy came aboard selling doughnuts. The one I bought was fairly palatable, but after a couple of bites I found something that looked suspiciously like snot. Uncle Six took the doughnut away from me and flung it overboard. He was getting ready to leave the boat and take a bus to Duong Dong, twelve miles up the coast, where he would sell his rice. We

wanted to join him there, but Binh was resisting our suggestion
that he find us a boat for the journey.

'Bus quicker,' he said.

'We don't mind; we're in no hurry.'

'Bus cheaper.'

'We've got money.'

'No boat go Duong Dong,' he insisted finally. 'The harbour
full of stones.'

The bus was so low that Dag had to bend almost double to
walk along the aisle, and he and I filled one of the hard plastic
benches designed to take three Vietnamese passengers. In the
seat ahead of us, a man held a fighting cock which for much of
the journey fixed me with a hard, bright stare. The windows of
the bus were jammed open, and the air blasting through them
was so hot and dry that it was like sitting inside a convection
oven. For six miles we travelled through fields of cassava and
coconut plantations, then took a side road leading back to the
coast. And a heavenly coast it was: long stretches of yellow
sand shaded by palms and papaya trees, and a shimmering
expanse of turquoise ocean. Strung along it were fishing villages, and in the largest of these Uncle Six stopped the bus.
While a couple of young men unloaded half his sacks of rice,
he was quickly surrounded by villagers who greeted him
enthusiastically, shaking his hand and patting him on the back.
Xa Duong To village stretched leisurely along the road. Its
houses had red tile roofs, shady verandas and gardens filled
with cashew and pepper plants. I wandered over to a food stall,
but found only dried fish for sale. The man with the fighting
cock, which he had tucked beneath his arm, walked past me
and into a house. I felt like following him; I could happily have
spent hours on a veranda, watching the surf roll onto the
beach. But the driver honked the horn, Uncle Six beckoned
and reluctantly I returned to the bus.

The gardens of Duong Dong's Soviet-style hotel were overgrown with weeds, and the swimming pool in front of it was
empty and coated with green slime. To all appearances, the
place was utterly deserted save for a receptionist who was reading a magazine. After a long and heated conversation with

Binh and Uncle Six, she slammed down the magazine and
stalked off.

'The hotel full,' said Binh.

'Full?' we repeated incredulously.

'They have Vietnamese tour group. We go guest house.'

Although it was more likely that the girl had refused to give
Binh a free room in return for bringing foreign guests, he was
in such a foul mood that we decided not to argue. We followed
him across a bridge that spanned a river chock-a-block with
fishing boats.

'I thought you said the harbour was full of stones,' I
commented.

'It is,' retorted Binh with a challenging glare. 'I tell you
before, I tell you *exactly*!'

The guest house doubled as a brothel, supposedly run by the
army. In the foyer, several young women in thick make-up sat
around a coffee table, languidly filing their nails and waiting for
custom. Our room had concrete walls and a barred window
opening out on a dank alleyway. The bed was lumpy and
smelled of stale sweat. When I sat on it, a cloud of dust rose up.

'It's the first time I've paid to spend the night in a prison
cell,' said Dag.

We escaped to explore the town, but found only a beach
where two dead pigs lay rotting and a scruffy market where we
ate a meal of rice and some extremely unpleasant fish.

At ten, the electricity in the guest house was turned off for
the night. The place was plunged into darkness, and the fans
slowed to a stop. We lay listening to rats squeaking and dogs
barking in the alleyway. It was so stuffy in the room we'd
decided against using the mosquito net, which anyway was full
of rips. The tiny bugs incessantly whined around our ears and
zoned in on the spots we'd missed with the insect repellent: ear-
lobes, hairlines, soles of feet.

'Shall I tell you a story?' I asked Dag, propping myself up on
one elbow.

'Do anything,' he said, 'to take my mind off this place.'

I recounted to him a Vietnamese legend which explains
where the mosquito came from. 'There was a poor farmer,
who worked in the paddy fields, cultivated mulberry bushes

and raised silk worms. His wife pretended to be happy, but secretly she longed for a life of luxury. During one monsoon season, the farmer's wife got a fever and died. The farmer was grief-stricken and set off with his wife's body in a sampan to find the genie of medicine. The genie agreed to return the woman to life, but warned the farmer that he would regret it. On the genie's instructions, the farmer opened the coffin, cut his finger and let three drops of blood fall on his wife. She instantly awoke. On the way home the farmer stopped at a port to buy provisions. While he was shopping a big cargo ship came in. The rich owner of the ship saw the farmer's wife, immediately fell in love with her, invited her aboard and set sail. For a month the farmer searched for this ship, but by the time he found it, his wife had grown to like her new life of luxury and refused to go back to him. Angrily, he demanded that she return his three drops of blood. As soon as she cut open her finger and the drops fell, she died. But she couldn't resign herself to leave the world. Taking the form of a small fly, she relentlessly followed the farmer around, trying to steal back the drops of blood. Every night she buzzed about him, begging for his pardon.'

'Why didn't he squash her?' asked Dag, slapping at a mosquito that was biting him beneath the chin. 'He'd have done us all a big favour.'

Dawn found both of us grumpy and despondent.

'I'm fed up with this place,' said Dag as we were packing our bags.

'We won't stay here another night,' I reassured him.

'I don't just mean *here*, I mean Vietnam.'

I looked at him in alarm. During our trips, it was usually me who was beset by an early attack of despondency, and Dag who cheerfully managed to dispel it. Unused to adopting the optimistic role, I racked my brains for something suitable to say.

'Things are bound to improve,' I told him. 'After all, we've got at least ten more weeks here.'

'Ten weeks!' he spluttered. 'That's *two and a half months* of restrictions and grubby hotels and sordid little towns! I didn't come here to stay in places like this, or to travel around by bloody bus!'

'I'm sure once we get back to Saigon we can—'

'We can get the next plane out of here, that's what!'

'I do have a book to write,' I gently reminded him.

'Exactly! *You* have a book to write! And it was *your* idea to come here!'

There was a knock on the door.

'Ready for breakfast?' called Binh.

Flies crawled all over the table of the market café, where we sat eating *pho*. Binh's mood, at least, had improved during the night, and he was eager to share some newly hatched plans.

'I think next year I bring the foreigner group to Phu Quoc,' he said. 'There is the airfield here, we fly from Saigon, spend three day in the hotel, take the boat back. What do you think?'

'Marvellous idea,' said Dag wryly. 'The foreigner group will love it.'

'So now we go beach, you swim?'

Dag made an odd choking sound.

'Actually, we'd like to leave,' I said.

'For where? The boat go tomorrow.'

'I wondered,' I said hesitantly, owning up to an idea that I'd been toying with since the day before, 'if perhaps we could spend the night at the village we stopped at yesterday. Uncle Six seemed to know people there, and maybe—'

Dag instantly perked up.

'Brilliant, Maria,' he said.

But Binh's mood plummeted.

'The people here hate the foreigner,' he said glumly. 'Later we go fishing village near Nha Trang, my uncle live there, he big Communist, no problem.'

I waited while he lit a cigarette.

'Uncle Six is a big man in that village,' I cajoled. 'Let's ask him.'

And Uncle Six, of course, was delighted.

By noon we were back in Xa Duong To village, and relaxing under the shade of a veranda. A hundred yards away, surf pounded onto the beach. There was too much wind for fishing that day, so the blue and green wooden boats were hauled up on the sand and tied to the bases of coconut palms. Wicker coracles lay next to them. Cows strolled along the road, the oblong bells around their necks making hollow clunking sounds. Once in a while, a bicycle went by, or scooter puttered past, but otherwise there was no traffic. We had been welcomed into the house of the village leader, Nguyen Van Minh, a handsome man with a strong profile and a placid nature. His wife Cuc brought us fresh coconuts to drink from, and plates of dried squid that we dipped into *nuoc mam*. Close by, two pot-bellied pigs snuffled about, their tails furiously waggling, and the family's youngest child, four-year-old Duc, had settled by my feet and was playing with a cartridge of spent bullets.

'These from Russian gun,' said Binh, when I bent down to examine them. 'Minh have Kalashnikov and M16s.'

A staunch Communist party member, Minh had recently retired from the army. He was the youngest and the only survivor of five brothers, all of whom had been soldiers. Two of his brothers had died in the American War, and two more during battles in Cambodia. In 1975, the forces of Pol Pot had begun incursions over the border into Vietnam. These incursions resulted in the deaths of 30,000 civilians, and the flight of many more. Three years later, Vietnam invaded Cambodia, ousted Pol Pot and the Khmer Rouge and installed a new government. Backed by China, the Khmer Rouge rearmed and rebuilt its army from Thailand. A ten-year war ensued, during which 80,000 Vietnamese troops were killed or wounded.

'He join the army when he fifteen,' Binh translated. 'He small, his rifle the same size as him! And he saw the terrible things. He tell me, in 1975 the Khmer Rouge came to Phu Quoc looking for Lon Nol. They no find him, they very angry. They go to Tho Chu Island, near here. They kill six hundred Vietnamese. He say they rip up the babies, they put the bamboo stake through the mothers. Six hundred people!'

Despite Minh's political leanings, he chatted amicably with Binh and was obviously devoted to Uncle Six.

'In the war, Uncle Six was South Vietnamese Army military

policeman here in this village and Minh was Viet Cong, hiding in the mountains,' explained Binh. 'They were enemies. But you know, we are all from the south, and men of the same blood. Now we can be friends.'

Minh showed off his bullet wounds – a huge scar across his stomach, and a nick in his skull. Then he brought out his medals, pinned them on his shirt and posed with Uncle Six for Dag's camera.

When we expressed a wish to go swimming, Minh and Cuc became very concerned. 'They say the water have bad spirits,' Binh warned us.

These *Ma Da*, they said, were the wandering ghosts of people who had drowned, ghosts that could not find peace until they found another victim to replace them in the afterlife. Sometimes they appeared as a mist on the water, but most often they lurked beneath its surface, waiting to yank people down. Children were believed to be most at risk from *Ma Da*, and, like Minh and Cuc's offspring, they often wore bracelets or necklaces to repel the spirits.

'Does Minh believe this, even though he's a Communist?' I asked.

'He believe very much,' Binh assured me.

A crowd of children followed us down to the beach, but nothing could persuade them to join us in the water. In the family's small thatch outhouse I'd changed into a swimsuit and covered myself in a long length of cotton which covered me from shoulder to knee. At the water's edge I dropped this wrap; letting out earsplitting shrieks of terror, the children fled, as if they'd come face to face with a *Ma Da*.

'Minh invite us to sleep here,' said Binh, over a lunch of omelette, squash and rice. 'What do you think?'

We told him we were delighted. He collected our passports, squashed onto a scooter with Uncle Six and Minh, and set off for the police station to seek permission for our overnight stay.

With the men out of the way, Cuc and her five children crowded around us for an impromptu language lesson. They pored over our phrase book, taking turns to read out the Vietnamese and try the English. We practised what we'd learned, and my rendition of one to ten in Vietnamese brought howls of friendly laughter. Then Cuc proudly showed me around her home. Like all the other village houses, it had three rooms and large verandas in front and back. One room ran the width of the house, and contained a bed base and a glass-fronted wardrobe. Behind it was a small, dark bedroom and a large kitchen well equipped with two charcoal burners, a food cupboard with slatted doors and pots and woks hanging from a low beam. I squatted next to Cuc as she carefully sorted through rice grains in search of stones and bugs. Little Duc joined us, rummaged in his pocket and presented me with a dusty, half-chewed piece of dried squid. Then he jumped off the veranda and chased a pot-bellied pig around the garden. Watching him, I crossed my fingers that we'd be allowed to stay in this delightful place for the night. Within half an hour, the men had returned, with a live chicken for dinner and the news that my wish had been granted.

The afternoon slid lazily by. While the men sat drinking rice wine on the veranda, I lay on the bed base in the main room, cooled by sea breezes, catching up on my notes. Twelve-year-old Hanh sprawled at my feet, chewing dried fish and reciting from our phrase book while, in the garden, Duc and his six-year-old brother Hien played with the cartridge of bullets. When Cuc and her eldest daughter Hong began preparing the dinner, my offers of help were firmly rebuffed. The food was served on the veranda, where I ate with the men while Cuc and her children retreated to the kitchen. Nothing I said would persuade them to join us and my attempts to sit with them only caused confusion. Binh was of no help in these interactions, as he was busy translating Minh's explanation of the village economy.

'They grow pepper, send it to Iran and Iraq. Now there is a problem with the price, it go down. But the village still rich – look at the roofs – all tile!'

Since *doi moi*, he explained, the villagers had been more motivated to work hard in their pepper and rice fields.

'Before,' said Binh, 'they must give most of pepper and rice crop to government. First to Diem and other South Vietnamese presidents, then to Communists. Now they can keep it. Before, the people don't work so hard and Vietnam import the rice. Now they work, and since 1989 we are the big exporter, the third biggest in the world US, then Thailand, then Vietnam.'

While Binh was translating for Minh, Uncle Six was choosing what he considered the best pieces of chicken and placing them in my bowl. Parts of the stomach came first, then the heart and finally a foot. I poked these around with my chopsticks until, when Uncle Six wasn't looking, I could pass them to Dag.

All day, it had been utterly peaceful in the village: no traffic noise, no music, no videos, no karaoke. But, at seven o'clock, the village generator was turned on. Suddenly radios and ghetto blasters crackled into life and someone began crooning a Vietnamese cover version of 'Yesterday'.

After dinner we went for a walk along the sandy road. One of the homes had been converted into a little cinema, with rows of chairs set up in front of a video screen. I couldn't see over the heads of the audience, but from the speakers came the unmistakable 'Ahhh! Urggh! Crash! Uuuuuh!' sounds of a Kung Fu movie. And at the far end of the village, on a purpose-built and extra long veranda, were a couple of French-style billiard tables, legacies of French colonization. The men playing wore only shorts and a glaze of sweat, and as they walked around the tables they stepped over children who were curled up and sleeping on mats spread over the ground.

While Binh set about teaching Dag how to play, I decided to go back to the house. It was less than three minutes' walk away, and the village felt entirely safe, but Minh insisted on accompanying me. The place was quiet – Cuc and her children were all sleeping in the back room, and had left the hard bed base free for me and Dag, and hammocks set up for Uncle Six and Binh. Before he left me to return to the pool game, Minh showed me one of his automatic rifles and a cartridge of bullets, assuring me I'd be safe that night. The ocean breeze meant there was no need for a mosquito net, and I stretched out, relishing the feel of wind against my skin. I woke briefly as the men returned. The village generator had been turned off and the last sound I registered, as sleep pulled me back, was surf crashing on the shore.

Towards dawn, a wind started blowing hard from the ocean and howling around the house. Lightning fizzled across the sky, and shortly afterwards came a deafening crack of thunder. Beneath the veranda the pigs made distressed snuffling sounds, and Hien and Duc both began to wail. The rain, when it came, was a deluge. Minh and Cuc unrolled hand-sewn canvas blinds that covered the front of the veranda, but they were of little use. The wind billowed them into the room and drove the rain through the house. Through the cracks between the blinds I could see the palm trees on the beach thrashing about, and pond-sized puddles forming in the road.

Then it was over as suddenly as it began. While the older children calmed the younger ones, Cuc swept water out of the house, Minh rolled up the blinds and Uncle Six sat in his hammock, combing his hair and grinning broadly at me.

Just after eight o'clock, a bus rattled into the village. Uncle Six flagged it down and we quickly climbed aboard. Minh and his family stood in a line, waving to us until they shrank out of sight.

'What would have happened if we'd stayed another night there?' I asked Binh. 'Would there have been a problem?'

His answer gave me cause for thought. 'No problem for you,' he said. 'But maybe problem for the family.'

We had time only for the briefest farewells with Fan, Thuan and Uncle Six, before we boarded the small fish cargo boat that was to take us north east to Ha Tien. Binh sat in the wheelhouse with Tu, the skipper, while we stayed on deck among sacks of fish and rapidly melting ice, shaded by a straw mat. Tu had been endearingly tenacious about rigging this up for us as a shelter, wrestling for half an hour with a complicated system of ropes and bamboo poles. When it was finally in place, he beamed with pleasure and ushered me to it as if I was a princess stepping into her carriage. I certainly didn't look like a princess. With the wind behind us there was not even the faintest cooling breeze, and it was desperately hot and sticky. As we headed into the open ocean I lolled about beneath the shelter, my legs askew, my loose cotton pants pulled up around my knees, drifting in and out of a troubled sleep. Then Dag was shaking me, and I sat up to see some pretty wooded islets slipping by, and a harbour ahead.

'We're here already?' I asked, incredulous.

'We've been going four hours. It turns out Tu has no permit to carry foreigners. When we get to the police post we've got to hide.'

Feeling like a pair of fugitives, we hunkered down in the wheelhouse and peered through cracks in the planks at Tu and Binh presenting their papers. But the policemen only gave them a cursory look, barely glancing up from the board game they were immersed in.

Many of the boats in Ha Tien's harbour were from nearby Cambodia. They had brightly painted, ornately carved wheel houses and the women working on deck wore long scarves cleverly wound around their heads. Until 1708, Ha Tien had been part of Cambodia. It was then made a fiefdom of Vietnam to protect it from the marauding Thais, but their attacks continued throughout the eighteenth-century. In more recent times the area had suffered murderous attacks by the Khmer Rouge, and between 1975 and 1979 tens of thousands of people had to flee their homes.

'There was no one left,' said Binh, as we went ashore. 'Tomorrow I take you to a place where the people remember.'

Although we were the only foreigners in town, Ha Tien was a popular spot for Vietnamese tourists. All the hotels and guest houses were full except one, a particularly decrepit place.

'I know how to find romantic spots for my wife,' joked Dag, as we surveyed our room, with its two lumpy beds, grime-smeared walls and a floor covered with grit and dust balls.

At the far end of the corridor outside was a large metal tank filled with cloudy water. Ten people stood in a queue, each with a jug of water they'd collected from the tank, waiting patiently for their turn inside one of two bathing cubicles. I joined them, feeling increasingly queasy as I listened to noses and throats being cleared inside the cubicles. When my turn came, I found things were even worse than I'd expected. There was green slime on the walls and black mould on the wooden door, and the drainage system was so poor that I was standing in the dirty water of the last occupant. After a rapid and ineffective wash I emerged looking like a wraith, with tousled hair and a badly crumpled dress. At the same time a girl stepped out of the adjoining cubicle. Her long hair was wet but immaculately combed, her skin looked polished, and her clothes were smooth and unwrinkled. She set off down the corridor, posture perfect, while I slopped behind her, pondering over the mysterious ability of this girl, and others before her, to emerge so well turned out from such dire conditions.

From Ha Tien we had hoped to find a boat that was heading around the coast of the Mekong Delta and up to Vung Tau. Such a boat, we soon discovered, did not exist. The fishermen we talked to through Binh said they ventured no more than twelve miles away from the harbour. Rach Gia, the nearest sizable port, was about sixty miles away. To get there would take us days, and involve changing boats several times. We were not helped much in our search by Binh, who quaked at the thought of more boat trips.

'Too many sea robber!' he insisted. 'No security! The fishermen ask too much money!'

After a morning of fruitless conversations down at the harbour, we gave in to Binh's suggestion that we should take a *xe Honda loi*, a six-seater trailer pulled by a scooter, to Duong Beach, twelve miles towards Rach Gia. There, he promised, we would find a fishing village, maybe a boat and also, he added with gleaming eyes, a comfortable hotel.

Finally, Binh found himself back in the role he relished – a tour guide, showing two foreigners the local sights.

'Take a look!' he cried, as the *xe Honda loi* rattled south out of town along a bumpy, rutted road.

Ahead, popping straight up from the paddy fields, were sheer limestone hillocks.

'Get out!' commanded Binh as we arrived at the foot of one of these mini-mountains. 'Take a look!'

At its foot was a statue of two clenched fists. Binh translated the simple inscription below it: 'In this village Pol Pot killed one hundred and thirty people, March 14, 1978.'

Scores of Vietnamese tourists were posing for photos by the statue before heading up the steep path towards Thach Dong Pagoda.

'Come on!' cried Binh.

We followed him through a series of caves connected by roughly hewn rock steps. The wind blew through them, making an eerie whistling sound, and carrying with it the scent of the hundreds of burning joss sticks stuck into crevices. In one cave a monk sat at the feet of a statue of *Quan The Am Bo That*, touting his wares. He had tapes of himself chanting, photographs of a revered five-legged dog and, incongruously, packs of Christmas cards showing red-cheeked children building a snowman.

As we carried on, the red dirt road became riddled with huge potholes, and several times we had to get out and help push the *xe Honda loi* through the mud. More limestone outcrops appeared, improbably steep and rising from the paddy fields like islands from a calm sea. Some of them were being mined to provide raw materials for the cement factory we passed. Smoke belched from its chimneys and electricity pylons marched towards it across the fields. We went through a couple of dingy towns and some raggle-taggle villages where people stared sullenly at us from their houses. I began to wonder where Binh was taking us, but then the ocean came into view and the *xe Honda loi* pulled off the road and into a compound with dusty flower beds and two wooden chalet-style buildings.

Apart from a pig which lay sleeping on its veranda, we were the only guests at the Hon Trem Guest House. It was a pleasant place, with clean, breezy, wood-lined rooms facing the beach, and I went straight in for a swim. The water was muddy, and very warm. A sampan was being rowed towards the shore, and crowded into it were seven fisherfolk, including four teenagers. Trailing behind it, buoyed by wooden floats, was a long green net. One man anchored the sampan with a stake driven into the sand and two women, their heads wrapped in cloth, slipped into the water and began pulling in the net. I went to help, and was probably more of a hindrance than anything else, but they smiled kindly at me. It took half an

hour of hard work to bring in the net, and the catch was pitiful – a small basketful of fish, the biggest only six inches long,
a tiny ray that the women gave to the youngest child to play
with, and a few translucent shrimp.

These people were from Binh An village, which straggled
along the road between the guest house and Duong Beach. It
was a poor place, dry and dusty and severely lacking in shade.
Washing was spread over cacti. Women sat on verandas mending nets, and pigs and their piglets wandered past them, in and
out of the open-fronted houses. A *nuoc mam* seller cycled past
us, with two buckets of the brown liquid sloshing about in a
crate on the back of his bike. Young men crooned karaoke
songs inside a thatch-walled café. The adults avoided our gaze,
but children ran from their gardens and trailed along behind us
yelling '*Lien Xo!*' Russians!

Beyond the village were more limestone outcrops. Some
rose from the bay, and inside one of them, towering up from
the land and blocking our view of the beach, was *Hai Son Tu*,
or the Sea Mountain Temple. Parked on the path to the temple were several rather battered buses, stuffed with luggage. A
man was sleeping in a hammock strung between two of them,
and people were stretched out on mats beneath the chassis.
These were tourists from Saigon, on week-long, budget trips to
famous Buddhist shrines around the delta. We followed a party
of them towards the temple, running the gauntlet of vendors
selling partly incubated duck eggs, heaps of black pepper
kernels and Ha Tien coconuts with hearts of sweet jelly.

Leaving the harsh sunlight, we stepped into a dim and dusty
shrine built onto the back of the cave, where shaven-headed
bonzes pottered about, setting down offerings at altars to several
different manifestations of Buddha. Linking this chamber to
the Sea Mountain Temple was a natural passageway, about
thirty paces long, with a ceiling that dipped low and let in a few
shafts of light through narrow cracks. As we shuffled along it,
feeling our way with our hands on the uneven walls, bats flitted
past my head, and I could hear water dripping, gongs resonating and the hum of prayers. The passage twisted, there was a
glow of light ahead and suddenly a lofty cave opened up before
us. Candlelight flickered in wall niches, and multi-coloured

neon halos glowed around the heads of several large and impressive Buddhas. Pilgrims were prostrating themselves before the statues, lighting incense sticks, dropping money into offertory boxes and tapping on brass gongs.

'Where you from?' a man asked Dag.

Our answer was passed around in echoing whispers: 'Can-a-DA . . . Eng-LAND.'

While Dag set up his tripod to take a photograph, I sat at the base of A Di Da, the Buddha of the Past. Promptly, eight people settled on the ground in front of me in two rows, observing me as if I was about to perform some trick. Behind the statues, and along all the walls of the cave, people lay sleeping with their belongings and their food gathered around them.

'No wonder the hotel's empty of tourists,' said Dag. 'They're all here.'

Another much longer tunnel led out from the far side of the cave to the beach. Small boys with flashlights grasped our arms and guided us along it. Fumbling for our sunglasses, we stepped out into dazzling sunlight at its far end where we stood on the warm sand, gaping in astonishment.

On the narrow strip of sand between the limestone cliff and the sea was a full-blown Vietnamese beach resort. Canvas deck chairs were arranged in rows under striped umbrellas. Thatch changing huts stood next to palm trees and thickets of bamboo. Children with buckets and spades, like the ones we'd seen being loaded off Kiep's boat in Long Xuyen, built sand castles. Old ladies in black pyjamas and conical hats stood waist deep in the sea, while young women wearing smart dresses and wide-brimmed straw hats posed for their husbands' cameras. Pop music crackled from speakers as Coca Cola signs swung in the breeze. There was ice cream for sale and inflated inner tubes for hire.

'It's like Blackpool,' I said.

'No donkeys,' muttered Dag.

I decided we should at least try an ice cream. I called to a boy pushing a wheeled cooler box along the sand, who took out a long tube of grey, frozen water and used a rusty knife to cut it into two pieces. He pushed a tooth pick into each of these and handed them over. Instantly they began to melt. I licked mine, and decided it might send me to bed for several days.

'It's only alginate and fruit,' said Dag. 'It can't hurt you.' But after only one taste, he flung the lolly over his shoulder.

Binh found us sitting in deck chairs, drinking beer and hoping to flush out the effects of the ice cream.

'Tomorrow we go with tourist bus to Saigon,' he announced.

'What about a boat?' I asked wearily.

'The people here are Cambodian. They don't speak Vietnamese. They are afraid.'

To prove his point, on our way back to the guest house he stopped at a couple of village houses where men were mending nets. Some of them looked at him uncomprehendingly as he spoke. Others simply shrank away into the shadows. We didn't have the energy to cajole Binh into looking further afield, and by seven next morning we were in a village café, waiting for a bus.

The roof of the café was supported by a live palm tree, and a cigarette lighter hung by a long string from a cross beam. Clouds of flies buzzed around our heads, Muscovy ducks waddled in and out of the doorway and once a cow stuck its head through a window and mooed at us. Next to me, Dag hunched morosely over his glass of green tea and Binh was making valiant attempts to cheer him up.

'Dag, how long you say this is?' he asked, pulling out the mole hair on his neck to its full length.

'Haven't got a clue,' answered Dag grumpily.

'Four inches, Dag! Confucius have hair like this, it very lucky!'

By eight forty-five there was still no sign of the bus. Binh went off to investigate, promising to return soon. An hour later, he hurried back into the café.

'Come on! Come on!'

The tour bus that came rattling up the road was full to the seams with a convivial bunch of people. To make room for us on the back seat, women cheerfully sat on each others' laps and consigned their children to the floor. Everyone was neat and tidy, with freshly washed hair and clean clothes, a remarkable feat considering they had spent the last few nights on the bus or on temple floors. We'd not gone far when, from the front of the bus, a plump young woman started clambering over bodies and luggage, pushing her way towards us. She was unconventionally dressed in bright pink satin leggings and a short black dress, and her raunchy comments set everyone laughing and turning their heads towards us.

'Dag, she say she want to be your number two wife!' chortled Binh.

Playing to the crowd, she plopped herself on Dag's knees and began stroking his beard and hair. The hooting and cackling reached a crescendo when she bent forward to fondle his knees and calves.

'She weighs a ton!' Dag told Binh. 'Can you get her off me?'

But Binh was too helpless with laughter to speak. Finally he managed to croak, 'Maria, she say, if you want the son, she make one for you!'

For hour after hour we rattled through dingy towns and past endless paddy fields. The road was rutted and bumpy, and on the back seat we were constantly thrown about.

'I'm beginning to wish that woman had stayed on my lap,' groaned Dag after one particularly brutal bashing. 'At least she would have anchored me to the seat.'

Halfway to Long Xuyen, there was a toilet stop. The men went to one side of the road and the women to the other. An old lady in blue silk pyjamas took me by the hand and led me into a banana grove with a stream of dark brown water running through it. It was a peaceful and pretty scene: amid the wide green leaves and the drooping purple pods, brightly clothed women squatted down, their faces covered by their straw, conical hats.

The rain fell in sheets during the evening. When we finally reached Saigon I clambered down from the bus and stepped up to my ankles into warm water. As we sloshed through this huge puddle, men draped in plastic, hooded capes descended upon us.

'Sir, madam, cyclo, cyclo! Where you want to go?'

Dodging them, we found a taxi. It was a tiny 1954 2CV. The roof was so low that even the Vietnamese driver had to hunch to see out of the windscreen, which was greasy and had only one, ineffectual wiper. During the six miles into the city centre, he swerved this way and that to avoid the dark-caped figures on unlit bikes and scooters that loomed up ahead. Somehow he managed to get us to Guest House 72 without killing anyone. Arranging to meet Binh in two days' time, we paid for the taxi as far as his house, then stood waving as the car drove off through puddles, drenching the people on the pavement.

It seemed that, in just two weeks, Saigon had changed. More tourists had arrived, more private hotels had opened around Pham Ngu Lao Street and, on the terrace bars of the city's top hotels, more foreign businessmen were sitting around tables discussing joint ventures and import regulations. The businessmen were from Malaysia, Taiwan, Japan, Hong Kong, Europe, America and Australia. Some of them seemed implausibly young. All of them had come to take advantage of Vietnam's brand new opportunities: cheap labour and raw materials. In their wake were eager young graduates, ready to work hard for the newly established companies, and hoping to make lots of money fast.

One of these was Phil Worthington, the man we had met in the Bat Trang pagoda. We went to visit him where he lived, in the city's university quarter. His directions led us down a narrow alley that took several sharp turns and had a confusing house numbering system. There was no chance of getting lost as everyone along the way presumed where we were going and pointed us in the right direction.

'We're the only foreigners living down here,' Phil confirmed, when we found him. 'We have to keep the curtains drawn all day, because otherwise there's always a row of faces staring in at the window.'

In his front room, the familiar strains of a Manchester rock band played from a ghetto blaster, two jars of snake wine were arranged on a sideboard between empty bottles of Gordons Gin and Bells Whisky, and papers waiting to be marked were spread over the table.

'I've just lost a parrot,' he told us. 'I bought it yesterday from an old guy who was selling them in cages off the back of this bike. When I got up this morning, it was gone.'

He lifted up a bamboo cage with an escape hole chewed through the bars. Our eyes drifted to the vents in the wall above the door.

'The old guy said it couldn't fly much,' said Phil hopefully.

Phil was disgruntled with his university teaching job, which paid only five hundred dollars a month, and was hoping to switch to something more lucrative. He shared the house with another Englishman called Neil, a market researcher working for companies which wanted to set up businesses in Vietnam. Through Neil, Phil hoped to get a job with a Malaysian company selling aluminium door and window frames.

'They give you a video and some samples and off you go. There's no salary, but the commission is ten per cent. And they say it's easy to get contracts worth sixty thousand dollars!'

From the corner of my eye I saw something small and green on the floor in the kitchen doorway. 'Look—'

'Parrot!' we chorused, sending the bird scurrying beneath the sideboard.

The three of us were on our hands and knees, trying to coax it out, when Neil arrived home.

'Shut the door!' cried Phil. 'The parrot has escaped!'

'I come home after a hard day at work and I'm yelled at because of a stupid parrot,' grumbled Neil, who was tall, slender and bearded, with blond hair flopping over his eyes. 'You'll never catch it,' he advised.

'Dag will,' Phil told him. 'He's a vet.'

The vet was lying full length on the floor, reaching beneath the sideboard.

'Got it – OUCH!' he cried, as the parrot sank its beak into his hand.

Quickly, he put it back inside its cage, and stuffed a towel into the escape hole. We all peered at it through the bars.

'Isn't it pretty?' cooed Phil.

'It looks pretty pissed off to me,' commented Neil. 'How do you make a parrot happy?'

'Give it freedom and a female parrot,' advised the vet.

'I know just how it feels,' said Neil. 'My girlfriend's gone to Hanoi and I've been cooped up in an office all day.'

Like Phil, he had first taught in Saigon, then learned to speak Vietnamese and branched out into the business world.

'Today I might as well have been back in London. But most of the time it's great. I go around finding out what kind of books Vietnamese people want to read, what sort of beer they like, that sort of thing. I'm always meeting people and making good connections.'

His general enthusiasm and optimism spilled over into the conversation we had about our forthcoming journey up the coast.

'There must be a way. How about Cesais Tours? They're connected to the university, so if you say you're students and you want to do research on Vietnamese fishing boats and coastal life, maybe they'll arrange something.'

As we left, he offered us a warning. 'The problem is that no one has done what you're trying to do. The police will be freaked out by you; they're not allowed to harass foreigners any more, so they'll use the excuse of your "safety" to haul you in.'

Cesais stood for the Centre of Economic Studies and Applications. Its tour operator, Gian, was a delicately built young man wearing a crisp white shirt. His command of English was excellent, and he listened carefully to our story about being research students with an interest in fishermen.

'We can help you rent a boat,' he said, when we'd finished. 'Prices start at forty dollars an hour.'

From a folder he pulled out a sheaf of paper filled with information about Nha Trang and Halong Bay, Vietnam's prime tourist spots along the coast. There were photos of hotels, and of purpose-built boats with company logos on the prow.

'We want to travel on local boats,' I reiterated. 'Fishing boats.'

'You will be happy in our hotels,' said Gian. 'Then for five hours a day you can go out on our boats, see many beautiful places, learn much about our country. Some of these boats take twenty tourists, others take fifty. They are comfortable, and very safe.'

We returned the sheaf of papers, thanked him and left. All day, we heard the same story, from travel agents, tour guides, expatriates. By mid-afternoon Dag was thoroughly disgruntled. Refusing to go a step further, he sat down in a café around the corner from our guest house, and ordered a large bottle of beer. I, however, was still resolute. I flagged a cyclo, and headed for the port.

Beyond the high walls surrounding the port area I could see the prows of huge container ships. Most of them had Russian names. They weren't exactly what I'd had in mind, but by now I was obsessed with the idea of just getting back on a boat, *any* boat. But the first problem was to find a way into the port. The gates were heavily guarded by men in brown uniforms. Deciding on an audacious approach, I strode past them, bestowing confident smiles on all. They stared at me, dumbstruck, but when I'd gone about fifteen paces one raced up behind me.

'Police!' he cried, guiding me over to a low building.

At a desk, a policeman was sorting through a pile of Cuban passports. Although his English was on a level with my Vietnamese, I managed to communicate to him that I was a tourist, and that I wanted to travel on a ship up the coast of Vietnam. He picked up a phone, spoke for a couple of minutes, then indicated that I should sit down. Before long, another policeman came in.

'You author?' he barked.

'No!' I cried, flushing with guilt. 'I tourist!'

'Author! Author!' he repeated impatiently, pointing at me and then the ship.

'Tourist,' I told him firmly. 'No author!'

'Yes!' he said, nodding as if I'd finally given the right answer. 'No author, no go!'

The penny dropped.

'Authorization,' I said.

'Yes! No go!'

The first policeman, meanwhile, had hurried through the doors to hail down a man who was heading out of the port on

a scooter. This man spoke fluent English and quickly sorted
out the confusion. The ships, he told me, were all heading to
Russia. There may be a ship going up the coast to Haiphong in
a week or so, but it had no authorization to carry passengers.
To get this I would have to contact the shipping company, the
police, the immigration authorities . . . and even then, in his
opinion, I would have little chance of success.

'The problem is that on the ship there is no security for the
foreigner. Down the road there is Saigon Tourism. Maybe you
should ask in there?'

'Never mind, Maria,' said Dag, when I returned to the café.
'And anyway, there's no way you'd have got me to spend three
weeks on a Russian freighter.'

Since I'd left him in the café he'd been joined by Binh and
several empty beer bottles. 'Maria, what you think, tomorrow
we take luxury tourist bus to Nha Trang?' asked Binh. 'My
uncle have restaurant on the beach. He know many big
Communists. For sure he can help you take a boat.'

I looked questioningly at Dag, who shrugged.

'Maria, I go no more by boat!' pleaded Binh. 'Our delta tour
was terrible, so hard. Tomorrow we go by luxury tourist bus,
much better, you will see.'

Lots of cyclo drivers were gathering around the café, hoping
to get some custom when the foreigners began leaving. One
was carefully scanning the faces of people sitting at tables.
Recognizing him as the man who had taken me to the port, I
waved.

'Hello! Madam!' he shouted, dismounting his vehicle and
hurrying over to me. He handed me the cheap ball-point pen
I'd been using to write notes with on the way back from the
port, and had left on the seat.

'Madam, you go cyclo tomorrow?'

'Yes,' I told him. 'To the bus station.' Next to me, Binh
grinned with relief.

5

NIGHT BUS TO NHA TRANG

Binh's promised 'luxury tourist Bus' turned out to be neither luxurious, nor for tourists, at least not for foreign ones. The seats were narrow, hard and so tightly packed together that when the man in front of me reclined his seat, he was practically lying in my lap. A low wooden bench ran the length of the aisle. Even when the bench and all the seats were full, more passengers came aboard, and soon a knot of angry people had formed around the driver's seat.

'Some people give the ticket man extra money and he give too many tickets,' explained Binh, who was sitting across the aisle from us. 'I know this exactly, so I tell you to come early.'

'Will some people have to get off?'

'No. Everybody stay. Maybe the policeman stop the bus and the driver pay something and the policeman put the money in the pocket.'

Two hours after the appointed time, we finally left. As we crawled through Saigon's evening traffic, the driver began sounding his horn every twenty seconds or so, something he would continue to do for the next fourteen hours. On the outskirts of the city he picked up speed. The luggage racks began vibrating, threatening to debunk their load of assorted boxes and bags. Hanging from the racks, and swinging wildly with the motion of the bus, were bunches of guavas, bananas and coconuts, a parrot in a cage, and a man in a hammock who lay suspended right above Binh. In the seat behind Dag was a young mother with a fussy baby boy. Like most babies in Vietnam, this one had never seen a nappy. When the need arose, the mother simply stripped off his wet clothes, used them to mop up the mess and dressed him in a clean outfit. I was wondering if she had enough clean outfits to get us all through the night, when the baby flung a well-chewed lump of banana in my direction, and hit me smack in the ear. The young man sitting behind me leaned forward and tapped me on the shoulder.

'Madam, I am a student of Economics at the University of Qui Nhon,' he said. 'Please tell me, why are you travelling by bus? It is so dangerous.'

Halfway through my explanation, the mother began making dreadful gargling sounds. Leaping to his feet, the Economics student yelled to the driver, and plastic bags were passed over heads to the woman. By the time they arrived she had already been sick all over our bags, which we had squashed between our seat and the aisle bench. Leaning back with an expression of relief on her face, she began breast-feeding the baby. She may have felt better, but others obviously didn't, for soon there were retching, gurgling and whooshing noises all up and down the bus. Before long there was a constant flow of plastic bags: empty ones passed over heads and full ones chucked out of the windows. I noticed Binh glancing nervously at the man swinging in the hammock above his head.

After a few hours, we stopped at a small market at the side of the road. The inside of the bus seemed to heave as passengers began disentangling themselves from their seats, the bench, their luggage and each other, and making for the door. Several other buses were parked outside the market, and crowds of people were busily buying, selling, eating and begging. One of the stall holders gazed up at Dag.

'How old?' he asked me.

'Very old,' I told him.

'But *very* beautiful,' he said, marvelling at Dag's dishevelled hair and beard.

I went to find a toilet, which was inside a very smelly thatch hut. Other women, wiser than me, walked past it and squatted in the shadows at the side of the path. Close by were troughs filled with water, where people washed their faces, cleaned their teeth and scrubbed their feet. After rinsing my hands, I joined Binh and Dag in a café. Unable to face the thought of food, I sipped on some bottled water while they wolfed down rice, pork and bamboo shoots doused in *nuoc mam*. As we stood up to leave the table, two transvestites wearing *ao dai*, jewellery, wigs and make-up came racing through the café, squealing at men and pinching them on their way past. As suddenly as they'd appeared, they were gone, leaving in their wake a lot of chuckling, but no real surprise.

'What was all that about?' I asked Binh.

'They queer boys,' he replied, shrugging as if there was nothing else to say on the matter.

As we set off again the TV screen above the driver crackled into life, and a series of music videos came on. Doll-like dancers and singers pranced about the screen, performing dreadful cover versions of banal Western pop songs. Around me, people threw up at regular intervals, and the air in the bus became increasingly fetid. I struggled to open my window. Sprays of rain and mud came through it. When I tried to close it again, it jammed. Glumly, I worked out that it was going to take at least ten more hours to reach Nha Trang. In the cir-cumstances this seemed like an interminable stretch of time, and I decided that the best way to deal with it was to break it down into shorter and more bearable sections. I told myself that we'd already done the first section of the journey. It had been bad, but it could have been worse. There were three more to go, but once we'd got this next section behind us, I reasoned, the journey would be half over.

'My God, *only* half over?' Dag groaned when I told him this. 'In that case, let's change seats for a while, mine's really uncomfortable.'

I soon discovered what he meant. In the aisle seat I was hemmed in by our now foul-smelling luggage and a young man on the bench who insisted on using my shoulder as a pillow. Right behind me was the vomiting mother and her baby boy, who had taken to being sick himself. As the bus rattled off into the night, I consoled myself that things couldn't get any worse. Then, from right behind me, came a loud squirting sound.

'WAAAHHH!' cried the young man, leaping up and pulling a disgusted face at the brown mess all over his trouser leg.

'Baby have bad stomach,' explained Binh, as rags were produced and apologies made.

Sighing deeply, the man once again nestled against me. He smelt of baby shit, but I didn't have the heart to shrug him off. After a while, deciding to make the best of the situation, I shifted my position until I was comfortably curled around this total stranger, and began drifting in and out of sleep.

'Waaah! Waaah! Madam! Madam!'

I was jolted awake as the man sprang up once again. This time it was the young mother who had erupted, spraying whatever she had eaten in that market place all over him, the bench and our bags beneath it.

'Thank God we brought waterproof bags,' commented Dag.

'This man say he make a mistake, because today unlucky for travelling,' said Binh from across the aisle, as more mopping up was done. 'He come late and have to sit on the bench. Then he sit by this woman and her baby, and they put the piss, shit and sick all over him.'

The poor woman and her baby continued to do the same all through the night. By the time dawn was approaching, I'd begun to wonder if I'd died and been consigned to this form of hell for eternity. But then the light came, revealing splendid vistas of the coast: a sparkling ocean, distant headlands and green, softly contoured islands. At last, Binh instructed us to collect our bags and stand by the back door, ready to get off. It took a good five minutes to squirm our way up the aisle, making apologetic noises all the way for the foul state of our luggage. Then Binh banged on the side of the bus to signal the driver to stop, and we climbed down outside the Huong Bien Restaurant.

Flowering vines grew over woven bamboo walls and a red-tiled roof. Chicks and ducklings darted through a pretty rock and cactus garden. There were hammocks to lie in, and cooling sea breezes. A few steps away was a protected cove, its yellow sand scattered with smooth grey boulders, its blue waters still and inviting. Taking our waterproof bags with us, we waded straight in, letting the warm ocean wash away the rigours of the night.

Binh's Uncle Chap and Aunt Lan were a hearty couple in their late forties, who ran a restaurant from the veranda of their home. They seemed unperturbed by their nephew arriving unannounced with two tousled foreigners, and quickly worked out with Binh an arrangement for our stay. Binh could sleep in a small thatch outbuilding near the restaurant. We could camp for free in their garden, and they would bill us for all we ate and drank. The fact that camping was technically illegal in Vietnam seemed not to concern Binh or his relatives.

'No one see you from the road,' said Binh, 'and my uncle know some big Communists.'

We ate breakfast at a sturdy wooden table, scrutinized by the couple's three sons. These boys, aged ten to seventeen, were the youngest of five children. They were dumbstruck by the sight of Dag, and at first hid behind the thatch bathhouse, peeping out at him. But as the morning progressed they gradually plucked up courage, and by the time we stretched out in deck chairs under the vines for a much needed snooze, they had gathered by his feet, which they were examining in great detail.

Around noon, a purple, bell-shaped flower fell onto my face and woke me up. Next to me, the three boys were gathered around Dag. They were tugging at his beard, pulling his nose, stroking the hair on his chest, counting the moles on his arms and legs, and giving him 'massages' by pummelling his shoulders.

'It's been going on for an hour,' he patiently told me.

As no other customers arrived at the restaurant that day, for lunch Lan served us with all she'd cooked: shrimp rolled in rice paper with onion and fresh basil, crab, fried fish and, for dessert, slices of unripe mango dipped into fish sauce and sugar.

'Hey youse!' the three boys cried repeatedly to Dag, feeding him with choice tidbits and topping up his glass with beer. There was never a moment when at least one set of hands wasn't patting, stroking or pinching him.

'They love you,' Binh told him. 'They say you look like Mr Rambo.'

That afternoon we walked with Binh to the fishing village of Thon Tan Thanh, half a mile away. All along the beach were narrow bamboo and rattan boats, painted blue and yellow and decorated with oval eyes and Yin Yang signs. Their sails were furled around their masts – no one was out fishing that day, and most of the villagers seemed to be congregated in a market that was taking place along a sandy lane. At food stalls women were preparing rice flour pancakes, which they filled with shrimp, dipped in fish sauce and fried until brown. We bought some, and made appreciative noises about how good they tasted, but the women and everyone else in the market ignored us. It was hard to gauge whether people were shy or unfriendly, but Binh seemed to be profoundly ill at ease. When we nudged him into asking about boats, he did so most begrudgingly.

'They say no one here pay the taxes, so they cannot get the travel permit to go far,' he told us after speaking to a couple of men. 'If the police take a look and see the foreigner on the boat, the fishermen get a problem. The police worry what happen to the foreigner if the ship was sunk, so they make the boat driver pay the money, and the foreigner have to get inland right away.'

'You said Chap had friends in the Communist party,' I reminded Binh as we walked back. 'Could he write a letter that we could show to the police?'

'For example,' continued Binh, as if he hadn't heard what I'd said, 'if you take a boat from company tourist in Nha Trang they take care for you everything. They go nine in the morning, take you to place to swim and buy fish from the fishermen, cook the food on the boat, come back at four o'clock. It very nice tour.'

Things were busy at the restaurant. Chap was feeding his chickens and ducks with a mixture of rice and green vegetables. Lan was hauling a block of ice from her 'refrigerator', a pit filled with rice husks and covered with sacking and a sheet of corrugated iron. The couple's two daughters were preparing the evening meal in a mud-floored kitchen, while their sons sat around a table, doing homework. Although it was the school holidays, Binh told us, their parents made them read and write every day.

'Hey youse!' the boys chorused when they saw Dag, scrambling from their seats and dashing towards him. He was saved by Lan, who shooed them back to the table.

As the day drew to a close, Chap began lighting the oil lamps that hung above the restaurant tables. Electricity lines ran along the road, less than ninety feet away, but the cost of connection was prohibitive. The family was saving hard to pay for it, and Chap was very apologetic that we were not able to sing karaoke during our stay, but promised that we could if we returned in a year's time.

We dined splendidly, on fried bean curd cake, roast pork, sticky rice and green papaya grated finely and mixed with green beans, lime juice and salt. The soft glow of the lamps attracted hundreds of large flying ants which whirred against the glass then fell to the floor and dizzily crawled around. The cat trapped them under her paw, but the dog was more interested in the frogs that were hopping in from the garden.

'*Con Coc! Con Coc*!' the boys yelled. 'Uncle Frog!'

As Lan went to and fro from the kitchen she carefully stepped round the frogs so as not to hurt any of them.

'My aunt believe the frog is uncle of Rain God,' Binh told us. 'She say when the frog croak, rain come.'

Despite a good bit of croaking, there wasn't a drop of rain that night. After everyone had gone to bed, Dag and I had a swim, then found a smooth boulder to lean against. We sat in companionable silence, watching fishermen from the nearby village row out in sampans and set their shrimp nets. Each net was marked by a ring of floating oil lamps, which formed necklaces of light on the water. Further out in the bay were the lights of police patrol boats, close to a restricted island where highly valued swallows' nests were collected.

'What shall we do if Binh can't arrange a boat for us from here?' I asked Dag.

He was silent for a while. 'Well, there's an airport in Nha Trang—' he said.

I began to protest.

'Okay,' he said soothingly. 'If you like, we could do the eight hundred miles to Hanoi on one of those lovely buses.'

It was my turn to be silent. By now I'd realized that we wouldn't be able to get all the way up the coast by boat. There were too many restrictions, not just on us, but on the people who owned boats and who lived along the water. So what was there left to do? How else did local people travel? By bus, I thought, and by scooter, and of course by . . .

'Bicycles!' I cried.

'Huh?'

'Let's buy a couple of bikes!'

'Bikes?' Dag repeated incredulously.

'When we get rides on boats, we'll take the bikes with us. And when we can't, then we'll just pedal on to the next fishing village.'

'Maria,' said Dag slowly. 'When were you last on a bike? I mean, *really* on a bike, for any considerable distance?'

I thought for a minute. 'I had my own bike when I was twelve. I used to go off on it for day trips.'

'That was thirty years ago.'

'So?'

'Coffey,' he said slowly. 'You are losing your mind.'

After two hours in a Nha Trang bike shop, I was beginning to think he was right. When we first got there Dag had examined a couple of ominously racy models, the like of which I'd yet to see on the roads of Vietnam.

'We're supposed to be travelling like local people,' I said, 'so we should buy the sort of bikes they use.'

Binh and Dag looked at me with pitying expressions.

'These are the best bike but the new model,' Binh told Dag, 'so the people have no parts to repair them.'

'I have a feeling we might need a few repairs,' said Dag.

He started looking through the other bikes in the shop. These were of the 'sit up and beg' design and bore a strong resemblance to the one I had when I was twelve.

Maria boarding Kiep's
boat in Cholon.

Alfresco supper afloat in the Mekong Delta.
From left: Kiep, Khue, Chi, Em, Di (on the tiller),
Maria, Sang (standing) and Binh.

A monk in the
Bat Pagoda, Soc Trang.

Dawn on Cantho's waterfron
in the heart of the Mekong Delt

Market in Cay Dua,
Phu Quoc Island.

Maria in a village bathhouse
on Phu Quoc Island.

Enemies during the American War, now friends.
From left: Binh, Minh and Uncle Six in Xa Duong Village.

A fishing boa
Xa Duong Village, Phu Quo

arly morning fisherman,
ear Nha Trang.

Bamboo fishing boats
in Thon Tan Village, near Nha Trang.

Maria and Lan watch the bikes being loaded on to
Toan's boat, outside the Huong Binh Restaurant.

Toan takes the bikes ashore
coracle on the Dam Mon Peninsu

The beach near Vinh Yen Village
on the Dam Mon Peninsula.

Leaving Vinh Yen Village.

Rest stop at a drinks stand on Highway One, north of Dai Lanh.

Maria, after cycling
to the top of the
Ngang Pass.

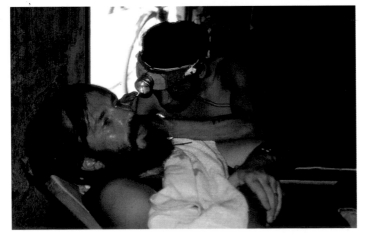

Dag having his ears
cleaned in Hoi An.

'I can't handle lots of gears,' I warned him.

He gave me another pitying look.

'You should be so lucky,' he said. 'None of these have any.'

After much discussion, he and Binh finally selected two Chinese-made 'Forever' bikes. Mine was purple, and had a black wire basket on the front, a narrow luggage rack on the back, and a shiny new bell.

'Try it out,' said Dag.

'Do I have to?'

'Maria,' he said patiently. 'As you're considering pedalling this thing for eight hundred miles, I think you should at least test it first.'

I wheeled it out onto the road, climbed on and began pedalling it in a wobbly fashion. Though I tried to hug the kerb, the traffic seemed to suck me in, and within seconds I was part of a mass of other bikes, scooters and cyclos. Three hundred feet from the shop there was a busy crossroad. As I approached it, I pulled on both of the brake levers, which were tucked under the handlebars. The bike continued to move. I pulled even harder, and although I slowed down, the wheels beneath me continued to roll. Briefly, I registered that none of the drivers around me had changed their speed or showed any sign of giving way to the vehicles heading towards us from left and right. Everyone was simply weaving their way around everyone else. Instinctively, I knew that the safest thing to do was follow suit, but my nerve failed. Putting one foot on the ground, I stopped dead. Instantly, organized chaos turned into mayhem. The weaving became frantic swerving and dodging, there was a series of near-collisions, bells rang tumultuously. The people whizzing past threw me puzzled glances, but no one shouted or cursed – except for Dag, who was testing his bike behind me.

'Get out of the way!' he yelled.

I did. I wheeled the bike to the pavement and pushed it back to the shop.

'You nearly caused a pile up!' cried Dag, when he arrived.

'*I* didn't!' I retorted. 'It was the brakes – they failed!'

I insisted we find bikes with more reliable brakes. For an hour we vainly worked our way through almost every bicycle in the shop.

'The owner he say you are the difficult customer,' Binh told me.

'Is it too much to ask for a bike with brakes?' I countered.

'All Vietnamese bikes are same,' he said patiently. 'So everybody learn to drive like this –' and he waggled his arms about in a good imitation of the weaving and dodging I'd seen on the crossroad.

Resignedly, I agreed to the purchase of two 'Forever' bikes. The Vietnamese price for each of these was, according to Binh, about forty dollars. The owner of the shop wanted to charge us a hundred. It took some hard bargaining to bring him down to seventy-five dollars for each bike, including wire baskets, bells and a pump. Finally we were all happy. The money was exchanged, the bicycles were handed over and we wheeled them to Binh's favourite restaurant for a celebratory drink.

'All my foreign friend like this place!' Binh claimed.

In the middle of the restaurant, men were standing on scaffolding, hammering at the ceiling and sending dust and plaster chips flying in all directions. We ordered a mid-morning snack of spring rolls, which were so horrible even the emaciated cat mewing round our feet rejected them. But from where we sat we could see the full sweep of Nha Trang's famous crescent beach: sparkling white sand and emerald, clear water which was being churned into white capped waves by a stiff onshore wind. This natural beauty was somewhat marred by several rows of beach umbrellas, and the young foreign tourists who were sprawled on loungers beneath them. Happily, Binh sat drinking beer and surveying the women, most of whom were blonde, beefy and wearing very little.

'They look like this because they eat the cheese and the milk,' he informed us. 'Vietnamese women are skinny because they eat only rice and fish.'

Local women, covered up in pants, long-sleeved blouses and conical hats, were circulating the tourists, collecting money for rental of the loungers and umbrellas, selling fruit and cakes from baskets attached to their shoulder poles, or delivering drinks and food from the restaurants lining the beach. One came over to our table, and presented us with colour snapshots

showing her massaging foreigners on the beach. She was kneel-
ing on their backs and pummelling their sun-reddened
shoulders. Her clients looked far from comfortable.

'I give you massage, madam? Only five dollar!'

'I don't think so.'

'You have hair!' she cried, peering down at my legs. 'In ten
minutes, I pull it out!'

'How?'

'Like this!'

From her pocket she produced a reel of cotton. Breaking off
a long piece, she put one end in her mouth, and wrapped the
other end around her fingers in a complicated cat's cradle.
This she ran along my arm at high speed, plucking out
individual hairs and bringing tears to my eyes.

'The barber do like this on my neck,' offered Binh. 'It very
painful.'

'Manicure, madam!' she persisted. 'Your nails not nice, I
make them beautiful, only ten minutes!'

I may have been tempted, but there was something else I
wanted to do before we left Nha Trang. During my research for
our trip I'd come across the translation of a paper written in
1945 by Gustave Langrand, about a village on the coast of
Annam, as Central Vietnam was named by the French. It was
described as being just south of Nha Trang, located at a river
mouth and protected from storms by nearby islands. Its official
name was Thuong Dong, or Western Village, and the popular
name was Cua Be, or Little Port. The article gave precise
details of the village, including a description of a temple to the
whale god, *Ong Nam Hai*, in the village *dinh*, or communal
house. I was eager to see how the village had fared over the past
five decades, and to find out if the temple was still there. Since
reunification of North and South Vietnam, however, most of
the country's place names had been changed, and I was unable
to find Thuong Dong, or Cue Be, on any map. But Binh's
uncle was convinced it had to be Vinh Truong, which was now
on the outskirts of Nha Trang. When Binh had finished his
beer, we asked the owners of the restaurant to look after our
new bikes, and set off in a *xe Honda loi* to find the village.

The road hugged the beach, passing a cluster of tourist bungalows, which Binh craned his neck to scrutinize, and then the small airport, which Dag looked at longingly. After a few miles we turned onto a dusty track. All along it, houses were under construction. Piles of iron girders were heaped up at the building sites, and bricks and bags of cement were being delivered in bullock carts. Beyond them were newly completed houses, tall and skinny, and freshly painted in ochre, blue and yellow. It was only when we reached the centre of the settlement that I began to recognize it as the place described by Langrand.

We clambered down from the *xe Honda loi* outside a house with stone colonnades, ornately carved wooden pillars and a tiled roof overgrown by lichen, the type of house Langrand recorded as having belonged to a merchant or head fisherman. In its front room, which was open to the street, a wooden screen was set up in front of the ancestral altar. This, according to Langrand, was to confuse the evil spirits which the Vietnamese believe always travel in straight lines. I asked the owner of the house, who looked as old as the building, if this was true. He said it was, and asked why I was interested in such things. When Binh explained he smiled, and said he remembered the foreigner who used to come to their village so long ago, when France still ruled the country. And he said the *dinh* was still where Langrand had described it, beyond the market, at the base of a cliff covered with trees.

Peeking above the canopied market stalls were two dragons, yellow and red, facing each other with snarls and curling tails, and standing on a pair of tigers. The early Vietnamese believed they were descended from a dragon king, who mated with the queen of the fairies to produce a hundred sons, one of whom became their first leader. Thus dragons were seen as lucky and protective, like these two, who stood above the gate of the *dinh*, the old religious and civil centre of Cua Be. These days, village *dinhs* are small, concrete shrines, where offerings are left to the guardian spirits of the village. But in former times they were large buildings, incorporating meeting halls and temples, and where the original deeds of the settlement were stored.

Cua Be's once impressive *dinh* now had an air of abandonment. Its courtyards were strewn with litter and its wooden doors and pillars, with their carvings of fish and dragons and sun motifs, were worm eaten. We found the custodian lying in a hammock. He yawned, swung his legs to the ground, slipped his feet into plastic sandals and shuffled over to meet us. Binh introduced us as students of Vietnamese religions, and asked if we could see the various altars around the courtyard. The custodian, though sleepy, was most obliging. He unlocked doors, switched on lights and swept aside cobwebs. In the first room he opened up there was an altar to the goddesses of metal, wood, water, fire and earth. Their statues were encased in glass, and each wore an embroidered robe adorned with pearls and gold nuggets. In the next room was the altar of Than Hoang, the guardian spirit of the village. High above it, in the rafters, was a box where records dating back to the thirteenth century were kept. But the custodian kept the best door until the end. It led to a fairly ordinary-looking altar, heaped with the usual gaudy decorations and offerings and surrounded by dusty fairy lights. Behind it were stacks of red wooden boxes. The largest one was about nine feet long, four feet wide and three feet high.

'*Ong Nam Hai*,' said the custodian, lifting its corrugated-iron lid.

Inside the box were the bones of a whale. Ribs that, standing on one end, would reach above Dag's head. Vertebrae as big around as his waist. A jumble of dusty bones, the remains of a huge whale that washed up near here fifty years ago. And in the other boxes, the remains of nineteen smaller whales.

Although nowadays only rorquals are seen off Vietnam, and rarely at that, the whale is revered all along the coast. People call it *Ong Nam Hai*, Lord Fish, or *Ca Ong*, Master Fish, because they believe that by speaking its real name they risk summoning up its power. It is believed to rule the sea, to rescue boats in peril or, if the sailors are in the whale's bad graces, to capsize them. The Cham civilization, which appeared in Vietnam around the second century, is said to have developed the cult of the whales, and various myths give it authority. The most popular one recounts that in 1792 the future Emperor Gia Long was shipwrecked while on his way to Phu Quoc. Whales carried him and his junk safely to shore and once on the throne he ordered that temples be constructed in their honour. For many years, whenever a dead whale was found along the coast the government would donate red silk for the burial ceremonies.

'This man,' Binh told us, 'he say that in the seas, when the storm come the fishermen on the boat shout out to the whale and the whale appear and help the boat. Sometime a whale die near here, and they believe a god come and they bury him respectfully. Then when he is just the bones, they take him out the earth and put him into the box and take him to the temple. Every year they have the three-day party, take the bones in a boat.'

The custodian showed us water-stained photos of red boxes aboard sampans with fringed canopies and elaborate decorations.

'I've read about this,' I said, paging through the notes I'd taken from Langrand.

The *dinh* may have been crumbling away, but it was exactly as he described. As we left, I asked Binh how much I should leave as a donation. He looked around the place, as if assessing what would be needed for its restoration.

'Give him the money for cigarettes,' he suggested.

As I was too tired for an inaugural bike ride back to the restaurant, we and the bikes were ferried back there in a tiny bus that resembled a cupboard on wheels. Over dinner we continued the discussion about boats, a subject that by now everyone seemed thoroughly fed up with. Spreading our maps over one of the tables, we showed Binh, Lan and Chap what we'd like to do. Forty miles to the north was a peninsula attached to the mainland by a sand causeway. According to the map it had a couple of villages and a small road that ran along the causeway for twelve miles and linked up with Highway One. Our idea was to get a boat to the village of Dam Mon at the tip of the peninsula. From there we'd look for another boat, and if that didn't work out we'd simply cycle up to the highway.

Lan and Chap seemed to approve of this plan, and promised to find us a boat that would take us to the peninsula. But not tomorrow, they said. Tomorrow was the official start of the monsoon season. It was a day when it was considered unlucky to work, when offerings were made to placate the spirits responsible for the cholera that used to be rife in the monsoon season, when taking a dip in the ocean would bring good luck for the rest of the year. And a day when Chap and Lan hoped their restaurant would be packed with customers from morning until night.

By eight next morning, several smartly dressed young couples had arrived on Hondas at the restaurant. While the men got stuck into some rice wine, the girls went into the water, wearing everything but their shoes, and began playfully splashing one another. When the fourth set of Hondas had roared up to the restaurant, and Lan and Chap were becoming harassed trying to meet everyone's orders, we decided to get out of the way. Clambering over the rocks that protected one side of the cove, we walked along the beach in the direction of Nha Trang. Half a mile away, a temple was built on the shore. In its grounds Buddhist nuns with shaven heads sat under the shade of a large tree, and giggled at us as we passed them. Close by, a massive white statue of *Quan The Am Bo That* gazed out to sea. In front of it some young Vietnamese women in tight jeans and high heels posed for each other's cameras. One of them held a lobster by the antennae and struck an incongruous Hollywood pose, her head thrown back and her breasts stuck out, while the nuns looked on and whispered to each other.

A few hundred feet offshore, beyond some shrimp nets, were two rocky outcrops topped by tiny thatch houses. A man appeared in the doorway of one of the houses and began waving and beckoning to us. Other heads popped out of the window, more hands beckoned. The man climbed down a ladder, untied the wicker coracle attached to the bottom rung and sculled over to us with a single oar. He was a rough-looking character, and obviously drunk, but we couldn't resist the chance of a ride in a coracle. Clambering in, we hunkered down and clung to the side. I felt like a character in a nursery rhyme, heading out to sea in a big, round basket. There were a few inches of water in the bottom, and pearl oyster shells and empty beer bottles swished around our ankles. When we reached the rock outcrop, I started up the ladder first. As I neared the top a man leaned out of the doorway, grabbed my arm and yanked me into the house. Suddenly I found myself surrounded by ten grinning and extremely inebriated fishermen. The room was in disarray, with empty beer bottles, crushed-up cigarette packets and lobster carapaces scattered everywhere. One man was grilling large oysters over charcoal, another was pouring beer into a cooler, a third was smashing lumps of ice against a wooden post then throwing the shards into the beer. When Dag appeared in the doorway, practically filling it up, all the men began chortling and hooting in delight. More bottles of beer were hauled up in a basket which had been floating in the ocean. We were ushered to sit on the mat, and from all sides food, drink and cigarettes were pressed upon us.

'Drink!' A beaker of beer watered down with filthy ice.

'Smoke!' A lighted cigarette.

'Eat!' A large shell filled with a fleshy oyster.

'*Don't* eat that,' cautioned Dag, and coming from him this was a strong warning indeed.

To fend off all the offers, I smiled apologetically and patted my stomach to indicate, quite truthfully, that it was upset. The man closest to me removed my rejected oyster from its shell and began lasciviously licking it, winking and grinning in our direction. Another of the fishermen was tenderly serenading Dag with a Vietnamese love song, while giving him longing looks. I felt a stab of panic – we'd made a terrible mistake – we were hopelessly outnumbered by these strongly built, drunk men. But then the fellow next to me dropped the oyster, picked up a battered guitar and began strumming and singing a familiar tune.

'Too-night you're mine, compeetey,' he sang, 'Yoo give you lub sue-weetly, Too-night, too-night the lie of lub is in you high . . .'

'Sing! Sing!' the others urged us, and we joined as he crooned: 'We you ste lub me, to-morrow?'

Our efforts were met by ecstatic applause. The guitarist was instructed to play the tune again. This time all the fishermen rousingly joined in with the chorus, 'We you ste lub me, too-morrow!'

We sang this, the only verse we knew of the old Chanterelles song, eight more times, with the fishermen's chorus getting increasingly louder. The noise drew the attention of the men in the hut on the nearby rock outcrop, and five of them paddled over to join us. They squashed into the little room, another basket of beer was hauled up and more oysters put on to cook. As the party looked like it was about to get very raucous, we decided it was time to leave. I expected a bit of an argument over this, but as soon as Dag pointed in our phrase book to the Vietnamese translation of 'Goodbye I must go now', all the men stood up to solemnly shake our hands. We climbed back down the ladder and into the coracle and were rowed back to shore. From a quarter of a mile away, as we walked towards the Huong Bien Restaurant, we could hear the fishermen's voices drifting over the water: 'We you ste lub me, too-morrow!'

All along the beach, groups of people were having picnics and going in for the ocean dips that would bring them luck in the coming year. But the cove was strangely empty and all the motor scooters were gone. We found the whole family sitting inside the restaurant, looking tense and worried.

'Where you go?' Binh angrily greeted us. 'I worry!'

But we weren't the real cause of Binh's agitation. While we had been enjoying ourselves with the fishermen, a girl had drowned in the cove.

'A lot of people they come here,' explained Binh. 'They go in water, they enjoy, everyone round here was drunk and happy. And then one girl, she talk with very big mouth, she say "Where my girlfriend? Where my girlfriend?" And they look, they see her girlfriend's hat on the water and they know she was sunk. About fifteen minute later they find her under the water and they pull her up. I help carry her here, everybody try to save her, they do everything, they hold her upside down, they bang on her body, but it too late. And people were drunk and shouting, and the girl she have sand all over her. And her face – so horrible, all green and the mouth blue and the eyes open. Her eyes look at me like the fish. We stop a car and the people they take her to hospital, but she dead already.'

For a while we sat in shocked silence.

'Didn't anyone realize she was drowning?' I asked finally.

'Nobody hear her,' said Binh. 'She walk into the water and she sunk and she say nothing! I think she fall down in a hole.'

During my swims in the cove, I'd noticed the steep gradient of the sandy bottom. I imagined the girl wading in, suddenly finding herself out of her depth and drowning, quietly and without a fuss.

'You know, my aunt she believe a ghost, a *Ma Da*, live under the water,' Binh continued. 'She say this *Ma Da* pulled the lady under. So now that lady is a *Ma Da* too, she look for someone to kill. That is why the people leave the beach and go home.'

After the drowning, Lan had lit some joss sticks on the beach to placate *Ba Thuy*, the goddess of water who had brought this *noi*, or curse, upon them. Soon, said Binh, she would build a proper shrine there, and next year at this time she would make special offerings to the *Ma Da*, and perform a special ceremony for anchoring a lost soul.

'She worry for her children, you know. The *Ma Da* like to take the children best. I think tonight she is afraid to let them go to toilet.'

As darkness fell, Chap lit every oil lamp in the restaurant. The flying ants arrived in droves, and the frogs hopped around, croaking their promise of rain. After dinner we played cards, and swapped ghost stories. Lan told us about the Spinster Spirits, the ghosts of women who have died unmarried and barren, and who wander around looking for a child to snatch away from its family.

'What about me, when I die?' I asked. 'I'm married but I have no children.'

'Better you have some quick,' said Binh.

Then he confided something he'd kept from us in Cantho.

'In hotel, first night I wake up three times. Someone push me and I fall out the bed! I alone, but still someone push and push me. In the morning I talk to the owner of this hotel.' He paused dramatically, and lit a cigarette. 'He tell me, two year ago a woman kill herself in that room. And now her ghost stay there.'

After this story, which he translated for the family, everyone seemed reluctant to go to bed, and the oil lamps were still

burning at eleven o'clock. Chap and Lan tried vainly to persuade us to move our tent inside the restaurant for the night.

'They say it safer,' said Binh. 'Otherwise the *Ma Da* throw
rocks at you.'

When Dag announced he was going for a moonlight swim,
everyone was plainly horrified. The family sat in uneasy silence,
straining their ears to hear him splashing about in the cove.

'Maria, you should come in!' he jubilantly shouted. 'The
bioluminescence is fantastic!'

'What this?' asked Binh nervously.

As best I could, I explained about living organisms in the
water emitting a sparkling light. Binh's translation brought on
some excited discussion.

'They say this light is the *Ma Da!*' he hissed.

Minutes later Dag was back, refreshed and exhilarated.
Reassured by his safe return, the family finally went to bed.
Dag and I sat up for a while, watching the lights of boats on
the water. Before we turned in, I had to argue long and hard to
stop him playfully chucking some rocks at Binh's hut.

'Did you hear something in the night?' asked Binh anxiously
next morning.

Only the occasional truck rumbling by, we told him, an outboard engine in the bay and, at dawn, the cockerel crowing
right next to our tent. He looked relieved.

'My family afraid. No one go toilet all night.'

Then he broke the news that he had decided to go home,
that evening, on the night bus to Saigon.

'First,' he assured us, 'I arrange your boat.'

After three days of equivocation over the boat issue, Binh
had it all sorted out within an hour. Uncle Chap set off on his
Honda to find a fisherman. He returned with a man called
Toan, who offered to take us to Dam Mon for a hundred dollars. Binh bargained him down to sixty five dollars, then wrote
out a contract stating what we would pay, where we would be
taken, and when. Toan said he would get a travel permit and
collect us at the beach at seven the next morning. He also said
he would help us find a place to stay in Dam Mon and, if
possible, another boat for us to carry on up the coast.

With everything settled, we could all relax. The day was extremely hot and sticky and we spent most of it in deck chairs under the shade of the vines. A few customers trickled into the restaurant. When they arrived, Uncle Chap would unearth ice from the rice pit for their drinks, and the chickens would flock around his feet, pecking at errant kernels. Binh announced that he wanted to buy a chicken to take back to Saigon, and pointed to one that was scratching about in the cassava patch. The family fanned out around the chicken, each of them with arms and legs spread as if guarding a goal post. Sensing danger, the chicken made a dash between Chap's legs. He turned and flung himself full length in an impressive rugby tackle, but succeeded in catching only a few tail feathers. For the next fifteen minutes the chicken led the family a dance around the cassava patch, then around the house, and once right through the restaurant where it fluttered, squawking wildly, over a table of people having their lunch. Finally, Lan captured the loudly protesting bird, tied its feet with pink string and left it lying on the floor.

After this excitement, the boys once again gathered around Dag to stroke and pat him and to laugh at his nose. We had written out some sentences that we thought might come in useful during our journey up north, and we asked Binh to translate them into Vietnamese and help us with the pronunciation. The boys listened with amusement, and Uncle Chap with increasing consternation, to this impromptu language lesson.

Could we speak to the local government official? *Lam on cho toi gap cong an xa?*

Can we spend the night in this village? *Chung toi co the ngu lai dem trong lang khong?*

We have a tent to sleep in. *Chung toi co leu va nem de ngu.*

Can you take us in your boat to – ? *Anh co the cho toi di theo ghe anh toi – ?*

'My uncle he worry,' said Binh when we'd finished. 'He say you end up in the prison.'

At five o'clock we stood at the side of the road, waving goodbye to Binh. As the Saigon-bound bus disappeared over the

hill, I felt a strong sense of loss. For three weeks he'd been our
close companion and our main link with the world around us.
Not only would we miss his company, from now on we would
have to manage with language, and anything else that came
our way, alone.

Uncle Chap had insisted that we should spend the night in
the hut where Binh had slept, so as the light faded we packed
up our tent and moved into our new home. There were two
single beds in there, both rigged up with mosquito nets. We got
our bags ready for an early start next day, then went over to the
restaurant for a final dinner. Once again, all the oil lamps were
burning and the ants had begun their nightly suicidal rituals.
The boys were at one table playing cards. Chap motioned for
Dag to sit with him, and for me to sit at another table, on my
own. Lan served the men with several plates of food and a bottle of beer apiece, then she joined me, setting down two bowls
of rice and *nuoc mam* and one bottle of carbonated water.
Chap came over to pour the water into my glass.

'Vietnam, Madam, no beer, no rice wine!' he said firmly.

Over the past few days I'd sensed Chap's disapproval of my
beer-drinking, modest though it was, and with Binh gone he
obviously now felt free to express it.

'What are you eating?' I asked Dag.

'Fried tuna, it's delicious,' he said smugly.

Lan was running to and fro, replenishing the men's bowls.

'This is ridiculous,' I told Dag. 'I mean, we're paying for our
food!'

Chap gave me a stern look and shook his head, and Lan
returned to the table and put a finger to her lips. The message
was clear: do not interrupt your husband while he's eating.
Dag had his back to me; his shoulders were shaking.

'You *wanted* to live like the locals, Maria,' he said.

When it was time to go to bed, Chap and Lan seemed intent
on coming with us. At first I thought they were just lighting
our way with an oil lamp. But they followed us inside the hut,
and climbed under one of the mosquito nets.

'Okay, no danger, okay,' Uncle Chap kept repeating, before
blowing out the oil lamp.

'What's all this about?' I whispered to Dag.

'Maybe they've come to guard us,' he whispered back.

'But they've left their boys alone in the restaurant!'

'Hey youse!' whispered Dag. 'Quit worrying and go to sleep!'

The bed was narrow and hard. And as the hut was close to the road, the lights of passing vehicles regularly swept over its one barred window. Sleep was hard to come by, but finally I drifted off, only to be woken around midnight by my bladder. I sat up, slipped out of the sheet sleeping bag and wriggled to the end of the bed. As I lifted the end of the mosquito net a truck passed and its headlights flooded over me.

'Waaaaaah!' yelled Dag, sitting bolt upright and grabbing me by the throat.

'It's me!' I croaked, trying to prise off his fingers.

'What d'ya think you're doing!' he cried, shaking me hard and squeezing the air out of me.

'It's *me*!' I gasped, desperately beating his head with my fists.

His hands flew off my neck.

'Maria?'

'I was going to the toilet – I never thought –'

'God, I thought someone was creeping in here to murder us. Are you okay?'

By now we had dropped our voices to whispers, but in fact there was no need for such caution. Uncle Chap and Lan were, as they had been throughout our frenzied struggle, deeply asleep.

6

UNDER ARREST

Our shiny new bikes were propped against the sun-bleached wicker coracle that lay upturned on the deck of Toan's boat. Beyond them, and across a stretch of calm water, four tiny figures still stood in the cove, watching us depart. After a final wave, Lan and her boys headed back up to the restaurant.

Uncle Chap had been nowhere in sight when we woke that morning, and he still hadn't appeared when Toan's thirty-foot wooden boat chugged up to the beach with black diesel smoke puffing from its funnel. His wife and sons waded into the water with us, helping us to hoist our bags and bikes onto the deck.

'Hey youse!' the boys had yelled repeatedly, as we pulled away.

'Hey youse!' we cheerfully shouted back.

But we were unsettled by Chap's absence, and it occurred to us that, as someone with connections to the Communist party, he might have thought it better not to be around when two foreigners hopped on to a fishing boat right outside his restaurant.

Toan, at least, seemed relaxed about the seven-hour journey ahead, and the morning passed pleasantly. We headed north, crossing a wide bay and rounding a mountainous peninsula. At its tip, steep hillsides covered with gnarled trees dropped to beaches of startlingly white sand and boulders covered with red and black lichen. The water was a deep blue, and clear enough to see the coral reefs, twenty feet below. Sometimes we passed other fishing boats, which were launching coracles from their decks like tiny satellites. In each of these little baskets was a lone fisherman, with nothing to propel himself but a wooden oar, and the prospect of hours at sea, checking on nets or setting new ones, before the mother ship returned to collect him.

By noon, on the horizon, we could see a shimmering ribbon of sand leading from the mainland to a steep and forested mountain. Dag was peering towards it with a worried expression.

'We're on the wrong course,' he said.

'We can't be.'

'We are. Look, there's Hon Lon Island. We should be skirting its southern tip and going through the passage between the island and the peninsula. Toan's heading towards its northern end.'

Leaning over to Toan, Dag tapped him on the shoulder.

'Dam Mon,' he said.

Toan smiled and pointed to where we were heading.

'Long Hoa,' he replied. Long Hoa was a town on Highway One, just south of where the peninsula joined the mainland. We shook our heads and waved our hands about to show Toan that we didn't want to go there. He smiled affably, but made no attempt to change course. Pulling out our map, we pointed to where we'd come from and where we wanted to go. Toan turned the map upside down and studiously examined it.

'I very much doubt that he can read maps,' groaned Dag. 'And I bet he only knows his local waters. The poor bugger's probably never been as far from home as this before.'

We pulled out the contract which Binh had written on a piece of school exercise paper. On one side, it read: Contract for boat hiring from Mr Nguyen Van Toan to: Dag and Maria. For taking a Boat Trip. From: Ha Chong Cat Loi To Loi to Dam Mon village. (70km) Amount due: 650,000 VD.

Toan studied the other side of the paper, which was written in Vietnamese, then looked up and said, '*Long Hoa.*'

'*Anh co the cho toi di theo ghe anh toi Dam Mon?*' Dag read out from his notebook. 'Can you take us in your boat to Dam Mon?'

Toan shook his head. '*Long Hoa*,' he repeated.

Dag started pointing towards the mainland and vigorously shaking his head, then pointing towards the general direction of Dam Mon and vigorously nodding his head. He kept repeating this sequence, until I felt dizzy just watching him. Toan regarded him indulgently, but made no attempt to change course.

'There's only one thing for it,' said Dag.

Gently but firmly, he took over the wheel and turned the boat in the direction we wanted to go. Toan nodded and sighed deeply, as if finally resigning himself to his fate.

It seemed inconceivable that anyone would not want to go to Dam Mon, for it was a place of astonishing beauty. Beyond some tree-covered islets lay a protected, aquamarine lagoon. Along its shoreline were groves of palm and papaya trees, and the red-tiled roofs of houses peeping over bamboo fences. A high gleaming sand dune which rose above the village was in turn dominated by a steep and lushly forested mountainside. As Toan motored slowly across the lagoon, Dag and I stood on deck, marvelling at the scene. Then we noticed the two men in green uniforms who were standing on the beach, watching our approach. Nervously chewing on his lip, Toan let down the anchor. We lifted our incongruously new and shiny bicycles off the coracle, so that he could lower it overboard. Before clambering into the wicker boat, Dag grabbed a pack of the cigarettes we'd bought for any police encounters, and I pulled some dollar bills from my money belt and slipped them into my pocket.

The policemen were like a double act: a hard-bitten sergeant, middle-aged, plump and stern-faced, and a young, skinny constable with a nervous tic in his cheek. The sergeant spoke sharply to Toan, who appeared to have shrunk several inches. Toan swallowed hard, gazed unhappily at Dag and crossed his wrists. We were, it seemed, under arrest. With the sergeant leading and the constable at the rear, we marched in a crocodile formation along lanes of soft sand between the bamboo fences. A Vietnamese proverb popped into my head: 'To love your neighbours, build fences and hedges.' Through gateways, faces peeped out at us and offered shy, bemused smiles. We smiled back, but Toan looked stricken.

'I don't think for a minute,' said Dag behind me, 'that he's got anything resembling a travel permit.'

The police station was a low L-shaped building with a tin roof. In one room a couple of men lay sleeping on cots, their AK-47s propped up next to them. We were ushered into a reception room and sat around a long wooden table. Green tea was poured and served, our passports and Toan's log were requested. For several minutes, there was silence in the room, save for the clicking of a grasshopper and the rustling of pages being turned. I sat wringing my hands beneath the table, and staring at a painting of Ho Chi Minh on the wall. The sleeping policemen had woken up, donned shirts, and were now peering at us through the doorway.

'Can-a-da,' the sergeant finally said. Then he pointed to our visas, which had been issued in London.

'Lun-dun. Why?'

Rather than attempting to explain that we had been temporarily working in England when it was time to apply for the visas, we shrugged and grinned, as if to say, 'Why not?'

Opening a drawer beneath the table, he pulled out a large blue ledger. On the first pages, several questions had been hand-written in pencil. Painstakingly, he read them out.

'Whoo-ah-iz-a-nem? Wh-ear-iz-a-fum? Whoo-ah-iz-do-in-Vietnam?'

Hopefully guessing correctly at what he'd said, we answered hesitantly. The fourth question, however, completely stumped us.

'Do-iz-lik-worz-Vietnamese?'

We paused, then spoke simultaneously.

'Yes,' I said.

'No,' said Dag.

There was another long silence. The sergeant stared at us, breathing hard, while the constable's cheek twitched faster than before. Toan was sitting very still and gazing fixedly into space, as if willing himself to dematerialize. When both policemen began firing questions at him he snapped out of this trance, but said nothing.

'Now I'm *sure* he's got no travel permission,' muttered Dag, as the sergeant flipped through the log, which was in a pink school exercise book.

Suddenly Toan launched into an impassioned speech, accompanied by a lot of hand waving in our direction, in which every fifth word seemed to be 'Long Hoa'.

'He's blaming all this on us,' Dag murmured. 'He's explaining that *he* wanted to take us to Long Hoa, but *we* insisted on coming here.'

'Which is true,' I murmured back.

When Toan finished speaking, both policemen looked at us with puzzled expressions. Turning to a clean page in his ledger, the sergeant drew the outline of a bicycle.

'Why?' he asked Dag, pointing to the sketch.

'We go Dam Mon to Long Hoa,' said Dag, also pointing to the picture.

The policemen and Toan stared at us as if we were insane. The drawer was opened again, and a topographical map pulled out and spread over the table.

Large scaled and highly detailed, it showed the southern end of the peninsula. The sergeant pointed to where we were, and then traced his finger across contour lines that ran close together, depicting a steep slope. He said something to the sergeant, who stood up and did an impressive mime of carrying a bike up a hill.

'*Con duong?*' we asked. 'Road?'

Heads shook. And light began to dawn. There was no road, only a mountain.

More tea was poured. The sergeant began interrogating Toan anew, while the constable copied into the ledger every single detail of our passports.

'Great,' muttered Dag. 'We're on a fishing boat with no permit to carry us, we arrive with two bikes at a village that has no road access, we're taken in by the cops and we speak hardly a word of the language.'

'What shall we do?'

'Start worrying.'

Our whispering drew suspicious glances from the two

policemen. Then the sergeant leaned over the map and pointed to another village. Vinh Yen was about three miles from Dam Mon by land, over the mountain, or ten miles by water, around a large headland. Beyond Vinh Yen, the map showed only sand and dunes, but the sergeant insisted that a road led from it to the mainland.

'*Con duong! Con duong!*' he kept repeating, jabbing his finger at the map.

'Go Vinh Yen,' he said finally.

'How?' asked Dag.

All eyes turned on Toan, who looked even more stricken than before and vehemently shook his head. It was quite clear that he'd already had more than enough of us. This suited the police, who had an alternative plan ready.

Police boat. $50, the sergeant wrote in his ledger.

'Bloody criminals,' said Dag, smiling broadly at him.

Holding out the pencil, the sergeant invited him to a bargaining session.

$15, Dag wrote.

The policemen laughed out loud, shook their heads and said something that probably translated to 'bloody criminal'.

$25, finish, Dag wrote.

'No,' said the sergeant firmly, and stood up. The rest of us followed suit, and we were marched back down the sandy lanes to the beach. The constable was still holding our passports, which he'd slipped inside Toan's log.

'Got some dollars ready?' asked Dag.

But a bribe wasn't necessary. When we reached the shore, the policeman returned the documents, pointed to Toan's boat and said, 'Goodbye!'

In utter misery, Toan paddled us back to the boat, started up the engine and headed out of the lagoon. We cheered him with the promise of extra money for his trouble. Then it was our turn to feel depressed, as we watched Dam Mon shrink away behind us, and regretted that we hadn't been able to linger in such a lovely spot.

Our disappointment was short-lived. Two hours later we stepped ashore on a tropical white sand beach that was lapped by azure water, shaded by leaning palms and lined with brightly painted sampans. A skinny young woman darted through the trees, had a brief conversation with Toan then tugged at my arm. The short walk to her village was kaleidoscopic: across a narrow strip of brilliant green paddy fields where iridescent blue dragonflies flitted about; through a shady grove of banana trees where huge drooping leaves brushed against our faces; past intricately woven twig fences surrounding gardens of flowering bushes and fragrant herbs and into the village itself, a neat arrangement of neat wattle and daub houses. All this was impressive enough, but towering over the settlement was a colossal sand dune, steep and shining and rising to over two hundred feet, like some ancient, talismanic monument.

Dumbstruck, we gazed up at the dune. The villagers who had carried our bikes and bags from the shore gathered around us, chattering excitedly. Tin, the skinny young woman, led us through a gate and into the sandy yard of her house. It was different in style to the open-fronted houses we'd seen elsewhere, with shuttered windows and solid wooden doors. Out back, in a courtyard shaded by thick vines, three dun-coloured dogs were eating cooked rice out of an aluminium bowl, and growling at the chickens trying to get their beaks between them. A whole crowd of us trooped through the house, along a narrow passageway towards a cool, dark room. Tin hurried around this room, pushing open shutters and a set of double doors, letting in sunlight and heat.

Eight men sat around the table by the doors, smoking the cigarettes Dag had handed out and taking turns to page through our dictionary. One of them was the young government official who looked after the village in lieu of any police. After a long conversation with Toan, he gave us permission to stay in the village and sleep in this house. But only for one night.

'*Sang mai* – tomorrow morning', Toan repeated, over and over until he was satisfied we'd got the message. Then he left – anxious, no doubt to escape us before we inveigled him into anything else.

Soon the conversation turned to our bikes, which were out

on the veranda, and being squabbled over by children who wanted to ring the bell and try out the pump.

'*Con duong*?' 'Road?' asked Dag, pointing to the bikes.

A puzzled silence fell over the room.

Then he tried, '*Lam on, chi cho toi duong quoc lo?* Can you tell me which is the way to the highway?' at which all the men turned and pointed westwards.

We pulled out our map, and pointed to the red line running the length of the peninsula.

'*Con duong*?' Dag repeated.

The men stared at the map as if it was covered with Egyptian hieroglyphics.

'Have you noticed how quiet it is in this village?' he asked me.

'I haven't heard a karaoke bar yet,' I joked.

'There's no traffic, Maria,' he said. 'No bicycles. No Hondas. Nothing.'

Before I had time to react to this, Tin was again tugging at my arm. She took me back to the courtyard, where she pulled up several buckets of water from the well and sent me with them into a roomy bathhouse. While I washed and changed, I marvelled over this magical village, built on sand, with lush gardens, flooded paddy fields and an obviously abundant supply of water. Delicious water, at that: at dinnertime I drank over a litre of it. We ate on the front veranda with Tin and her husband, who had one ear missing. Spread out on a mat between us were bowls of rice, a steamed green vegetable like spinach, some small bony fish and a weak fish broth. An oil lamp hung from one of the veranda posts, and neighbours gathered in the shadows it cast to watch us.

When we'd finished the meal, two men came forward and beckoned to us. Tin and her husband nodded their encouragement, so we followed the men through the gate and along the village paths. Lamps glowed softly in the windows of houses. There was no electricity, no generators, no radios, no videos, no karaoke. It was so quiet that we could hear the frogs croaking in the paddy fields, the whirr of insects, the gentle snuffling of pigs in their pens. The men called into houses as we went, and children and teenagers ran out, skipping along behind us and giggling softly. We passed beyond the village, through a patch of sweetly smelling bushes and to the foot of the immense sand dune. It rose sheer above us, gleaming eerily in the moonlight. The men began to climb it and we followed them, taking a crisscross route, sinking knee deep into the fine, warm sand. Children pranced around me, grabbing me by the hands to pull me upwards.

'Holy smokes!' I heard Dag cry from the top.

When I joined him, I was rendered speechless for the third time that day. The view was stupendous, a panoramic sweep of open ocean, etched softly with the dark outlines of peninsulas and islands, and twinkling with hundreds of fishing boat lights that were like a reflection of the star filled sky above.

'*Dep lam*!' we repeatedly told the men. 'Beautiful!' and they beamed with pleasure. This view was their pride and joy, something they showed off like people elsewhere in the country showed off their Hondas and their videos. For over an hour we relaxed at the top of the dune, caressed by a cool breeze. The younger children played around us, doing handstands, and tumbling backwards for soft, safe landings. The older ones wrote their names in the sand, and taught us how to pronounce them. And the men sat and smoked contentedly, the ends of their cigarettes glowing in the dark.

Back at Tin's house some old men had gathered and a card game was in progress. Dag joined them, rice wine was poured and more cigarettes were lit. Tin laid out a mat and a pillow on the wooden bed base close to the table, and I gratefully stretched out on it. My head was next to the window; a gentle breeze played on my face, carrying sweet scents from the garden. There was no need for a net, as this fairy-tale village appeared to be blessed with an absence of mosquitoes. An oil lamp threw strange, flickering shadows over the ceiling and the men's voices and laughter faded away into a distant murmur as I fell into the most peaceful sleep I'd had since arriving in Vietnam.

We woke at five, and lay still for a few minutes, savouring the quiet. Then we crept out of the house and went down to the beach for a swim. Already the dragonflies were hovering over the paddy fields, where a lone woman was working, knee deep in water, bending from the waist, her face hidden by her hat. The sea was still as a lake, and felt pleasantly cool. We swam far out, turning to admire the magnificent dune and trying to imagine the forces that put it there. My eyes followed the sweep of the beach.

'How far is it to Long Hoa from here?' I asked Dag.

He was floating on his back, with his chest puffed up and his hands behind his head, looking as relaxed as if he was lying on a sofa.

'About seven miles,' he answered.

'I can't see a road,' I said.

Flipping onto his stomach, he began a lazy breast stroke.

'We should get back to the house. The family will wonder where we are.'

We drank tea on the back veranda of the house with Tin and her husband. There was an air of tension, which we attributed to concern that we might not leave that morning, as the village organizer had requested. Soon, we were packed and ready to go, but how or by what route was still uncertain.

'Okay, let's head for the beach,' said Dag assertively.

We took our bikes from where they were leaning against a wall, and wheeled them through the yard. Strapped onto my tiny luggage rack was my bag, three feet long and about thirty-five pounds in weight which, as I'd feared, made the already wobbly bike even more unstable. Tin walked alongside me, looking greatly concerned.

'*Con duong*?' I asked her, but she shook her head.

'There *must* be a road close by,' I called to Dag, who was ominously silent.

Even getting along the path was a chore. The weight of the bag flopped the bike against my hip and sent the front wheel askew. To keep it going in a straight line, I had to twist the handlebars and hold my body in an awkward position. I managed to get through the village and across the paddy fields, but when we hit the beach the wheels sank into the soft sand and I ground to a halt.

'*Con duong o dau*?' I asked Tin. 'Where's the road?'

She pointed to the sand and vehemently shook her head. Then she grabbed my arm and pointed to the ocean.

'*Ghe! Ghe!*' she cried. 'Boat!'

'Tin says there's no road,' I told Dag, when he appeared behind me. 'She says we have to go by boat.'

'Her husband says the road starts two miles from here,' he countered. 'That's not far.'

'*Not far?*'

'Even at snail's pace, we can cover two miles in a couple of hours. It would take us that long to arrange a boat ride. And we've got to start using these bikes sometime.'

'I can't do two miles along this beach!' I wailed. 'I can't even do two feet!'

'We'll be all right as long as we keep very close to the water's edge, where the sand is firm,' coaxed Dag.

Tin, her husband and a crowd of villagers watched incredulously as we wheeled our bikes down to the water's edge. The sand was indeed firmer there, but not firm enough to stop our heavily laden bikes from sinking into it.

'I'll go ahead,' suggested Dag, 'and you follow in my tracks.'

With any other bike, this may have been possible, but the front wheel of mine seemed to have a mind of its own and constantly veered off to one side. Two teenage boys ran down to join us, and began helping me to push my bike. The beach curved, and soon the village was out of sight behind us. Ahead was nothing but an expanse of sand, with dunes on one side of it and ocean on the other. It was seven o'clock and already unbearably hot. After ten minutes we reached a small water channel. The boys helped me to ford it, lifting the bike and its heavy load between them. Tired by this, they stopped pushing and walked alongside me, staring at me as if I had two heads. At every step, the sand seemed to get thicker and softer.

'*Con duong o dau?*' I asked them.

'*Duong?*' they repeated incredulously. 'Road?' and began to laugh.

'*Duong!*' they cried, pointing to the beach.

Realization struck. This was the road – it wasn't two miles away, it was here. And it was no place to start my first cycling trip in thirty years.

'*Stop!*' I yelled at Dag.

He turned, took one look at me and wheeled his bike back.

'I was just thinking,' he said, 'that we've got no food and no water, and that seven more miles of this might just kill my wife.'

As soon as we came back into view, Tin hurried over to meet us.

'*Ghe! Ghe!*' she cried, and pointed to where a small motorized fishing boat lay at anchor.

This time, Dag didn't argue, and a deal was struck. For five dollars, a man and his wife would take us over to Long Hoa, an hour's ride away. We climbed aboard, the diesel engine spluttered into life and we set off into a headwind and a choppy sea, waving goodbye to Tin and her husband.

'We might not come across anywhere else in Vietnam as pristine and peaceful as that place,' said Dag ruefully.

'Don't be so pessimistic,' I chided him.

But I stared resolutely at the beach and the dune behind it until they sank back into the horizon, trying firmly to imprint on my memory all the impressions of the last twenty hours.

Two hundred yards from the shore of the mainland, our boat ran aground. The skipper seemed unperturbed, as all around us other flat-bottomed fishing vessels were also sitting on the sand. He and his wife rolled up their pants, jumped into the water and carried our bikes ashore, while we followed with our bags. We'd arrived at a village called Tu Bong, a mile from Highway One. On the beach was a muddle of fishing nets and a bony, fly-ridden donkey was hitched up to a trap and tied to a palm tree. There was also the ubiquitous police post, to which the couple took their pink school exercise book. The young policeman inside the post wrote something in the book and handed it back, looking suspiciously at me and Dag. We leaned our bikes up against the palm tree and turned to invite the couple for a drink at a nearby stand, but they were already gone, hurriedly wading back through the murky water to their boat.

We were joined instead by the effete young policeman. He

arrived from his post with an AK-47 slung over his shoulder, and ordered a bottle of Coca Cola that we were obviously expected to pay for. His thick hair flopped over his eyes, and he repeatedly pushed it back with long, limp fingers. Staring at us, he frowned deeply and his lips moved as he tried to find English words.

'Where from?' he managed.

'Canada,' I told him. 'England.'

'Ca-na-da,' he painstakingly repeated. 'Eng-Land.'

Minutes of mouthing and frowning led to his second question.

'Du-iz-a-sueist-ralatave?'

He stared at us, fingering his rifle and waiting for an answer.

'I think he wants to know if we have Swiss relatives,' said Dag.

Truthfully, I answered, 'No!'

He seemed satisfied by this, but immediately began practising another sentence.

Before he had time to form it, we drained our drinks and left.

7

A PAIR OF DA TRANG CRABS

Highway One, the coastal road linking Saigon and Hanoi, is the country's most important artery of transportation. During the American War, it was heavily bombed. Since then, there have been few resources available for its upkeep. We joined it a mile away from Tu Bong, and found a highway that was about as wide as an English country road. It was buckled and broken and riddled with potholes. It had no marked lanes, and its shoulders were narrow strips of gravel crumbling away into the paddy fields. And what we didn't know, but were soon to find out, was that this was one of its better stretches.

The traffic, though not heavy, was manic. Trucks and buses roared past, forcing us onto the shoulder, deafening us with air horns, belching exhaust fumes over us and spraying us with water. Few of the buses and trucks along Highway One have working radiators. Instead, on their roofs they have tanks from which water trickles down hoses and runs through the engine, collecting heat and dirt on its way. Then it squirts out – more often than not over unfortunate cyclists. But at least these vehicles passed quickly by. Scooter drivers, however, often insisted on slowing down and puttering along right beside us for a 'chat'.

'Hello! Whazza name?' they'd yell, as clouds of blue smoke from their low-grade fuel formed around us. 'Where you from? How old you? How many children? What your job?'

But none of this could yet dent our spirits, or rob us of an immediate and heady sense of freedom as we set off northwards, and independently, along Highway One.

After a few miles, the road began to climb towards the Co Ma Pass. It was a fairly gentle gradient, and Dag shot off ahead of me. Valiantly, I pedalled after him, and soon caught up with a girl who was pushing her bike.

'Stop!' she commanded me.

I promptly obeyed. Side by side, we plodded upwards for an hour. She was sweet and demure in a blouse with a Peter Pan collar, white cotton gloves and a varnished straw hat with fake flowers tucked into its brim. While I toiled and sweated, she remained cool and poised, and pushed her bike without apparent effort almost to the top of the pass.

'You are beautiful,' she said solemnly, before turning off on a track that led to a small, mud walled farm house. 'But not strong.'

Dag was waiting for me at the top. Below us lay the settlement of Dai Lanh. Tucked beneath a steep, green hillside, and strung along a crescent beach lined with casuarina trees, it looked an enticing place to rest after our first day, and our first twelve miles, of cycling. We free-wheeled down, enjoying the wind in our faces. But there was only one hotel in Dai Lanh. It had been half built then abandoned, and was a hulking, rotting three-storey shell. Behind it, on the beach, there was a deserted restaurant where three waitresses lay stretched out on the drinks bar, fast asleep. The toilet in the restaurant was appallingly squalid. We contemplated a swim, only to discover that the water was infested with jelly fish. Then we sat on the sand, discussing what to do. It was now almost three o'clock, and Tuy Hoa, the next settlement of any size, was twenty-eight miles away. Pitching a tent on the beach was out of the question: as well as camping being illegal, some very unsavoury characters had begun wandering along it, watching us intently. Finally we decided simply to carry on, and to see where we got to by dark.

We had just set off along the highway when a teenager cycled up to us. He was well dressed in a crisp white shirt and grey pants, and wore his thick hair in a brush cut. He introduced himself as Linh, and said he was a student of English. Patiently, we let him work through the familiar barrage of questions about our names, ages, marital status, jobs and children. Then we explained our situation, and asked if he knew of anywhere we could safely spend the night.

'You can sleep in my house,' he said. 'But there is no bathroom. And we are very noisy. All night we sell beer.'

His house was on the opposite side of the road, across the railway tracks and at the foot of the hillside.

'This house new,' said Linh. 'Last year, the big storm come in monsoon, and the sea come on the land and cover the old house. We run to the mountainside and when we come back the house is gone.'

The new, two-roomed building had a large veranda wrapped all the way around it. Part of this veranda had been converted into a small bar. Bottles of beer and soft drinks were displayed on a glass counter. There were no customers, but a dog lay sleeping on each of the three low tables.

'Your parents?' I asked Linh.

'Nha Trang,' he told me. 'Funeral.'

I got washed and changed in the thatch bathhouse next to the well, then wandered off into the scrubby undergrowth behind the house, where my nose led me to the toilet area. Then we invited Linh for dinner and went with him to the deserted restaurant, where he woke up one of the waitresses and persuaded her to bring us a meal of fried fish, rice and vegetables. When we returned to Linh's house we found his parents, just back from Nha Trang, staring with deep suspicion at our tent, which we'd erected on the veranda along one side of the house. Nervously, Linh introduced us.

'I tell them you are teachers,' he said. 'They want you to buy drinks.'

His father swept a dog off one of the tables and served us

with glasses of iced beer. All three of them sat and watched us drink it.

'They say you must go to bed,' Linh told us when we'd finished. 'Soon people come, get drunk, very noisy.'

By eight we were lying in our tent. We could hear traffic passing on the road, a freight train going by, music playing from a ghetto blaster in the house and the wheezy snoring of one of the dogs, which had settled down close by.

'I don't believe this business about customers,' said Dag. 'They're just paranoid about the police, and they want us out of sight.'

Within the hour he was proved wrong. A couple of Hondas rolled in and parked twenty feet from our tent. The couples on them spread mats on the ground behind the house, and were soon drinking beer. A Filipino remake of 'My Boy Lollipop' blared out of the ghetto blaster. More scooters arrived, their headlights on full beam and strafing our tent. The music got louder, beer bottles rolled around, there was coarse laughter, people staggered to and fro past the tent and sometimes faces peered in at us. I feared it really would go on all night, but at eleven o'clock sharp the lights went out, the music stopped and everyone began speaking in low voices. Finally we fell asleep – only to be woken two hours later when fifteen Hondas spluttered into life feet away from our tent, sending clouds of dust through the insect screen.

Next morning, Linh showed no sign of having had his sleep disturbed. His hair was coiffed, he wore a freshly ironed shirt, and he had prepared a farewell speech.

'When you return to my country and pass by this house again, please honour me with a visit.'

As his parents were still asleep, we asked him to thank them on our behalf, and to pass on some dollars to repay them for their hospitality. Linh looked relieved, and blurted out the rest of the speech, which he had obviously been holding back to the last minute.

'My family very poor, my schooling very expensive, one day I will work for foreign company, for now if you can help me thank you.'

We stopped for breakfast at the first *pho* stall we came to. While we slurped our soup, an elderly man came to join us. He told us that he had fought against the Communists during the American War.

'I was a colonel,' he said proudly.

'Afterwards, did you go to re-education camp?' I asked him. He shook his head, and smiled.

'I was like you, I cycled fast from place to place and no one could catch me.'

It would have been easy to catch us that morning. We were now heading into the Central coast, which suffers its hot, dry season while the rest of the country is hit by monsoons. By eight, the air temperature had already begun to soar. And, after we'd pedalled for less than half an hour, the road began snaking up the side of a mountain that rose steeply from the coast. Before long, we were pushing our bikes. It was a long, steep and gruelling haul, but the discomfort of getting up this pass in such sticky heat was compensated by the riveting scenery. Clouds of dragonflies hovered around our heads. At the sides of the road, clumps of incense burned at little shrines and herds of long-eared goats chomped on scrubby bushes. On the slopes beneath us, villages of ochre mud houses sprouted from red earth. Far below them, yellow beaches were speckled with brightly painted boats hauled up out of the tide's reach. And beyond the beaches was the vast, glittering sweep of the ocean, dotted with forested islands.

It took us two hours to reach the top of the pass. Dag got there first, and I found him with his camera glued to his face, clicking away.

'These vistas are stunning!' he cried.

Then he lowered his camera, and looked at me with a puzzled expression on his face. 'It's weird, but I can smell shit everywhere.'

'That's because you're standing in it,' I said.

His eyes followed mine, and he groaned in despair. The large pile of wet and unmistakably human faeces had begun to curl over the sides of his sandals, and some had found its way between his toes. He hopped around, looking for something to clean himself up with. The only water in sight was the stuff in our drinking bottle, which I refused to hand over. And all the foliage around was sharp and prickly. Finally he resorted to using something resembling a cactus leaf, gaining an impressive and deeply embedded collection of thorns.

The road leading down the pass swept around the mountain, giving us tantalizing glimpses of a jewel-green sea of paddy fields stretching across the huge flood plain below.

'Don't use your brakes!' yelled Dag as he flew past me.

It was superfluous advice, because they barely worked. The back brake, however, still gripped a little and soon the knuckles of my right hand were white from me squeezing the lever and vainly trying to slow my progress. As I whizzed around the steep winding curves, the whole bike began to rattle and shake beneath me. I felt utterly out of control, and prayed that I wouldn't meet a bus coming up and taking a bend on the wrong side. Images of horribly broken bones and appalling hospital wards started flashing across my mind. Several times I passed Vietnamese people walking their bikes downhill, and it was only when I had reached the plain and slowed to a breathless stop that it occurred to me why they had been doing this.

'That was insane!' I protested, when I caught up with Dag, who was grinning with pure enjoyment. 'One mistake, one truck coming up on the wrong side, and we'd have been finished.'

'How's your bike?' he asked cheerfully.

'It feels as if it's falling apart,' I said.

'Don't worry, from here to Tuy Hoa it's only nineteen miles and totally flat,' he said, looking at the map. 'We should easily make it in a couple of hours.'

The road ran straight as a rule across the plain. On either side of it, paddy fields stretched away until they disappeared into a shimmering heat haze. Raised dykes criss-crossed them like a chequer board, buffalo plodded along hauling ploughs, family tombs popped up here and there. Women bent over in the fields, or walked along the dykes with heavily laden shoulder poles. It was a calm, almost soporific scene and we cycled along enjoying the views and our slow, easy pace. Then the wind picked up. It came from mountains to the west, flowing down their slopes and funnelling through the river flood plain. It whistled towards us and hit us side on at thirty miles an hour, blowing me off my bike.

'Lean into it!' yelled Dag, as I picked myself up.

I leaned as much as I dared, but three more times in the first half hour I ended up lying on the gravel with my bike on top of me. Finally I started pushing instead of pedalling. Local people were doing the same, plodding alongside bikes heavily laden with pots, live ducks, sacks of rice. They pushed with their faces turned from the wind, keeping up a steady, labouring pace. Ahead of me, Dag had also dismounted.

'This is hell,' I told him, when I caught up.

'You said you wanted to travel like the locals,' he said sanctimoniously. 'And you can't get any more local than this.'

Slowing down, I let him get ahead of me, so that I could be miserable in peace.

After an hour we reached a settlement, and stopped for a drink under a shady veranda. Immediately, a gawking crowd formed around us. The owner of the place was a charming man, who spoke good English.

'You must excuse us,' he said. 'It is only since a few years that we see foreigners like you, and can speak to them.'

Speechless with exhaustion, I let Dag take over the conversation. People in the crowd giggled at me and nudged each other. I couldn't blame them, I was a horrible sight. The grime and sweat on my skin had mingled to form a crust that I could scratch off with my fingernails. My spectacles were tied onto my head with string to prevent them from constantly slipping down my sweaty nose. My hair had escaped in clumps from its pony tail and was sticking out of my head like a haystack. But the kind restaurateur didn't seem to mind my ridiculous appearance.

'Madam, you are beautiful,' he said, as I stared at him, stupefied. 'So, *so* beautiful!' All morning my straw hat had been constantly blown back off my face by the wind. Dag fixed it by tying a long string around the brim, pulling up its sides to lie flat against the crown, and leaving the front of it sticking out.

My once elegant hat now looked like a bastardized base-ball cap. Dag clamped it onto my head and tied it around my chin with string.

'There,' he said fondly. 'Now you're *really* beautiful!'

The temperature had reached thirty-five degrees and the wind was so strong that, even just pushing the bike, I had to lean into it to stay upright. My left ear felt as if it was filling up with sand and my throat was dry and raspy. There were no trees, no drinks stands, nowhere to escape from the scorching sun. From time to time I stopped and leaned on the bike, my head on the handlebars, in a pose of pure exhaustion. Dag's spirits, however, were strangely high, and he egged me on with promises of treats ahead, as if I was a three year old. I hated him for his cheerfulness. I hated Vietnam. I hated myself for having such a stupid idea as buying these bikes. I hated the bus and truck drivers who blared their horns at us, and the scooter drivers who slowed down to yell at us. I particularly hated the young foreign tourists who sped by in an air-conditioned minibus with 'Kim's Café' written on the side, craning their necks to gape at us in wonder.

The road stretched on, interminably. The wind showed no sign of easing up, nor the sun of cooling down. Dag urged me to try cycling instead of pushing.

'The faster you go, the sooner you'll be out of this hell hole,' he'd say, but I would manage only a few revolutions of the wheels before being knocked over by the wind. During the early afternoon my progress got steadily slower, and Dag's patience began to wear thin. He would wait for me to catch up with him, then wait for me to rest and drink, but minutes after we set off together he'd be pulling ahead again. I could sense his growing frustration and I bitterly resented it.

'STOP ROLLING YOUR EYES, YOU BASTARD!' I once yelled at his retreating back.

He stopped, and turned with an amazed expression on his face. 'How did you *know*?' he asked.

At last, a tiny drinks stand came into view. It offered shade from the sun but no shelter from the wind, which was whistling right through it. A quarter of a mile further on was the start of a settlement, the first for miles, with trees along the road which would give some respite from both wind and sun. I knew Dag would be thinking it was pointless to waste time at the stand when we could carry on to the settlement and have a long rest there. And I knew that if I didn't catch up with him, he'd just sail past it. Climbing onto my bike, I cranked the pedals, cycling faster than I had all day, trying to close the distance between us. He had almost reached the stand, and showed no sign of slowing down. Pedalling like fury, and summoning every vestige of breath, I screamed, 'WE'RE STOPPING HERE!'

It came out as a strangulated croak, but Dag got the message. He dismounted outside the drinks stand and watched my approach.

'No questions, no discussions – an order – right?' he said, as I caught up with him and tumbled off my bike.

Despite my hat and the sun block I was slapping on at regular intervals, during the afternoon my skin began to burn badly, and I imagined I could feel it turning to parchment.

'Never again,' I kept muttering, like a mantra. 'Never, never again.'

I was beginning to feel desperately sorry for myself when we came across a young woman at the side of the road. Pitifully thin and dressed in black pyjamas and a brown top, she lay curled up in a foetal position. Her hair was full of dust. Even from a distance, she looked lifeless, yet other cyclists plodded by her without even a glance, and motorized vehicles passed without slowing down.

'Is she dead?' I asked anxiously, as Dag knelt to take her pulse. The wrist he held was absurdly frail.

'No,' he answered. 'But she's very, very sick.'

A crowd quickly gathered, but to stare at us, not at the girl.

'Anyone speak English?' asked Dag.

The people looked at each other expectantly, and giggled shyly. Pushing through them, Dag started flagging down vehicles. First a car, whose driver slowed down, caught sight of the girl and put his foot on the accelerator. Then several scooters. On one of them was a man who spoke English.

'Where you from?' he cheerfully asked Dag. 'What your name?'

'This girl must be taken to hospital,' Dag told him. 'Is there one in Tuy Hoa?'

The man shrugged helplessly and set off again.

The girl coughed and moaned. A gust of wind swirled through the green rice shoots, pushing them into pretty patterns and rippling the water in the irrigation channels. It struck me how strange it seemed for someone to be dying next to such a lyrical scene. We waited for an hour. People gathered to stare at us, moved on, and were replaced by others. No one seemed even to notice the girl.

Finally a minibus stopped. Several men were inside it and loud rock and roll was playing on the stereo.

'Where you guys from?' called the driver, leaning out of his window.

He had Vietnamese features but an American accent, and he was chewing gum. In the seat behind him were two men wearing lots of gold jewellery.

'My name's Joe, I live in Santa Barbara!' he continued, reaching out to shake Dag's hand.

'We need to get this girl to a hospital,' Dag told him.

Joe conferred with the men in the back seat.

'We can't take her, it would be big trouble. But we'll go and get the police.'

He spoke to one of the farmers who was staring at us, and pushed some money into his hand.

'It might take a couple of hours for the cops to come. This guy will look after her until then. Don't worry, okay?'

He drove away, waving through the window. We sat by the side of the road for another half an hour.

'There's nothing else we can do,' said Dag finally. 'We should get going.'

I heaved my laden bike to an upright position, and started pushing it. Then, wanting to get away as fast as possible, I climbed on and began pedalling against the wind. Only once did I look back. The girl was lying perfectly still, and the farmer was standing next to her. They looked like figures in a painting. Nothing had changed. And nor did we see a police vehicle go by during the rest of our hot, dusty and exhausting ride into Tuy Hoa.

There was only one hotel where foreigners could stay in Tuy Hoa. Government-owned, it was a grim, Soviet-style building, set in a compound surrounded by a high concrete wall. In the foyer, a large sign above the reception desk read, 'Bedroom Foreigner $15'. All the staff were sitting around a television, watching one of the first football matches of the World Cup. One man reluctantly dragged himself away from the screen to show us a room. I sank onto the bed, grateful that I didn't have to move another inch. A notice on the wall close by announced that: 'Bicycles, motorbikes, pets, firearms, explosives, inflammable things, stinking things and even prostitutes are not allowed here.'

Dag pulled out his camera.

'Right now you look a bit like a stinking thing,' he said. 'I have to take a photo.'

Unable to find the energy to protest, I gaped at the lens and listened to the shutter click.

The hotel restaurant was a cavernous place, empty of customers except us, with floor to ceiling windows looking out at the compound walls. French muzak was playing from speakers set in each corner, and on one wall hung a large tapestry depicting a deer with a full rack of antlers standing in a snowy, Alpine landscape. From time to time, a girl teetered past the kitchen doorway on high-heeled sandals, but she never glanced our way. Eventually Dag went to the doorway and called to her. Looking deeply resentful, she brought us a menu. Before she could teeter away again, we ordered steak, rice and beer. The steak, when it came, was chopped up into slivers of meat that were the consistency of old leather. All day, Dag had remained cheerful in the face of relentless wind, heat, traffic and the sheer physical discomfort of the journey, but this awful meal finally brought his spirits crashing down.

'You cycle all day and end up in a dump like this,' he complained, pulling yet another piece of inedible meat from his mouth, and adding it to the pile on the side of the serving plate. 'I can't stand it. This trip is going to drive me bananas.'

A Honda pulled up outside the glass doors of the restaurant. Two men dismounted, walked in and came across to our table. Both were wearing sunglasses, tight polyester trousers and nylon shirts, and had their hair slicked down with grease. One of them was barely out of his teens, and he hung back uneasily while his older friend addressed Dag.

'Sir, can you dancing with my friend?'

Confused, Dag looked around the room, as if to see who else the man might be talking to.

'Dancing with my friend!' the man repeated, pointing to the embarrassed young man.

Dag stared at him, wide eyed.

'Your friend?'

'Yes, very nice, not so many dollar.'

'Ah, er, no . . . sorry . . . thanks very much,' stuttered Dag.

'Okay!' cried the man, turning on his heel and walking out of the restaurant, with his friend in tow.

'Let's go back to our room,' suggested Dag, looking a trifle worried.

We had to hunt down the waitress so we could pay for the meal. Eventually we discovered her behind a counter in a room off the restaurant. She was hunched on a stool, reading a magazine and eating biscuits. When we coughed to get her attention, she reached for a receipt book and crossly paged through it, as if she'd had scores of bills to settle up that night.

The next day began badly. A few miles out of Tuy Hoa, Highway One disappeared altogether, and was replaced by a rough sand track. Buses and trucks slithered dangerously along it, their wheels spinning. We got off our bikes, and once again started pushing. The track led us through scrubby hills and fields of cassava, marshes and sand flats and an impromptu market. Trucks and bikes were parked in a higgledy-piggledy fashion on either side of it and at least fifty women were lined up with baskets heaped high with cucumbers. Sensing a less than friendly atmosphere, we headed quickly through the crowd – but not quickly enough to avoid the sellers who reached out to pinch our legs, or the young woman who slapped each of us hard on the arm with the flat of her hand, leaving us with stinging red marks. As if to make up for this, a man ran out to tell us that Germany had won that day's World Cup match.

To help pass the time and break the monotony of the land-scape, we played a game of spotting the most bizarre cargo on the backs of scooters. Pigs in conical baskets were disqualified, simply because these were so commonplace. The basket filled to the brim with silk worm larvae was a strong contender, and the flat basket with a neat arrangement of pigs' heads vied for an award with the large, old mortar shell strapped onto a lug-gage rack. But the outright winner was declared when a scooter loaded with three bamboo cages full of writhing green snakes went zipping by us.

'Imagine colliding with *that*,' shuddered Dag.

When the game was over, we swapped to spotting bizarre things at the side of the road. I saw a completely featherless chicken pecking in the dirt outside a house. Dag saw a family having lunch on a veranda with a large pig which was eating from a bowl. We drew even when we both claimed the Christmas tree, complete with lights, in the little café where we stopped for lunch.

During the afternoon we passed through pretty villages built right along the beach. The houses had saddle-shaped thatch roofs, and outside them crude salt and fish were spread along the side of the road to dry. Around the fortieth mile of the day, we reached the outskirts of Song Cua. First came salt flats, evaporation tanks, fish farms in muddy lagoons and an army base. Then the town itself, a shabby place which had no guest houses that would accept foreigners. The nearest hotel, we were told, was in the small port town of Qui Nhon, twenty-five miles away and over a pass. We were anxious to get to Qui Nhon, which was the home of my friends Hanh and Tuyen, and from where we thought we might be able to get a boat. But it was too late, and we were too tired, to reach it that day by bike. We were standing in the road, wearily discussing what to do, when a bus rattled by then braked to a halt a few yards ahead of us. Although it was full, and its roof was heavily loaded with sacks, the young man hanging out of the back door beckoned to us to come aboard.

'Qui Nhon?' Dag asked him.

'Bien Dien,' he answered.

Bien Dien was on Highway One, twenty miles north. From there a road led off to Qui Nhon, five miles away at the tip of a peninsula.

The man jumped down and grabbed my bike, making the decision for us. There followed a slight delay as he and Dag haggled over a price. Five times the cost of a local ticket was asked for. Three times the local price was offered and accepted. Then there was a dispute over the charge for carrying the bikes. Finally the two men agreed on five dollars for both bikes, which were duly hauled onto the roof, while we clambered up the steps with our bags.

There were no free seats on the bus, so we stood at the back, hanging onto a rail, hunched over because of the low ceiling. Each time the bus swerved we were thrown against each other and lurched into other passengers. Dust poured through the open doors and windows, and the driver appeared to be resting an elbow on his horn. Despite the discomfort, I was glad to be where I was rather than pushing my bike up what turned out to be a very long pass. We had almost reached the top of it when the man hanging from the back door began asking us for more money.

'Muoi dollar!' he insisted. 'Ten dollar,' all the while pointing up to the roof, as if to say this was the charge for the bikes.

Dag stood his ground, insisting that we would not part with a single dong more.

'Muoi dollar! Muoi dollar!' the man kept insisting.

The dispute was still unresolved when the bus stopped at the turn off to Qui Nhon. The driver kept the engine revving while our bikes were passed down – mine without its bell, Dag's without its pump – then at a sign from the man on the back it pulled away fast, leaving us in a cloud of dust and dirt.

There was a dream-like quality to our arrival in Qui Nhon. The light was fading and the air was filled with dust. A layer of wind-blown sand covered the main street and along the pavement

were numerous pairs of sand-coloured, copulating dogs. We
checked into the Duong Phong Hotel, one of the few places in
Qui Nhon licensed for foreigners. The walls of its foyer were
decorated with pink and blue paper doilies cut into the shapes
of kissing couples. Above a doorway covered by a bead curtain,
a bright neon sign read: 'Massage.'

After forty-four miles on a rattling bike, a massage seemed
like a wonderful idea. My attempt to book one, however,
caused considerable confusion. 'Massage?' repeated the hotel
receptionist, his eyes widening in alarm. 'For madam?'

He composed himself, then said, 'Massage lady busy now.
Please come back later.'

I came back later to find three young women wearing tight
dresses and lots of make-up sitting on a bench beneath the
neon sign.

'Take your choice, Maria,' said Dag cryptically.

The bead curtain parted and an older woman appeared.
Long ringlets framed her face, and when she smiled invitingly
at Dag, several gold teeth flashed.

'Let's go to the bar instead,' I suggested.

In the hotel bar and restaurant, four men were sitting around
a table loaded with empty beer bottles, watching a World Cup
game on a wall-mounted television.

'Hey! Hello!' one of them yelled across to us. 'Wazzanem?'

As we had been asked that question at least two hundred
times since the morning, I couldn't really blame Dag for
wearily answering, 'My name is Godzilla.'

'Mr Godzilla!' cried the man joyfully, grabbing a full beer
bottle and hurrying over to join us. 'How you do?'

His friends watched with great interest as he proceeded, in
a happily drunken fashion, to hold a one-way conversation
with us in English.

'I have three daughter. One doctor. In Cana-da. To-ron-to.'

He paused, and held his fine nose between a thumb and
finger while he searched for words.

'To-ron-to. Big. Cold. Snow. Beautiful.'

By now he had ordered another round of drinks for himself,
his friends and, despite our efforts to dissuade him, for us.

'I doctor Vietnamese,' he said.

Gently, he took one of my wrists and held three of his fingers and a thumb against it. His forehead deepened into a frown as he felt my pulse. Then he began patting my hand, as if to comfort me, while speaking urgently – and quite incomprehensibly – to Dag.

'What's he saying?' I asked worriedly.

'Probably that you should go and see a doctor,' said Dag.

From his trouser pockets he pulled out various bits of paper and a ball point pen.

'Mr Godzilla – address!' he instructed Dag, handing him the pen and a piece of paper.

After a meal, several more beers and a friendly tussle with the good doctor, who tried hard to pay our bill, we bade him and his friends good night. As we left the restaurant we met a young Western tourist coming in. He wore his hair in a pony tail and had both ears pierced. With him was one of the girls who had been sitting beneath the 'Massage' sign. We stood to one side to let them pass through the doorway, and the tourist responded to my quizzical stare with a sheepish smile and a nervous clearing of the throat.

Despite the efforts of a ceiling fan, it was hotter inside our room than outside on the street. When we opened the one small window, the strains from a nearby karaoke bar drifted in. At the beginning of the trip, Dag had eschewed any suggestion of us ever staying in air-conditioned rooms, arguing that they were bad for the health and that we needed to acclimatize to the heat and humidity. I saw his point, but after such a long hard day, the prospect of a hot and noisy night was not a happy one. And, as I'd feared, the mosquito net had several large rips.

'This will be like sleeping in a swamp,' I said. 'Let's get a different room.'

'Maria, it's too much trouble, and they're all the same.'

'We'll take an air-conditioned one.'

'We will not!'

Ignoring him, I stalked out of the room and slammed the door. Down in the foyer, I caught a glimpse of the doctor heading out of the hotel. The girls on the bench were gone and in their place were two of the doctor's friends, each of them holding a ticket.

I asked at the desk about an air-conditioned room, and was told it cost eight dollars more.

'Perfect, I'll take it,' I said.

The receptionist was reaching over to the keys hanging from a board, when the lights went out.

'Electric cut, madam,' he said, fumbling for matches and candles. 'Very sorry.'

I made my way back to our room by the light of one candle.

'At least there'll be no karaoke for a while,' said Dag.

Cursing his cheerfulness, I joined him in bed.

The power was still out at six, when we got up. In the hotel foyer, we met the same tourist we'd seen the night before. He was paying his bill by Visa while his girlfriend leaned on the reception desk, smoking a cigarette, and leafing through his New Zealand passport. She looked more elegant than the night before, and wore gold-rimmed spectacles, tight-fitting jeans, a cotton shirt and high-heeled, wedge-soled sandals. Her face was carefully made up and she reeked of cheap perfume.

'Was it too hot for you last night as well?' I asked conversationally.

With a disdainful look, the girl blew smoke in my direction.

'Ah, yes, very hot, very uncomfortable,' stuttered her friend, blushing to the roots.

Along Qui Nhon's waterfront was a narrow strip of parkland with manicured flower beds and café tables shaded by striped umbrellas. Beyond it, a quarter of a mile away, fishing boats were hauled up on the beach.

'I'll bet that's Hanh and Tuyen's village down there,' I said. 'We should go and look for the whale temple, and ask about boats.'

'Let's have some breakfast first,' suggested Dag, propping his bike up beneath an umbrella.

While we waited for coffee and baguettes to be served, he spread our maps on the table.

'Look how exposed the coast of Binh Dinh Province is,' he said. 'I can't see a harbour that would be a natural place for a boat to head for.'

'Someone in that village must have an idea of where we could go,' I suggested.

'You think so?' he said. 'Remember what happened when we left Nha Trang? The fisherman only knew his local area and couldn't read a chart. And I doubt anyone here can get authorization to take us to the next province.'

'You're giving up before you've even tried,' I snapped.

'Okay, you go and find a fisherman!' cried Dag. 'You try bargaining and making him understand why the hell we want to go on his boat.'

A waitress arrived with our breakfast, and Dag bad-temperedly swept the maps off the table. 'You leave everything to me! You couldn't even be bothered to find your way around Qui Nhon this morning, I was the one who had to look at the map and work out where we were going!'

'That's not the point—'

'Yes it is! I'm fed up with arguing over prices and trying to make myself understood while you just sit back and let me do it all!'

He ripped off a piece of bread and started chewing it, staring out at the ocean. I sat in silence, thinking about what he'd said. His anger was justified. I had been leaving a lot to him, partly out of laziness but also because the guides, bus drivers, fishermen and bicycle salesmen we'd encountered so far had gravitated towards him, and not me, for bargaining and striking deals. And, I had to admit, during our trips I always depended on his skills, and his consistent drive and good humour to keep me going. But now, for the first time in all the travelling we'd done together, that drive and good humour was beginning to seep away. It was alarming, and it made me wonder if, this time, we'd perhaps taken on more than we could deal with.

'We're like a pair of Da Trang crabs,' I said finally, breaking the silence between us.

Dag rolled his eyes. 'What the—'

'There's a Vietnamese proverb about people who pursue

impossible tasks,' I said quickly. 'It comes from a legend to explain why those little crabs dig holes in the beach at low tide.'

His expression softened, and I told him about Da Trang, the man who owned a magic pearl that allowed him to understand what animals were saying. He treasured the pearl, and always kept it in his mouth. Once, he overheard some ants discussing a big flood that was soon to occur. He told this to the king, who moved his subjects and all his possessions to higher ground just in time to escape the biggest flood in history. After this, Da Trang was made advisor to the king and went all over the country, passing on information he heard from animals and birds. One day, the king wanted to listen to the fishes. He and Da Trang sailed out into a bay until they saw some squids. The squids were singing, and Da Trang thought this was so funny that he laughed out loud. The pearl fell out of his mouth and into the water, and was never seen again. Da Trang spent the rest of his days on the beach, sifting through sand, looking for it. After he died, his soul became a sand crab that would endlessly turn over every grain of sand in search of the magic pearl.

'So do you think we should give up?' Dag asked, when I'd finished.

'Absolutely not.'

He shaped his fingers and thumbs into imitations of pinchers, and waved his hands around like a crab's claws.

'Okay, Coffey, one way or another we'll get up this coast.'

We were wheeling our bikes through the park when a neatly turned-out young man approached us and began speaking in English.

'My name is Thang. I am so happy to meet with the foreigner. In my school we have teacher from New Zealand but she give three lessons a week and is too busy to talk with me.'

He was thrilled to discover I was from Manchester.

'Ah, Manchester United! You like football?'

I was equally thrilled to find him. Could he, I asked, spare a little time to act as our interpreter in the fishing village nearby?

Thang's face tensed up. 'I am third year English student at Qui Nhon College. My parents are poor. I have scholarship of only fifty-nine thousand dong a month. Sometimes my family send me a sack of rice from their farm.'

Once I'd assured him that we would pay well for his services, he relaxed. Then I tried to introduce the subjects of whale temple and boats, but Thang wasn't listening.

'In two days time, I have speaking exam. Can you help me? I tell you questions, and you say answers slowly and I write. Okay?'

He pulled out a book and a pencil from his bag, and we sat down on the edge of a concrete flower bed.

'First question,' he said, reading from the book. 'What are the ingredients for a successful life? Second question. What makes a good teacher? Third question. What are the advantages and disadvantages of foreign investment in Vietnam?'

While Thang scribbled my answers, I gazed towards the village.

'We want to find the temple of *Ong Nam Hai*,' I told Thang.

'You know *Ong Nam Hai*?' he cried. 'How is this possible?'

The village was a jumble of shabby houses, in a labyrinth of narrow, sandy alleyways. People stared suspiciously at us from doorways and dogs bared their teeth. I decided against trying to find a friendly fisherman in this place. And, much as I wanted Thang to ask if anyone remembered Hanh and Tuyen, I decided against that as well, remembering how unwilling they'd been to give me the addresses of their relatives. The whale temple, however, was easy to find. Situated just off the main road, it was built of brick and had two dragons sitting atop its tile roof. The windows were shuttered and the double wooden doors were padlocked. From behind it, an old man appeared, and introduced himself as the custodian of the temple. He was hunched over, and so skinny that folds of loose skin wrinkled around his knees. Inviting us to take tea with him in his house, he led us along a narrow dark corridor to a small room with a dirt floor. On the wall was a picture of a young man in uniform.

'It is me,' said our host. 'A soldier with Viet Minh.'

This old man had been in the army for forty years of his life, and had fought against the French, the Japanese, the Americans and his own countrymen. His son, he told us, had also fought against the Americans and the South Vietnamese Army, as well as the Cambodians and the Chinese. Medals were brought out, and more pictures of men in uniform.

'Is he happy with what has happened in Vietnam since 1975?' I asked Thang.

There was a very brief exchange.

'He work for the government and he is very busy,' said Thang evasively. 'He will show you the temple now.'

At first glance, it looked more like a school room than a place of worship. The walls were covered with a pale green wash, and tables and benches were set out on the red-tiled floor. But at the far end of the room three steps led up to an altar shaded with yellow parasols. Piled up behind it, reaching to the ceiling, were fifteen large, red wooden boxes. And propped up against these, forming a frame around the altar, were two enormous bones, each one eight feet high and nine inches across. I stood staring at these, trying to imagine the size of the creature they had come from.

'Bones very old,' said Thang.

I remembered Hanh telling me how the site for the temple was chosen by a geomancer over a century ago, when a whale was washed up on the beach. But the building we stood in looked fairly new.

'The local government believe in the whale,' said Thang, when I asked him about this. 'So they rebuild the temple.'

'But the local government is Communist,' I said.

'Yes. The fishermen support society with very much income, and the whale help the fishermen, so the government look after the whale.'

The old custodian was staring up at me.

'He want to know how you hear of *Ong Nam Hai*,' said Thang.

Wary of mentioning Hanh and Tuyen by name, I explained as briefly as I could about friends of mine in Britain who had left this village fifteen years ago.

'He want to know if they escape.'

I nodded.

'He say that one year ago, twenty-two people escape here on a boat. A big storm come, and they shout out for help. Two big whale appear and get close and make the boat not upside down. After one week, an American boat come and pick up the Vietnamese people. Now they are in America, they send a letter to this man, they tell how the whale save them, they say one day they will send a lot of money and rebuild this temple very bigger.'

It was a confusing scenario – a Communist party member and veteran NVA soldier who not only believed in a whale god but also happily accepted donations for the upkeep of the temple from anti-Communists who had fled the country.

'It is the way it is,' said Thang sagely.

Before we left the temple, we gave the custodian a donation for the temple. As an afterthought, I added an extra few dollars.

'From our friends in Birmingham,' I told Thang.

We invited Thang to have lunch with us in a nearby café. He ate slowly, and put a baguette into his bag for later.

'When I finish my exam I must go home to help my family with the rice harvest,' he said. 'After one month I will return to Qui Nhon, but I will be very thin, because my family do not have enough to eat.'

Before he left, we practised for his oral exam.

'What are the ingredients of a successful life?' I asked.

Carefully, he read out, 'Good health, happy relationships and love of one's work.' Then he paused, thought for a minute and looked up. 'And I want to say as well, money and freedom to travel, is this okay?'

8
QUA ROI

At twelve miles an hour, we cranked our pedals due north all the way through Binh Dinh province. But if we thought we were working hard, our efforts were little compared to what was going on in the paddy fields stretching away on either side of the road. Months earlier, I'd read about rice culture in books translated from French, published four decades ago and illustrated with drawings dating from the turn of the century. And what struck me, as we ground along on our bikes, was how little had changed in this landscape since 1900, and per-haps since long before that. In the southern half of Binh Dinh province, women were uprooting seedling rice plants from the mud, gathering them into bundles and carefully placing them into sacks which they carried away on shoulder poles. In adjoining fields, men and boys guided harrows yoked to water buffalo, preparing the soil for receiving the young rice seedlings. The replanting was done by teams of workers who moved forward in rows through the mud, working fast, bend-ing from the waist, faces hidden by conical hats. Technology certainly hadn't entered the lives of these people, or of the couple I watched when we stopped to rest. They were shifting water from an irrigation channel to a field, using a conical basket sealed with lacquer and attached to a double rope. Standing either side of the channel, they dropped the basket into the water then stepped back and tightened the ropes, swinging the brimming basket up into the air and dumping the water into the field. This they did rhythmically, quickly, steadily, over and over again without a break. According to the old French books, this operation is called *viec tat nuoc* and can be used by two people to shift eight hundred gallons of water an hour. And, according to more recent statistics, rural workers employed thus earned an average of eighty cents a day.

Somewhere around the fortieth mile of the day we started cycling through an area where the rice was ready for harvesting. The scene here was even busier and more labour intensive than further south. Whole families were out in the fields, cutting the paddy with sickles, feeding the stalks into threshers worked by foot pedals, stacking up the straw like conical hats. On the side of the road, women were winnowing the rice, tossing it into the air from large flat baskets, then spreading it out to dry on the highway, forming long white strips that covered a third of the asphalt. They didn't seem to mind when the passing traffic forced us to cycle right through these neat strips, and patiently smoothed out our tracks with hoes.

There was more than rice at the side of the road: beans, copra, nuts and salt were also spread out to dry, rice paper was stretched on racks and occasionally, in the shade of trees, sugar cane juice stands stood waiting for customers. Around mid-afternoon we stopped at one of these stands and sat on low wooden stools next to some farmers. They were gently curious about us. The men examined our bikes, and assured us we'd been grossly overcharged for them. The women tried on my hat and glasses, and showed concern over my skin, which was sunburnt and pouring with sweat. Meanwhile, the girl who owned the stand fed long lengths of sugar cane through a diesel-powered mangle. A murky green juice ran down a plastic pipe and into a bowl. She mixed this with shots of orange juice and lumps of ice, and served it to us in grimy glasses. It was delicious and refreshing, and as I drank it I imagined I could feel new energy coursing through my veins. The farmers grinned, pleased that I was enjoying this local drink and amused that we had chosen to travel, like them, by bike. Foreigners, they said, didn't stop here, but drove past in their cars. I thought about what people I knew had told me of the beauty of Vietnam, scenes they had witnessed through glass, from inside air-conditioned compartments. From where I sat, I could see small boys riding on the backs of water buffaloes, leading them into ponds where they wallowed to escape the heat of the afternoon. Farmers rested in the shade of palm trees whose wide leaves gleamed in the sunlight. Fishermen stepped through the irrigation channels, trapping fish with upturned baskets. It was, undoubtedly, a picturesque scene, but it belied the months, years and whole lifetimes of back-breaking work that had gone into creating it.

Around five o'clock, when the steep hills on the horizon were turning purple and gathering blue black clouds on their peaks, people in the fields began finishing up the day's work and heading home. Men pedalled bicycles heaped with tools and sacks, women carried heavily laden baskets swinging from their shoulder poles. They set off across the dykes towards villages tucked away out of sight behind groves of bamboo. Exhausted, and not wanting to face another soulless hotel, we were tempted to follow them, to ask if we could put up our tent and spend the night in one of their gardens. But, despite their shy smiles and their curious glances, we decided against it. By now we knew that the unbidden arrival of two foreigners, especially foreigners who could not speak enough Vietnamese to explain who they were or what they were doing, would cause alarm, and even fear in a village. Without an interpreter, or someone like Linh who had confidently invited us to his home, it seemed unfair to hoist ourselves upon an unsuspecting family, not knowing what repercussions there might be for them after we'd left.

And so, instead of a village, we ended up in a government-run motel, on the outskirts of Sa Huynh, just north of the border of Binh Dinh and Quang Ngai provinces. At first sight the place seemed to be deserted. The rooms, which ran around two sides of a large garden, were all in darkness. In the foyer of the main building, a night watchman was fast asleep on a table, his head resting on a pillow, his cigarettes and flashlight behind him. And the receptionist was snoozing behind her high desk. She was slender and pretty in an *ao dai*, and her long eyelashes trembled slightly on the fine skin of her cheeks. I was tempted to lean over and take a key from the board without disturbing her, but thought better of it. Gently, I touched her shoulder. She sat up with a start, then fumbled for a ledger and started paging through it.

'Yes, we have room to offer,' she mumbled, before I'd said a word.

The room had large flying ants, electricity that was cut off at eleven and a wash basin that dumped its water onto the bathroom floor. But the air coming through the windows smelt of salt, and carried the welcome sound of rumbling, rushing surf. Beyond the compound wall was a huge, curving beach. The sand was soft and warm beneath our feet. The lights of a fishing village and of boats twinkled to the north. Stars filled the sky, bioluminescence sparkled in the breaking surf. We swam and floated for an hour, then lay on the sand letting the breeze dry our skin. We forgot about the road, about buses and trucks with blaring horns, about the rigours of the journey ahead.

'You want massage?' said a voice early next morning.

A woman was standing at our window, talking insistently through the bars.

'My name Win, I give massage Nha Trang, Dalat, Hue, Hanoi, Danang. One hour, two dollar.'

We were easily persuaded, as our muscles were sore and stiff from the cycling. Win was strongly built and clearly a no-nonsense sort of woman.

'*Only* massage!' she firmly reminded Dag, as he lay down.

Squatting above him on the bed, she began by kneading his shoulders. He groaned in pleasure. As if to nip this enjoyment in the bud, she flipped him over, moved down to the other end of the bed, put his left foot over her right shoulder and then pulled back hard. CRACK! went his knee. After giving the other knee the same treatment, she flipped him over once more and clambered on top of him. Standing with one foot on his shoulder blades and the other on his buttocks, she steadied herself, then executed a little jump, landing with her full weight on his back.

'Ouch! Ouf! Urgh!' protested Dag, his cries muffled by a pillow. 'Stop! Enough!'

It wasn't enough as far as Win was concerned. Next came fifteen minutes of pummelling up and down Dag's body and then on his skull, where she managed to produce a sound like maracas being played. As a final touch, she grasped hold of his ears and, with accompanying splintering and crunching sounds, gave his head a sudden twist.

'YE-OUCH!' protested Dag.

'Finish,' announced Win, nudging him in the ribs.

With a stunned expression on his face, he rolled off the bed and fell into a chair.

'For God's sake don't let her walk on your back,' he said hoarsely.

I didn't, but it still took me a couple of hours to recover from the massage. We dozed and read in our room, went for a swim then dozed and read some more.

The beach was deserted, the hotel compound remained empty of any other guests, and we saw no one all morning. By eleven we'd decided to stay for another night. But I couldn't entirely relax. I kept thinking about the nearby fishing village. For all the difficulties I knew it would bring, I couldn't dispel from my mind the thought that we should try to get a ride on a boat to Quang Ngai, thirty-eight miles up the coast. When I suggested this to Dag, he pulled a face.

'Quang Ngai is seven miles inland,' he said.

'But it's on a river,' I countered.

'Yes, and look at the map – the river mouth is full of islands and the land all around it is marshy. It's the dry season here, so the river will be low. It might not be navigable for a boat. We might end up being dropped off far from a road, and having to push our bikes across rough ground. Do you want to try that again?'

'Maybe we should just go and talk to someone about it,' I wheedled.

'Fine,' he said, 'as long as *you* do the explanations and negotiations.'

After lunch, we cycled into Sa Huynh, which stretched along either side of Highway One for quarter of a mile. It was a bustling little place, with all the usual open-fronted shops and cafés from where people waved to us in a friendly, but not overly curious way. Yet when we left the highway and pushed our bikes along a sandy lane leading to the beach, we could have been a couple of aliens from outer space. Instantly, an excited crowd gathered around us. More people streamed out of the tiny passageways that led off the alley, and by the time we reached the water's edge we had become separated from each other by a press of men, women and children. Bodies were squashed up against me, little fingers were plucking at my clothes and patting my skin, someone was constantly ringing the new bell on my bike and someone else was trying to tug my notebook out of my hand. Determined that I should indeed take over the negotiations, I tried out a couple of the sentences in the notebook on one of the women next to me.

'*Anh co the cho toi di theo ghe anh toi Quang Ngai?* Can you take us in your boat to Quang Ngai?'

'*Chung toi muon di ghe boi vi bo bien cua viet nam dep lam.* We want to go by boat because the coastline is very beautiful.'

Not understanding a word of what I'd said, she leaned over to read the sentences, then relayed them to the crowd.

'Hung!' cried several people, pointing back towards the houses. 'Hung!'

Several children were dispatched, and presently Hung arrived. He was a rough and ready-looking chap, and he went straight over to Dag.

'He speaks a bit of English,' called Dag across the crowd. 'He says he'll take us to Quang Nhai for a hundred dollars!'

'Wait!' I cried.

Nudging people with my bike, I inched my way over to the two men. But, by the time I reached them, they already had an agreement. At seven the next morning Hung would meet us on the beach, and he would take us to Quang Ngai for fifty dollars.

'I thought I was supposed to be negotiating!' I said crossly, as Hung waded through the crowd and strode away.

'You weren't quick enough,' countered Dag. 'But you can come down here tomorrow and check out his boat.'

Back at the hotel, things had livened up. In the garden an enthusiastic game of volley ball was being played by eight local men, whose bare torsos were slick and gleaming with sweat. A white car was parked outside the reception building, and in the foyer the receptionist, Van, was giggling and flirting with two Americans.

'She's going wild over my belly,' said one, a smiling man with a generous paunch. 'It always works – the guide books should advise tourists in Vietnam to carry a strap-on stomach with them.'

Gregory Johnson and his friend Mark were touring the country by chauffeur-driven car. Mark was serious and rather tense, but Gregory had an easy bantering style, and appeared to take nothing and no one seriously.

'You're not going to join us, are you?' he asked me in mock astonishment, when we all sat down in the restaurant that evening. 'Surely you're going to serve us, then sit at another table and watch us eat and drink? And maybe give us all a little massage when we're ready? Or have I been in this culture for *too* long?'

He teased us mercilessly about our venture. 'By boat and bike up the coast? But didn't I hear you say you threw a bus in there somewhere? So if you've got three B's why not add a B.S – as in back seat? We're going to Hoi An tomorrow, and we've got lots of room in the car. And if that's going to mess things up for what you write in your book, we can always pretend the car's a boat. The way our driver swings around those potholes, you're bound to get sea sick anyway.'

It was a tempting offer. My intestines were once again in bad shape, and the thought of a long haul on a craft with, at most, very basic sanitation arrangements, was not appealing. But having made such a fuss about arranging a boat ride, I now felt duty bound to go through with it.

As I was locking our room early next morning, I discovered that the key I'd been using for the past two days was one we'd inadvertently brought with us from the hotel in Tuy Hoa. I tried using it to unlock the doors of a few other rooms, and they all swung open without a problem.

'That's global efficiency for you,' remarked Gregory, who was carrying luggage out to his car. 'Now, look, we've got plenty of room for you and your bikes. Are you sure you won't change your mind and come with us?'

I was sure. Shaking his head in bemusement, he watched me cycle away, my front wheel wobbling about and my chain ominously clanking.

In Sa Huynh, the alleyway that led down to the water was blocked by a busy market. Leaving Dag at a roadside café with our bikes and bags, I went to find Hung and check out his boat. The alleyway sloped steeply to the beach, and from the top end of it I looked down onto a sea of conical hats. Plunging into this, I elbowed my way through the crowds of women buying and selling bananas, oranges, herbs, leafy green vegetables, eggs, piglets, flowers and fish. Voices jabbered around me, hands plucked at my arm, there were squeals of surprise and coarse laughter. By the time I got to the village *dinh*, near the bottom of the alley, I was hot and breathless. I leaned against the wall of the *dinh*, which was emblazoned with carvings of fish and dragons. From the house opposite, an old couple sat staring at me, their bowls of *pho* frozen mid way to their lips.

'Hung?' I asked them. '*Ghe?* Boat?'

The old man barked some orders into the back room of his house, and a small child ran out. She was a tiny waif, with tousled black hair and shy eyes, but she had a determined little stride and led me off the main alley and into a maze of passageways. The houses were tightly packed together; incense burned on pedestals in front of each one, and cooking smoke rose from the back rooms. People peered out at me and called to the child for an explanation, but she marched on, speaking to no one. We went around so many twists and turns I began to wonder how I would ever find my way back. Finally, we stepped into a courtyard where three women sat on a veranda mending a nylon fishing net. At the women's bidding an old man appeared, and then Hung, who folded back the wooden doors of one of the rooms off the courtyard, and ushered me to a chair on one side of a large table. He sat opposite with the old man, and the three women gathered behind me.

'The boat?' I asked Hung.

He was ready for this, and handed me a piece of paper. On it was written:

It's very expensive to buy a boating. Talk to the landlord if you have boating from Sa Huynh to Quang Ngai for $150.00 total. Take your money buy oil, diesel. Follow me please my direction go you give me money. Have to pay. What did you do in your country? What are you doing now? Please come into my home. You have to pay. Get a lower price. No I not. Make sure she like the boating.

I read this, then looked up in puzzlement at Hung. Taking it back, he turned it over and wrote, Sa Huynh to Quang Ngai 150.00 US dollars.

'But yesterday, you said . . .' I began.

He nodded.

Oil diesel expensive, he wrote, and handed me the pen.

$150 – too expensive, I wrote.

One of the three women had started fanning me vigorously with her hat. The other two were examining my earrings. The old man was muttering away to Hung, as if egging him on in the negotiations.

MISS NYUGEN THI LUONG, wrote Hung.

I looked at this, mystified. Who was Miss Nyugen Thi Luong?

Okay $100, wrote Hung.

'Yesterday, $50,' I said.

He frowned and pouted.

No, Miss Nyugen Thi Luong, he wrote.

There was an impasse, as we both sat and looked at each other. One of the women pressed a glass of water into my hand. Another wiped the sweat off my neck with a cloth. Hung took up the piece of paper and scanned the original sentences.

'What did you do in your country, what are you doing now?' he read out.

'Teacher,' I said.

His face flooded with alarm and he reached once more for the pen.

Identification. Police post necessary. Insurance, he wrote.

I squirmed around, trying to get my passport out of the money belt I wore beneath my clothes without revealing too much skin or underwear. This involved some considerable contortions, which sent the women into a paroxysm of giggling. By the time I'd got the passport, Hung had lost interest in it, and was writing something else.

She go boating sea sick?

I shook my head.

No, he wrote. She go tourist boat. Beautiful mountain.

By now the old man was complaining loudly.

Father need tobacco, wrote Hung. Give money food and drink. I go boating $80.

I crossed out the 8 and wrote a 6 above it. The old man made a cackling comment and Hung crossed out the 6 and replaced it with a 7. Then he gave me a searching look.

'Your husband?' he demanded, getting to his feet. 'We go!'

I followed him back through the maze of streets and to the road, where we found Dag sitting outside a café nervously chewing his nails.

'I was getting really worried about you!' he cried.

'I've been negotiating,' I said proudly. 'Hung wanted $150 to take us to Quang Ngai—'

'Maria, I've been looking more carefully at the map,' he interrupted. 'I really doubt he'll be able to get up the estuary at Quang Ngai. You know how it is with these guys, they only know their local waters and he probably doesn't realize how low the river is right now. If he runs aground he'll be stuck there until the monsoon.'

Hung was listening intently, trying to follow the gist of the conversation.

'I got him down to seventy dollars,' I said weakly. 'And I'm sure he'd take sixty if we pushed for it.'

Hung nodded.

'It would be really unfair on the poor bugger,' said Dag, shaking his head. 'And I don't want to get stuck out in the middle of nowhere. I don't think we should go with him.'

'No go?' asked Hung in alarm.

'Sorry, mate,' said Dag.

'Nothing?'

'Nothing.'

Hung gave me a withering, disdainful look.

'I'm sorry—' I began, but he was already stalking away.

'After all that, you change your mind!' I fumed at Dag. 'I feel an absolute heel!'

'You might not when we reach Quang Ngai,' he said soothingly, and went to buy me a bowl of *pho*.

It was almost a relief to get back on the bikes, and to be travelling without any complications. We pedalled hard for a couple of hours, then stopped to investigate a small temple at the side of the road. A large eye was painted above its doorway and a red, yellow and blue flag hung from the roof. These are the symbols of Cao-Daism, an eccentric religion founded in the Mekong Delta in 1926. It preaches that God's word is brought to the world through messages from the spirits of deceased dignitaries like Victor Hugo, Joan of Arc, St John the Baptist, Louis Pasteur and Lenin. The Cao-Dai Holy See, in Tay Ninh Province, is renowned for its garish sumptuousness, but this was a humble little temple, with a mud floor and a ragged curtain covering an altar set with incense and a framed picture of an eye. The man who cared for the place invited us to his house to have tea with him and his family. His adult daughter was badly afflicted with palsy, but still managed to competently hold and breast-feed her small baby. As we stepped into the shade of their veranda, I noticed her and her mother looking at me in alarm. While travelling by bicycle, I had swapped my loose dresses, pants and shirts for a pair of knee-length shorts and a tight, sleeveless T-shirt that I'd bought in Nha Trang. These ugly but practical garments had so far caused little concern or offence, except to worry people that I was exposing myself too much to the sun. But now, I suddenly remembered that Cao-Daists have strict rules about dress, especially for women, who they believe should be respectfully attired. Quickly, I retreated to

my bike, and rummaged around in my bag for something to
cover up my bare arms and legs.

While we drank the green tea, the old man proudly showed us
a battered, leather-bound book. Written in French in the
1950s, it was an explanation of the tenets of Cao-Daism: the
belief in one God, the communication with God through spirits and mediums, vegetarianism, priestly celibacy, the cult of
ancestors and active proselytizing. What the book didn't tell of
was the demise of Cao-Daism. Under French rule it had been
a strong force in Cochin China, the area now covered by the
southern provinces of Vietnam, and had a formidable private
army. The French tolerated the movement because it was anti-
Viet Minh and helped to split up the nationalist front. During
the Franco-Viet Minh war, and then the American War, its
soldiers became incorporated with the South Vietnamese
Army. As punishment for this, after reunification the
Communists confiscated all Cao-Dai lands and executed some
of its members. In 1985, the Holy See and several hundred
temples, including the one we sat next to, were returned to
Cao-Dai control, and since then the movement has slowly
begun to gain strength once more.

'*Ong theo dao nao?*' the man asked. 'What is your religion?'

When we shook our heads to indicate we had none, his eyes
lit up. Remembering what the book had said about proselytizing, we drank up our tea, made our goodbyes, and quickly left.

We were now on our way through Quang Ngai Province, an
area with a long history of revolution. Early insurrections
against the French colonizers were followed by active involvement on the nationalist side during the Franco-Viet Minh War
from 1946 to 1954. During the US-backed regime of
President Diem, the Strategic Hamlet programme was instigated in the area in an attempt to curtail further guerrilla
activities. People were forcibly moved away from their villages
along the highway and into fortified settlements, where they
were closely guarded. This was anathema to the villagers, for it
took them away not only from the land where they had always
lived, but also from the graves and shrines of their ancestors. If

these were left untended, they believed, their relatives in the spirit world would suffer. Consequently, the programme only served to harden people's hearts against Diem, and soon the Communists were infiltrating the hamlets. As American involvement in Vietnam increased, Quang Ngai province suffered some of the bitterest fighting of the war, and the worst massacres of civilians, including those at My Lai, Binh Hoa and Bien Khe Ky Beach.

So far in our journey, when we'd asked people about the effects of the war on the countryside they'd usually said, '*qua roi*, past already', and changed the subject. But as we cycled through Quang Ngai province, we could see the effects for ourselves. In some areas, the fertile rice fields gave way to a sandy wasteland covered with patches of scrub that local people refer to as 'American grass'. This is the only plant able to flourish in soil made permanently toxic by the chemicals used in defoliation. When we stopped to rest I paged through my notes to find some information I'd scribbled down about the war: eleven million gallons of herbicides had been sprayed over Vietnam, thirteen million tons of bombs had been dropped on it, over two million hectares of its forest were destroyed and every one of its major roads had been stripped of foliage. Once, these figures had been nothing but statistics; now, as I looked around, they began to take on a horrible reality.

On the outskirts of Quang Ngai we crossed a bridge spanning the Tra Khuc River. On both sides of it were the remains of other bridges, blown up during the American War. Below us, a shallow stream of water flowed around dozens of little sand islands, and people poled their way along it in sampans. Dag was cycling ahead of me. Halfway across the bridge, he stopped to pump air into his tyre, which had developed a slow leak. I came to a halt behind him.

'You were right about the river,' I said.

'What river?' he replied with a grin.

As often as Dag had to stop and pump up his tyre, I had to scuttle off to look for a private spot where I could relieve myself. For days, Dag had been saying he thought I was suffering from giardia, an intestinal parasite that is notoriously difficult to shift. Not wanting to believe this, I'd rebuffed both his diagnosis and the course of strong drugs he recommended. Now, the grinding sensation in my guts, and the smell and consistency of what regularly emerged from them, made it clear that Dag was right. It was, of course, utterly foolish to be pedalling a clapped-out bike for hours on end in 35-degree heat while suffering from giardia. But, in my weakened state I began to think hard about what life was like for the people who cheerfully waved to us in greeting from the paddy fields. To truly understand, I should, of course have spent years bent over in the mud, planting rice, have lived through a devastating war, had my village razed to the ground, my land poisoned by chemicals, and my country brought to its knees by subsequent trade embargoes. As it was, all I could do was be a sick tourist on a heavily laden local bike. But at least I could imagine a little of what life was like for the woman ahead of me, pedalling five miles from her village to the nearest town with a fully grown pig strapped to the rack over her back wheel.

Unlike the woman, however, when I finally grew too weak and weary, around three o'clock that day, I was able to hail down a bus, pay for my bike to be put on the roof, and escape the sun and the effort of cycling for a couple of hours. As we waited to climb onto the bus, a sack was thrown from the roof. It hit the ground close to my feet and began thrashing and writhing about. The snake inside it, a very big cobra, was far from happy. A woman jumped off the bus, grabbed the sack by the neck and dragged it to the side of the road, then returned to collect a large cage that was being carefully handed down from the roof. The bamboo bars of the cage were rein-forced with mesh; inside them were a dozen skinny snakes, with shiny green bodies and bright red eyes.

'The small snakes are very poisonous,' explained Thanh, the young woman sitting next to me on the bus. 'They are going to China, for medicine.'

I was having difficulty in concentrating on what Thanh was telling me, as our bus was in the hands of a psychopath. Hunched over the wheel, he was treating his vehicle as if it was a weapon, swerving wildly around bikes, scooters, bullock carts and pedestrians. I began shutting my eyes each time he veered towards the edge of the road or into the path of an oncoming bus. But this only let my imagination run wild, as the sounds of horns blaring, gears crashing and brakes squealing summoned up pictures of horrible collisions, and of my head snapping forwards to meet the metal rib around the seat in front.

'I'm scared silly,' I told Dag, hoping he would say I was being irrational, and so dispel my fears.

'Me too,' he admitted. 'This is far more dangerous than being on a bike.'

Thanh, however, seemed totally unperturbed. She chatted away, telling me that she spoke fluent French as well as English, and worked as an interpreter for a French company that was building a hydro electric dam near Qui Nhon. Her annual holidays had just begun and she was on her way to Danang to visit her family and her fiancé. When I asked her if she enjoyed her job, she was politely disparaging.

'It is a strange situation. The French supervisors earn seven hundred dollars, and the French workers three hundred dollars – every day! And they have free accommodation and cars. We Vietnamese earn fifty dollars a month. It is the same for all of us, because we work for the government, and not the company. When the company employs us, they must pay the government a fee. The government gets more than we do. Even a Vietnamese civil engineer gets only fifty dollars a month, yet he works harder than a Frenchman.'

'Are the French workers friendly to you?' I asked

She thought for a minute.

'Only so-so. They are rich and we are poor, so we do not mix. I think these people are, what is the word –?' She pulled a dictionary from her bag and paged through it. 'How do you say this?' she asked.

'Arrogant,' I read out.

'Yes! Arrogant. What a good word. I like it!'

The bus stopped for half an hour at a restaurant. While the passengers tucked into bowls of rice and meat, a blind man and his son wound their way through the tables. The man played a guitar and sang into a microphone clipped onto his shirt, while his son led him round by the cord of the megaphone which amplified the songs to a deafening pitch. I got the feeling that most people were giving them money simply to encourage them to go away.

'What is he singing?' I asked Thanh over the din.

'Soppy songs,' she shouted back. 'He learned them when the Americans were here.'

At the back of the bus was a young man who spent most of the journey leaning out of the door, squinting against the bright sun and the hot, dusty wind, on the look out for more customers. When some appeared at the side of the road he signalled the driver to stop by yelling and banging on the roof. After he helped people aboard, he let the driver know when to start up again. Every fifteen minutes or so he scrambled onto the roof to check that the water from the cooling tank was flowing freely. It was desperate work, and I wondered at how he managed to retain his obvious good humour. When the bus had dropped us at the turn off to Hoi An and was driving away, he hung precariously out of the door to wave at us, grinning through clouds of dust and oily-black smoke.

After the harshness of Highway One, the narrow road to Hoi An was a delight, shaded by old and leafy trees and almost empty of traffic. On either side of it, paddy fields glowed golden in the late afternoon sun and stretched towards the purple folds of steep hills. The seven miles to Hoi An took us well over an hour, as we had to stop repeatedly for Dag to pump air into his back tyre, or for me to hop behind a tree. Now that the end of the day was in sight, I was feeling increasingly weak, and longed for somewhere cool to rest, with a bathroom close by. The paddy fields gave way to sleepy suburbs where charming old houses were fronted by gardens filled with mulberry bushes. Then we reached an intersection, and negotiated our way through a few other bicycles and scooters to join a wider but still unhurried street. Alongside us was a high wall topped with barbed wire. My legs were starting to feel decidedly wobbly, and the horribly familiar grinding sensation had started up once more in my guts.

'I have to stop soon,' I called to Dag.

'How about right now?' he replied, steering his bike through gates in the high wall, and towards the Hoi An Hotel.

Parked in the grounds of this government-run hotel were half a dozen white minibuses disgorging young tourists. These tourists streamed up the steps of a three-storeyed building and into a foyer with mock crystal chandeliers. There they besieged several young receptionists in pink *ao dai*s.

'Why are there no screens on the windows of our room?' an Australian woman was demanding.

'Screams, madam?'

'*Screens*. S-c-r-e-e-n-s. You know? To keep out bugs.'

'Mosquito nets, madam, we have those.'

'But we want a room with screens!'

Two Italians were shouting at another receptionist.

'You cannot keep our passports!'

'But, sir, madam, the police insist—'

'What if the police stop us, and we have no papers, and there is big trouble . . .'

While Dag tried to get some attention, I leaned against one end of the desk. Next to me was a stone pillar set with mirrored tiles. I looked with detached interest at my reflection. I was weather beaten, gaunt and the colour of dust. A stick insect came to mind. A stick insect on a bike. I giggled to myself at the thought.

'And where have you come from today?' said a voice close by.

A young American man was leaning on the desk next to me. An arm reached over between us and put a key on the counter, and a posh English voice cried, 'Excuse *me*, can you possibly tell me when check-out time is?'

The American was fresh faced, and smelled of soap.

'Where have I come from?' I repeated, wracking my brains to try and remember.

'Talk about a scam!' growled a girl behind me. 'We paid extra to travel in two minibuses so that we could have some empty seats to stretch out on. Twenty minutes out of Nha Trang one of them stopped and the driver insisted it had broken down, so we all had to squeeze into the other for the rest of the journey.'

'I can't remember where I've come from,' I admitted. 'We're cycling you see, and . . .' my voice trailed off, as I cast back through the memories of the day, the bus, the desolate stretch of road, the temple, the negotiations with Hung, the hotel.

'Sa Huynh!' I croaked, relieved that my memory hadn't entirely been wiped out. 'I've come from Sa Huynh!'

The man's eyes had filled with surprise.

'You're *cycling*? Where from? Where to?'

I gave him a brief run-down of our journey across the Mekong Delta, the bus to Nha Trang, the boat rides to Tu Bong.

'And from there we've cycled about two hundred and ninety miles, give or take a couple of bus rides,' I concluded.

'Wow! That sounds really rugged!'

'It's hell,' I told him. 'Don't ever consider doing it.'

'God no,' he said. 'I thought the minibuses were bad enough.'

'How old are you?' I asked.

'Twenty-one,' he answered.

Exactly half my age. As we left the foyer, and wearily pedalled off into Hoi An's old quarter to look for a less chaotic place to spend the night, I decided it really should be me who was being ferried around Vietnam like a senior citizen, and not the young American.

9

FULL MOON IN HOI AN

'Enchanté, madam,' said Thap, bowing as he took my hand.

The feeling was entirely mutual. This charming, French-speaking young doctor was almost ridiculously handsome, with brown-black eyes, chiselled cheek bones, shining hair and perfect teeth. Dag had met him the day before, when he'd called at his surgery to ask for advice on my condition. Since arriving in Hoi An I'd been flattened by giardia, and the hefty dosage of Flagyl I was taking against it had joined forces with my malaria medication to give me bouts of dizziness. For two days I hadn't moved from our small guest house, and Dag was beginning to worry if I ever would. But Thap had assured him that he was treating me correctly, and that I would soon recover. He had also invited him out the following evening for a sampan ride on the river, to watch the rising of the full moon. This was a tradition for the people of Hoi An, he told him. It was also an enticing enough prospect finally to get me off my bed and out into the streets.

We met Thap at his house, which was like something from a film set. Built a hundred years before by his Chinese grand-father, its long narrow rooms had stone-flagged floors, walls with a natural 'distressed' look that interior designers in London spend fortunes trying to reproduce, and arched ceilings supported by hefty iron wood pillars set in marble bases. I was a little embarrassed by having to ask for the whereabouts of the toilet the moment I stepped through the door, but Thap was quietly sympathetic.

'Ah, oui, ce n'est pas le problem,' he kindly replied. 'But it is a simple place – I am a poor man.'

He led me through the long narrow room towards a shadowy inner courtyard. On the way we passed a woman sleeping on a bed base.

'My wife,' said Thap, speaking softly so as not to disturb her. 'She is sick, like you.'

When I emerged from the small toilet cubicle, Thap was standing in the courtyard by the stone well, placing sticks of burning incense in a brass holder set at its base.

'I make an offering to *Than Gieng*, the spirit of this well,' he told me, 'so that our water is always sweet.'

Moonrise was not until around eight, so first we had dinner with Thap at one of the small restaurants along the river bank. Long sampans with slender eyes on their prows were being rowed across the quietly flowing water to Cham Kim Island. Geese paddled around in the back eddies, pecking through the reeds and water hyacinths. Bamboo cages of ducks hung from house boats moored to stakes in the mud and lines of washing flapped above them like bunting.

'Once big ships came here,' said Thap. 'From China, Japan, Portugal, India, Britain. Can you imagine?'

Since Cham times, there had been a harbour in this vicinity. In the sixteenth century, to help foster economic growth in the south of the country and support the cost of their battles with the Trinh Lords of the North, the Nguyen Lords established the port of Hoi An. It quickly grew and became a prosperous, bustling place, trading in silk, areca nut, tobacco, sugar, gold, sea swallows' nests, cinnamon, molasses, elephant tusk and rhinoceros horn. Junks of up to ninety feet in length were locally built. Trade routes developed along the coast of Southern Vietnam and out into South East Asia. From China and Japan, ships sailed south with the northwest monsoon and stayed until the summer, when the southwest trades blew them home. The merchants developed communities in the town and intermarried with local women. Soon Hoi An had Japanese and Chinese quarters, temples and meeting halls. Some Europeans settled here also. In 1688 the British trader William Dampier wrote, 'Among the Western merchants . . . many owe their prosperity to their Viet wives, to whom they entrust money and commodities . . . These women know how to buy in at propitious moments and, as soon as they have built up a little capital, to increase it quickly.'

The town's heyday was in the seventeenth and eighteenth centuries. By the nineteenth century, the Thu Bon River had begun to silt up. Then Da Nang developed as a commercial port, overshadowing Hoi An, which became the sleepy backwater of twenty thousand people that it is today. The merchants and the traders, however, left an indelible mark. Houses like Thap's are common all over Hoi An; some are even older. The big ships have gone, but an atmosphere of time long passed still clings to the town.

The evening light was becoming softly tinged with blue. Across the road from where we sat was a two-storey stone house with hints of Portuguese influence: yellow-washed stone walls, a tree heavy with pink flowers growing around a doorway leading into a courtyard, pale green shutters over windows. I imagined sitting on the balcony of this house each evening and gazing out over the darkening river.

'I want to live here,' I told Thap, in jest. 'Could we rent that house?'

'I am sorry, in Hoi An this is not possible for the foreigner,' he said apologetically. 'The police will not allow it.'

Because his family had supported the American-backed Republic of Vietnam before 1975, Thap was now forbidden to work in any of the state-run hospitals. Instead, he had set up his own private practice, and ran a surgery from the front room of his house.

'Before, it was a big struggle,' he said. 'But now since *doi moi* things begin to get better.'

Taking my note book and pen, he drew Chinese ideograms on the back page. 'This sign means "stop",' he said, 'this one "the Knife" and this one "into the Heart". The three signs together mean "stop the knife in the heart", and stand for one word in your language. Can you guess what it is?'

'Mercy,' I guessed.

'Rescue,' ventured Dag.

He shook his head.

'It means patience. This is an important word for us in Vietnam. Now we must have much patience. We have the chance of big change, but the old men in the government do not want us to change fast, it is not good for them, because with the old system they can be very corrupt. We must be patient and wait until they are gone.'

As darkness fell, restaurant owners came out to light small oil lamps on the tables, and soon the faces of people sitting around them were softly illuminated. Our dinner was exquisite: minced pork wrapped around strips of peeled sugar cane; rice paper parcels of shrimp sprinkled with nuts; fish cooked with lemon grass, sesame seeds and coriander. When we'd finished eating, Thap called to a couple who had been hopefully watching us from the sampan moored close to our table. They helped us into their unstable craft, then paddled it downstream, past a settlement of small, narrow houseboats. Rising incongruously from the low, woven canopy of one boat was a large television aerial. Beneath it several figures were outlined by the light of a black and white screen.

'World Cup!' cried Thap, and there was a pause in our journey as we stopped to find out the progress of the game.

Soon we stopped again while the boatman baled out his sampan with an old army helmet. Thap leaned companionably against Dag and draped one arm around him.

'The first time I saw you,' he told him, 'I thought you were Ernest Hemingway!'

Other sampans passed us, their paddles making satisfying splashing sounds, and with joss sticks glowing and sparking in their prows. There was an air of expectancy and excitement; everyone was waiting for the moon. Heralded by a halo of soft light it appeared, huge, yellow and majestic, rising above the

palm trees of Cham Kim Island. *Chi Hang* – Sister Moon –
was greeted with cries of delight, with offerings tossed into the
water, with fire crackers and clapping. Suddenly I was transported back, fourteen years and thousands of miles, to another
moonrise, the one I'd watched in Manchester with Hanh.
She'd been filled with nostalgia for her country that night, and
as we drifted along the river, bathed in the light of a spectacular moon and with warm air on our skin and the scent of
flowers and incense in our nostrils, I understood why.

Early next morning, I sat on the rooftop garden of our guest
house, gazing down into Tran Phu Street and trying to imagine how this place must have looked in the seventeenth and
eighteenth centuries. Some things, surely, had barely changed.
The doorway of the old Chinese house across the street had
been sealed up the night before with three sets of horizontal
planks slipped into notches on wooden pillars. As I watched,
someone inside the house began removing the central section
of planks. The first one came down, then I saw a hand reaching up to dislodge the other planks one by one. Gradually, an
elderly woman revealed herself – first her grey hair, then her
old and elegant face and finally her black pyjamas. When the
doorway was uncovered she shuffled onto the street and placed
burning joss sticks in the brass holders attached to the outside
of the pillars. Then she stood on the pavement, speaking to the
sellers going by, checking on what they had to offer in the baskets hanging from their shoulder poles: *gio*, minced pork
wrapped in banana leaves, *banh ran*, sweet rice paste balls and
pho. Swinging from the *pho* seller's pole was a complete
kitchen, including a charcoal burner filled with glowing coals,
all the ingredients needed for her soup, bowls, spoons, chopsticks, glasses and a kettle of tea. As I watched her sway down
the street, and heard her cry of '*Pho-OH*' echoing behind her,
I was easily taken back three hundred years. Then a scooter
buzzed by, and I remembered that this was 1994, and there
was no more rhinoceros horn to be traded in Hoi An, and no
more sailing junks to take it away to China.

As our bikes were in dire need of an overhaul, we set off to
look for a repair shop. Across the road from the Hoi An Hotel,

a man was sitting beneath the shade of a large umbrella, replacing the inner tube of a bicycle wheel. Next to him was a woman dressed in biscuit-coloured cords, a white cotton shirt and a floppy white sun hat. She darted across the road to us.

'You want to rent a scooter?' she asked, furtively glancing towards the hotel gates.

We told her we only needed help with our bikes.

'Yeah? Come here, see my friend!'

Mai spoke excellent English, with a strong American accent.

'I learned it from my daddy's friends,' she told us.

We sat with her beneath the umbrella while her friend began work on the bikes.

'My daddy was a Lieutenant Colonel with the South Vietnamese Navy. We lived in Danang, we had picnics with his American friends, and sometimes they took me water skiing. But we didn't know all about his work. He was more important than we knew. In 1975 the government say they will put him in prison – for ever. So my daddy kill himself.'

From one trouser pocket she pulled out a small wad of dollars, stared at it absently, then transferred it to the other pocket.

'Since then me and my family are punished. I was a teacher, but now I can't work for the government. So I help this guy get business mending bikes and renting out motor cycles to tourists. You see those guys over there, leaning on motor scooters? They are party members, so they can work in the best place, right by the hotel. They get mad if they see me close to the gates.'

A couple of young foreign tourists walked by. Mai jumped to her feet and ran after them. They stopped and listened to her, but gave her no business.

'This government is Communist,' she said as she sat down again, 'but it does not help the people. I have to work night and day to pay to send my three kids to school.'

She explained how, in 1987, the government had allowed people to set up private businesses, but at the same time had cut state funding of health and secondary education. I told her about the woman we'd found lying at the side of the road, and how no one had stopped to help her.

'That's because the hospital would have asked them for lots of money.'

'We should have somehow taken her,' I said guiltily.

'Are you crazy? You'd still be there, they'd find all sorts of excuses to make you keep paying money!'

I was surprised by how openly Mai was speaking, out here on the street. And she was only warming up.

'Once, no one could speak on the street like this! Two years ago, there was an Englishman here. He used to be my teacher in Danang in 1970. He came back to Vietnam for a holiday. I wanted to invite him to my house for dinner, so I ask the police but they say no, not possible. So I meet him in a café, and we talked for three hours. That night, the police came to my house and took me to the police station. They gave me a pen and a paper and they said I had to write down everything I had discussed with my teacher. They said perhaps he is FBI or CIA. I tell them we have no secrets, but they make me pay money. After that, they watch me for weeks. Now the police let me talk to the foreigner on the street, but I cannot let you stay in my house – if I do I will be fined twenty dollars.'

'Why is the government still so strict?' I asked her.

'Vietnam looks at Russia and is afraid of changing too fast,' she said.

I told her about the government calling for an end to the discrimination against Southern intellectuals and professionals who had served the pro-American regime, and that it now wanted to harness their expertise to aid the country's growth.

'Yeah, maybe,' said Mai reluctantly. 'But it happens very slowly.'

We continued to sit and chat for an hour, while her business partner worked on our bikes.

'How come these bikes are in such bad shape?' asked Mai.

I told her about our journey across the delta, and our attempts to get up the coast by boat and bike.

'I can't believe it! You travel on these boats? No tourist does this! Are you crazy?'

'I'm beginning to think so,' I said ruefully.

She looked carefully at Dag's yellow, waterproof camera box.

'Your husband, he's a journalist, right?' said Mai.

'I'm writing a book,' I admitted.

She was silent for a minute. 'So you want to get a fishing boat from here?'

It was our turn to be silent.

'We thought about trying to get one up to Lang Co,' said Dag uncertainly. 'And then from there to Hue. But we haven't done anything about it yet.'

'My husband will find out about this for you,' she said, without hesitation.

'But what about the police?' I asked.

Her eyes gleamed. 'Right now, all day and night the police watch the World Cup. While there is this football, we are free to do anything we want.'

At six that evening we met Mai and her husband Hoang for dinner in a restaurant run by some of their friends. Hoang was a handsome man with twinkling eyes and a mischievous grin. Although he spoke some English, he was shy about doing so around his wife. We were served our meal by a tall, dark-skinned and startlingly beautiful girl in her late teens. Thick, shiny hair fell to below her waist, and she moved with the grace of a fawn.

'She is the youngest daughter of my friends,' said Mai. 'Many tourists fall in love with her.'

In one corner of the room, two young Frenchmen were doing exactly that, staring dreamily at her over their menus. She glanced back from time to time, smiling shyly, seemingly unaware of the effect she was having on them.

'There is an English man called John,' continued Mai. 'He is thirty-seven, he was here one week. He asked her to marry him and she agreed. He pay me to teach her some English, so they can talk. Now he is in Hanoi, to do the paperwork. He is very afraid. He know many foreigners love her. I didn't tell him what happened last week. A Dutch man came here with a tour group, he fell for her and he left his group! They went on to Hue without him. But next day he left, he was crying, because I told him she will get married.'

The girl put bowls of food before us. Her eyes ranged over Dag's face.

'What do her parents think about her marrying John?' I asked Mai.

'They are very happy! They are worried that no Vietnamese man will marry her.'

'*What?*'

'Maria, look at her skin! See how dark it is. Vietnamese men like pale skin. And she was born in the Year of the Tiger. The tiger girls are very difficult, and men are afraid to marry them.'

Another couple had come into the restaurant. One was a young foreigner with fashionably ripped jeans and bleached hair. Accompanying him was the girl we had seen with the New Zealander in the hotel in Qui Nhon. Mai leaned across the table to us.

'You see this girl? I talked to her today. Last night she checked into the Hoi An Hotel. Her boyfriend told the receptionist she was American. They asked for her passport, then they called the police. The police told her to go away. All night she walked around the streets. At four this morning she came to this restaurant, and the family let her sleep here.'

'What will she do tonight?' I asked.

'I don't know. But she tell me this man give her five dollar a day, and all her food. I say to her, don't you want to get married? No man will marry a prostitute. She said she doesn't care.'

Finally, after all the gossip, we got around to discussing our travel plans.

'This afternoon my husband went to the fishing village near here,' said Mai. 'He talked to five fishermen. One says he will take you all the way to Hue, for ninety dollars.'

We sat in stunned silence, staring at her.

'Is this too expensive?' she asked.

'No – not at all! It just seems too . . . easy.'

'Tomorrow we go with you to the village. We talk to the fisherman and make a contract. I think you can leave in a couple of days. And maybe me and my husband come with you – we've never travelled like this! It is an adventure.'

'We must pay you for your help—' began Dag.

Hoang, who had been smiling throughout this conversation, shook his head vehemently.

'No!' cried Mai. 'Maria, when I first saw you on your bike I really liked you. I don't know why. It was something about your face. I feel I know you from sometime before. We do this for friendship only.'

The fishing village was on the banks of the river mouth, four miles from Hoi An. We cycled there along a country road behind Mai and Hoang, who were sharing a bicycle. Mai sat sidesaddle on the luggage rack, her sun hat pulled down over her eyes, turning to grin at us from time to time. After crossing a bridge, we left the lane for a sandy track that ran alongside the river and through the village. Palm trees leaned over the water, and boats were tied up to their trunks. The houses were well hidden behind fences made of thatch and bamboo. Behind one of these fences we were introduced to Luc, the fisherman who had offered to take us to Hue. He was wearing a yellow hard hat and he sat on a bed base in the shade of a veranda. Close to his feet, chickens scratched around heaps of blue and red fishing nets. Hovering around behind him was a tiny old lady. She had sparse grey hair and betel-stained lips, and her teeth had been blackened with a mixture of tannin and ferrous sulphate, an old custom, done for the sake of beauty, that was now dying out. She seemed bothered by our presence and kept up a cackling diatribe during the introductions.

'Luc will show you his boat and my husband will go with you,' said Mai. 'I will stay here with Luc's mother.'

The boat was roughly built, but sturdy. It had a tiny cabin amidships over the engine, and a low wooden canopy on the deck. As usual there were no life jackets aboard, no life raft and no navigational instruments except for a couple of home-made oil lamps. There were, however, the remnants of many joss sticks stuck between planks all over the forty-foot-long boat, and fresh offerings of fruit and flowers on the prow. At the very least, I thought, we'll have the spirits on our side.

'You like this boat?' asked Hoang.

'We like it very much,' said Dag. 'Tell the captain we agree to his price.'

Hoang nodded.

'So we go to Lang Co, sleep one night on the boat, then go on to Hue in the morning.'

'What about the police?' I asked. 'Does Luc need a travel permit?'

He lowered his voice. 'Round here, the police very strong. If the captain ask permission, it will be very difficult, very expensive. So we leave early, in the dark. Maybe the police don't see us. If they do, I will talk with them, give them money and cigarettes.'

Back at the house, with Mai translating, we discussed when we should leave.

'Today is Sunday,' said Dag. 'How about we leave on Tuesday?'

'Luc is going fishing on Monday and Tuesday.'

'Okay, how about Wednesday?'

'He say he cannot go on Wednesday, because it is not an auspicious day.'

'Thursday?'

Thursday was agreed upon, but Luc's mother was still far from happy. In a shrill voice, she cross-examined Mai, waggling an admonishing finger at her.

'This is very difficult for me,' sighed Mai. 'The old lady is worried about the danger for her son on this long journey. She says he is her only son and she cannot lose him.'

I assured her that Dag was my only husband, and I had no intention of losing him on the way to Hue.

'She also ask me about money,' continued Mai. 'She say that you should pay one hundred dollar, because the risk to her son is so great.'

'Tell her,' said Dag, 'that if all goes well and the trip is a success, we will pay a hundred dollars.'

When this was translated the old lady treated Dag to a blackened grin, but still continued to complain.

'Now she talks of the police. She say we must leave very early, at least by four in the morning.'

We said this was no problem for us and, thinking that it might be helpful towards an even earlier start, we suggested camping in the yard of the house the night before we left. This wasn't well received. Heads shook vigorously, and voices rose.

'They say that if you do this, the police will fine them. It is better if you come here on your bicycles very early.'

Before we left, Luc's sister shyly asked if she could sample the mineral water I had with me in the basket of my bike. She'd never tried it, she said, because it was too expensive, but she had seen many tourists drinking it and had always wondered how it tasted. I handed her the bottle; she unscrewed the top and took a mouthful. '*Waaaah!*' she cried, spitting the lot out onto the sandy ground. '*Xau!*' Bad!

It was no problem to while away some time in Hoi An. We explored the fish market along the river bank, where women vendors smoking fat hand-rolled cigarettes squabbled nastily and noisily with each other. We sat in a café watching the World Cup on television with cyclo drivers who had left their vehicles abandoned and cluttering up the narrow street outside. We visited Japanese graves and Chinese pagodas, the boat-building yard on Cam Kim Island, a cotton mill that was straight out of Dickens and houses built by Chinese merchants two centuries ago and now declared by the government as 'living relics'. We wandered over a seventeenth-century wooden bridge built by Japanese merchants who believed it would incapacitate the giant dragon that lay stretched out from India to Japan and caused earthquakes in their homeland by flailing its tail. We even took a day trip, hiring Hoang and his friend Vinh to show us around the local area on the backs of their Hondas. Our first stop was the Marble Mountains, which rise sheer from the coastal plain, are indeed made of marble and are riddled with caves. Over the course of time these have been the site of Cham shrines, Buddhist temples and the hiding place of the Viet Cong; now they are a major tourist attraction. 'Guides', clutching trays of marble trinkets, descended upon us the moment we stepped into the site.

'Madam, sir, you buy?' these women whined. 'Pleeese, madam, sir, you buy? One statue? Cham statue, madam, sir, you buy?'

They followed us up and down hundreds of rough marble steps, and through caves where incense drifted across shafts of

light and statues peeped from rocky niches. The most spectacular of these caves was *Huyen Khong*, used by the Viet Cong as a
field hospital. It boasted sheer, lichen-covered walls, red-skinned
mandarin statues flanking its entrance, a large Buddha sitting
high on a rock ledge and a stone bench with Cham engravings.
Chinese tourists stood beneath its impressive stalactites, holding up cupped hands to catch the dripping water that is said to
come from heaven and rubbing it over their heads. Their children raced around them, playing tag and squealing loudly. A
brown-robed monk strode over to one of these children and
crossly hit him on the head with a packet of joss sticks. I felt
like doing the same to the four women who were clustering
and whining around me, and making it impossible quietly to
take in the powerful atmosphere of the place.

We had a brief stop at China Beach, a lovely stretch of coastline marred by an unspeakably ugly Soviet-built hotel with a
sign at its gateway saying, 'Have a good day' on one side and
'Have a good trip' on the other. It wasn't a place to linger, and
soon we carried on to My Son, Vietnam's most important
Cham site. For miles we bounced along a rough red dirt track,
through pot holes and puddles, and into an area that had been
badly defoliated in the war. Popping up from the desolate plain
were some brand new and empty houses. They were built of
concrete and painted in pastel colours, and the dirt around
them had been flattened out as if someone was about to
bravely attempt planting a garden.
  'Who owns these houses?' I yelled to Hoang.
  'Party cadres,' he yelled back.
  The track narrowed and began to climb. Soft green-clad
hills rose up around us, and wild goats skittered along their
steep slopes. A stream tumbled down through the narrow valley, and we had to dismount and push the Hondas across it. I
felt as if we were entering another country, an untamed jungle
landscape worlds away from the defoliated plain and the managed rice fields of the coast. We came across no settlements
until, close to My Son, there was a thatch booth to buy tickets
for the site, and a tiny open-sided café. Leaving the scooters
here under Vinh's care, we followed Hoang along a path that

wound through bamboo groves and clumps of papayas, bananas, coffee and taro plants. Mimosa spread over the ground, purple flowers bloomed all over bushes and bright butterflies fluttered around our heads. The air was still, hot and filled with the ringing of bird song and the burbling of a stream. Hoang caught a cicada and held the furiously whirring insect to his ear.

'What is name of this? See-car-dah? I like it VERY much!'

Then he stopped, and pointed ahead. 'Look!'

Peeking from the jungle were the ancient red brick towers of My Son.

The Hindu kingdom of Champa survived along the central coast of Vietnam from the second to the fifteenth century, when it was all but wiped out by the conquering Viets on their steady move south. Through commercial relations with India and the immigration of Indian literati and priests, the Chams adopted Hinduism, used Sanskrit as a sacred language and borrowed much from Indian art. My Son, which they occupied from the fourth to the thirteenth centuries, was their religious centre and possibly the burial ground for their monarchs. It remained almost intact until the American War, when Viet Cong guerrillas used My Son as a base and the Americans subjected it to devastating bombing. Hoang led us around the few towers still left standing. They were dark windowless places with vines, bamboo and cacti sprouting from between bricks that were cemented together in a process that is still a mystery. Inside and around them were carvings of Shiva, Ganesh, Vishnu, a headless statue of a male figure with a snake curling around his torso, tablets of stone inscribed with Sanskrit and lingams bigger and more phallic than any we'd come across in India. A large billy goat came up behind us while we were examining one of these lingams. It gave Dag a friendly butt then curled up on the stone slab and went to sleep. Peeking from a temple doorway close by was its mate and two newly born kids, their legs wobbly and umbilical cords still hanging from their undersides – living symbols of fertility to match the ancient ones all around us. By now it was late in the afternoon. The towers were a deep

glowing red, and from behind a mushrooming cloud the sun
sent out an ethereal halo of pale gold, green, pink and purple.
The atmosphere was eerie and unsettling; Hoang, Dag and I
looked at each other and decided it was time to leave.

We've never been good at sightseeing, and by Wednesday we
were becoming restless. Dag, for want of something better to
do, decided to go to the barber's to have his ears cleaned.
Traditionally, the Vietnamese believe that ear wax is actually
the faeces of worms, and must be periodically removed.
According to a French book I'd read, this is done with 'spat-
ulas, hooks, soft brushes, porcupine spines and the breath'.
The more assiduous barbers went on to 'clean the eyes by
returning the superior lids and scraping the internal faces'.

'Are you having that done as well?' I asked Dag in horror.

'No,' he said blithely, 'just my ears.'

The barber's shop was close to our guest house, on Tran
Phu Street. It was open onto the pavement, with a low wooden
ceiling and green paint peeling from the walls. In front of a
stained mirror was a shelf of pots containing greasy combs
and messy shaving gear. The barber was small and weasel-
faced, and wore a dirty overall and a head torch that looked
huge on his narrow forehead. Resting on his lap was a tray full
of long, sharp instruments. He picked up what looked like a
narrow spatula, inserted a good inch of it into Dag's left ear,
and started waggling it from side to side. Dag lay frozen still on
the reclining chair, his face set.

'What's he doing?' I asked in horror.

'Scraping the inside of my ear,' said Dag through gritted
teeth. 'With something sharp. I'm scared to move in case he
cuts me.'

The word AIDS came to my lips. I pursed them and held it
back.

The spatula was replaced by what looked like a kebab
skewer. Almost two inches of it disappeared inside Dag's head.

'I didn't know my ears went in that deeply . . .' croaked Dag.

I was beginning to feel nauseous. The skewer came out and
a long pair of tweezers went in. Then, very delicately, the
barber removed a large piece of wax.

Dag's eyes were round as marbles. 'The inside of my ear is really hot,' he whispered.

'Dag, for god's sake, he's picking up a porcupine quill—!'

'Okay, that's it!' Dag cried, suddenly coming to life and trying to struggle out of the chair. The barber leaned his elbows on his chest to push him back, still attempting to get the quill into his ear. For such a little man, he appeared remarkably strong.

'No, please, thanks – get *off*,' cried Dag, finally getting free of the barber and scrambling to his feet. 'It's okay, I'll pay you the lot—'

He shoved a fistful of dong into the hands of the puzzled man, and fled.

In the post office, I wrote a long fax to my publishers in London, with news of the journey so far. As it was lunch time, there was only one clerk on duty, a smiling girl dressed in a red and white *ao dai*. She disappeared with my fax into a back room, leaving me to gaze up at a picture of Ho Chi Minh on the wall above the counter. It showed him in middle age, with his hair just beginning to recede from his temples. He was reading a newspaper, holding it away from him as if he was longsighted. Not once had I heard anyone say anything derogatory about Ho Chi Minh. Even the people we'd met who had supported the Republic of Vietnam before 1975 showed nothing but respect for his memory. Binh, our guide across the Mekong Delta, and now my new friend Mai were vocal in their condemnation of the government, yet they both fondly referred to the man in the picture as 'Uncle Ho'.

'He was a good man,' Mai had said. 'He loved our country and our people.'

The girl reappeared. 'Your fax has gone to London.'

I handed her ten dollars. In return, she gave me a transmission report.

'The fax?' I asked. She was holding it in her left hand.

'We keep it,' she answered.

'Why?'

'To show the police.'

She nodded to a pile of fax sheets on a nearby table.

My mind raced through the information I'd just consigned to paper. Most of it was fairly innocuous, except for the closing lines about our forthcoming illicit trip on a fishing boat from a village near Hoi An.

Reaching across the counter, I took hold of one end of the fax sheet. 'I need this,' I said, giving the paper a slight tug.

The girl's grip on the other end tightened.

'It is the regulation,' she said.

'I need it for my records,' I told her.

'It is private?'

'Of course!' I said, forcing a smile and trying not to let my voice give away my concern.

'I can photocopy it?' she suggested.

'No!'

I tugged hard on the paper, but she wasn't giving way.

'You keep the transmission report,' I suggested, 'and I'll take the fax.'

'The police –' she said, glancing around the empty room. 'I am not allowed—'

'My *husband* wants this fax,' I told her.

I'd said the magic word.

'Ah, your *husband*!' she cried softly, letting go of the paper. 'I understand. But next time, I have to keep it.'

Mai was not in the least surprised to hear this story.

'My foreign friends who make business here tell me the same. Their phone calls are listened to and their letters are opened.'

We were at her house for dinner. Her two children, aged eleven and ten, had come to collect us. They sat on one bike, like replicas of their parents, and led the way off the main street and along narrow dirt tracks where houses crowded together. The family's small home had a thatch roof, stone walls and glassless windows. A wide doorway opened from the street onto a living room where a blue plastic three piece suite was arranged around a glass-topped coffee table. On one wall were shelves crammed with dog-eared books. There were twenty-year-old dictionaries and English grammars, several of Enid Blyton's Famous Five stories, a collection of Charlie Brown cartoons and a battered copy of Nietzsche's *Zarathustra*.

'Have you read Nietzsche?' asked Hoang. 'He is my favourite writer. I am his follower!'

'He's a very free thinker,' teased Dag.

'Of course! I read many philosophers. Do you know Jean Paul Sartre? I have read all his books too – but many years ago.'

Mai began serving out a delicate fish soup. 'Before 1975, our families had many books,' she said. 'Then the police came and searched our houses. They took all the books from my father's house in Danang. They put them in a big pile outside and burned them. And then some party cadres moved into our house. We had to leave. I spent four months in prison. I was a teacher then, but I lost my profession.'

She talked compulsively about her life since 1975, as if the words could somehow help to alleviate her pain. Although I had always sympathized with the nationalist struggle in Vietnam, I listened with unanimity. Mai and I had liked each other immediately. We were the same age and we shared the same sense of humour, but something more inexplicable existed between us, something that had created an instant sense of friendship and made me vividly able to imagine all the things that had happened to her. As if I, at forty-two, had also experienced a war, imprisonment, the suicide of my father and the loss of my home, my career and all the freedoms I took for granted. Whatever the rights and wrongs of the side she and her family had taken in the war and since, she had been cruelly punished.

'Not so long ago,' she said, as she served up beef, onions and rice, 'if you bought meat in the market the police would follow you home and search your house, they would say you were hiding money.'

For all her bravura on the street, Mai was still afraid of the police. Over a dessert of pineapple, she told us she had decided not to come with us on the boat ride.

'My mother is ill, I can't leave my children with her,' she said.

I knew there was more to it than that. Earlier in the day, she'd agreed to let me tape a conversation with her, talking about her life before and after 1975. Now, she told me this wasn't possible.

'I trust you, Maria. But my husband said that if the police stop you on the boat, they might take the tape and listen to it. This is a small town, I would be in a lot of trouble.'

I looked around their house, a simple place that they were struggling, bit by bit, to improve. Old curtains hung over the doorways, a few frayed rugs were thrown on the concrete floor. Mai was watching me; she knew what I was thinking.

'You know, Maria, I can stand almost anything,' she said. 'But losing my daddy, and having to watch while they burned all my books, from these I can't recover. Because of these, I will never completely find my life again.'

Before we left, we agreed to meet Hoang and Mai at four o'clock by the bridge next to the fishing village.

Mai warned us not to tell the hotel staff of our plans. 'Say that you are leaving so early because you are cycling to Hue. If the police stop you on the way, tell them you are going to the beach to do photography.'

'In the middle of the night?'

'Yes – they know tourists do strange things like this.'

By three fifteen we were cycling along Tran Phu Street, passing a few other early risers who swung their heads in surprise at the sight of two foreigners already up and about. Soon we were out of the town and heading along the narrow, unlit lane that led to the village. The moon was up, but shadows cast by trees threw deep pools of darkness across the road. Our bells tinkled as the bikes hit unseen potholes, and dogs rushed out from houses, snarling and snapping at our wheels.

'Don't be so paranoid,' whispered Dag once.

'I'm not paranoid,' I lied.

'Yes you are. I can tell by the way you're hunched over the handlebars.'

We found Mai and Hoang dressed all in black and skulking in the shadows.

'Sssh! No speak!' whispered Hoang.

Though we crept like thieves along the riverside path towards Luc's boat, it seemed that every dog in the village had smelt us and was barking at full volume to announce our presence. Quickly, we waded through the water and hauled ourselves and the bikes aboard.

'Sit here, where no one can see you,' said Mai, pointing to the front of the small cabin.

With much furtive shuffling and whispering, Hoang, Luc and another man stowed our bikes and bags into one of the holds. On the bank, the dogs still yapped and howled, and several roosters had begun some full-throated crowing. As Luc started up the engine, Hoang lit three joss sticks and placed them in the prow of the boat. Mai crouched down beside me.

'I have to go,' she whispered, her voice catching. 'Please be careful.'

Unable to find the words to thank her, I hugged her hard. She felt very small, and frail.

'Don't forget me, Maria!' she said, then she slipped away and was gone.

As we chugged into the wide mouth of the Thu Bon River, light began to spread across islets and thick groves of water coconuts.

'All this was VC,' said Hoang. 'The Americans bombed and bombed, but the VC hid under the ground. They were everywhere here.'

And now there were police everywhere. As we approached their first post, Hoang instructed us to hide with him in the engine compartment. It was a tiny, cramped space with a very low ceiling and an exposed engine pumping away in the middle of the floor. As we squeezed inside, it was all we could do to avoid touching the hot, oily metal. Hoang pulled the wooden shutters across the three small windows. The air was so thick with fumes that I was convinced I would suffocate within minutes.

'But you can look!' Hoang reassured me, pointing to a crack between two planks.

What I saw were the stilts of a dock, and bright lights above it. We felt a bump as the boat came alongside the dock, then the door of the engine room opened a few inches, and Luc peered inside and hissed something at us.

'No speak! No move!' translated Hoang.

The engine was still turning, and for what seemed like an age we were trapped in the hot, fetid compartment, with pistons pounding and spluttering only inches away. As my eyes grew accustomed to the dark I saw that Hoang had neatly and comfortably folded himself into one corner. By contrast, Dag was awkwardly squashed against the bulkhead. His chin appeared to have buried itself in his chest and his knees were somewhere around his ears. I was sitting with one side of my body against the planking and my legs folded beneath me. It was a foolish position to have taken, for soon my legs had lost all feeling.

'No move!' hissed Hoang from time to time.

I didn't bother to tell him that I couldn't.

At last, the boat pulled away from the dock. Five minutes later, Luc opened the shutter on the window facing the prow, and we gasped at the rush of fresh air. Hoang clambered through it onto the deck, but told us to stay where we were.

'Still no safety,' he warned.

We rearranged ourselves as best we could, trying to bring blood and life back into our limbs. Through the window we could see Luc making offerings to the spirits of the boat and the water. After placing new joss sticks in the prow, he tossed overboard slips of red and white paper, each printed with prayers. Some were whipped up by the wind and blown back onto the boat, and Hoang ran around like an excited child, gathering them up and dropping them over the gunwales to complete the offering.

After an hour, Hoang told me to come onto the deck.

'Are you sure it's safe?' I asked, peering around at the boats that were within hailing distance.

'You, yes,' he said. 'You skinny, look like Vietnamese. But Dag no, he big, with too much hair!'

Finally, as the sun peeped over the horizon, it was deemed safe for the big hairy Westerner to be released from his captivity. We sat on deck, enjoying the fresh breeze and celebrating with green tea our escape from the clutches of the police.

'You know, if the police catch Luc with the foreigner, they take away his boat for three month,' said Hoang conversationally. 'They only give back the boat if he pay them much money.'

We gaped at him.

'Three *months*?'

Luc had saved for years to buy this boat, and his entire extended family depended on the livelihood it provided. Without it they would have no income. Combined with a heavy fine, this would be a devastating blow from which they might never recover. I sat in silence, pondering over our whimsical notions of travelling up the coast, and the enormity of the risk Luc had taken for the sake of a hundred dollars.

'Maria, cheer up! Have cigarette!' cried Hoang, pulling from his pocket a rather squashed packet of Jet. 'I no have to give them to police! Now we smoke them! They are liberty cigarettes!'

When I declined, he passed the packet to the man who was steering the boat.

'He is Dinh, brother of Luc,' explained Hoang.

'Brother?' Dag queried. 'I thought Luc's mother had only one son.'

'Three day ago she have one son,' said Hoang. 'Now she have two.'

'That was quick work!'

Hoang paged through his battered Vietnamese-English dictionary, searching for a word.

'You know? Vietnamese women very – creative!'

We were twenty miles off shore, passing the steep green slopes of Cham Island. The water was flat calm and a shimmering gold, reflecting the newly risen sun. A fishing boat passed us, its prow heaped with offerings of flowers, and at the helm a slight figure in pyjamas and conical hat silhouetted against the pink and amber sky. The glory of the morning overcame my misgivings about the wisdom of our venture and I began to enjoy where I was and what I was doing. Then the engine spluttered a few times, and stopped. Luc pulled furiously at the starter rope, but nothing happened. He disappeared into the engine compartment with Dinh and Hoang, and a great deal of hammering and muttering ensued.

'I think there's something wrong with the propeller shaft,' said Dag. 'There's quite a bit of water leaking in.'

Peering down into the compartment, I was alarmed to see the three men sloshing around in a foot of water. Luc appeared on deck, stripped off to his shorts and dived overboard. The water was so clear we could see him turning over to face the hull, like a seal. He surfaced with a worried expression on his face and yelled something to the men in the engine room. Several more times he dived down, and each time he came up he looked increasingly concerned. Finally he hauled himself back on deck and hurried, dripping, into the engine compartment.

'Looks like we're going to drift right back to the police post,' said Dag glumly.

But at last Hoang emerged, holding aloft the source of the problem, a badly corroded bolt.

'In Hue, we buy new one,' he announced.

Although it remained unclear how we were going to get as far as Hue without this bolt, the three men seemed happy enough with the results of their work. Luc started up the engine while Hoang and Dinh rigged a makeshift hand pump for the bilge water. For half an hour they pumped steadily. Oily water gushed all over the deck, and our gear, before trickling out through holes in the gunwales.

As the sun got steadily hotter, the three Vietnamese men squatted under the low wooden shelter on deck, from where they could take turns on the tiller. Hoang kindly rigged up a sacking tarp for us, and we stretched out beneath it, watching the coastline slip by. The Marble Mountains rose dramatically from the coastal plain, and then a haze of pollution heralded the city of Danang.

'Sleep!' commanded Hoang.

'We will only see this once,' I told him. 'We want to stay awake and look.'

Grinning broadly, he pointed past me to Dag, who was snoring gently and twitching his way through a dream.

'Over there is the Lady of Stone,' said Hoang, as we passed the pink-grey cliffs at the end of a long, mountainous headland. 'You know this story?'

He was lying on his stomach under the shelter, wearing

Luc's yellow hard hat. I turned over and we faced each other, with our chins in our hands, as he told me the legend.

A girl called Ba was the only daughter of a fishing family. When she was very small, her older brother Hai hit her on the head with a piece of sugar cane and she lost consciousness. Thinking that he had killed her, he ran away, never to be seen again. When Ba was a teenager, both her parents were caught in a typhoon while they were fishing, and drowned. So she was alone, and very sad. But after some years, she met and fell in love with a young fisherman. They married, had a baby and were very happy. One night, when a storm was raging outside and Ba's husband couldn't go out to fish, he helped her to wash her hair. For the first time he noticed a scar on her scalp and asked her about it. She told him the story of her brother who had hit her then run away. While she spoke, a very strange look came over his face. All that night, his thoughts were in a turmoil. He wrestled to convince himself that this was a mere coincidence. But in his heart, he knew the awful truth. He was the little boy who had run away. He had married and fathered a child with his own sister. Filled with remorse, he sailed off into the storm. The next morning, Ba looked everywhere for her husband. When she saw the boat was missing, she realized he had gone to sea. Every day, she watched for the boats to come in, but he never returned. Heartbroken, and not knowing why her husband had left, Ba climbed to the top of a mountain with her baby in her arms, and stood gazing over the ocean, looking for him. She stood there for weeks and months, until the winds turned her and the baby to stone.

'And you know? She is still there,' concluded Hoang. 'When the fishermen are coming home in a storm they call out to her for help.'

Tears had welled up in my eyes. Feeling foolish, I wiped them away, and looked over to the peninsula where, dwarfed by the high cliffs, a fleet of small fishing boats was pulling in nets. In the distance, a huge container ship was steaming towards Danang.

'You know, Maria, it is only a story!' cried Hoang, alarmed by my reaction. 'Don't cry! I make you breakfast!'

Within minutes he'd set out beneath the tarp three

blackened pots full of food that Dinh's wife had prepared the night before. There was rice, fried fish and a squash and beef soup. To wash down the food, we passed around a large and very battered tin mug of green tea. When the pots, bowls and chopsticks were cleared away, Hoang and Dinh again pumped the bilge. The sounds of the rushing of water had the unfortunate effect of activating my guts once more. Desperately, I looked around the boat for a place where I could hang over the side unseen. Dag suggested behind the tarp, which was stretched along the port side, between the roof of the shelter and a long sculling oar tied onto the gunwale. Bracing myself on the oar, and with Dag standing guard in case I went overboard, I leaned out as far as I could, my relief mingling with embarrassment. But Hoang, Luc and Dinh were the perfect gentlemen, fixedly staring away from me and towards the coast for long after I'd finished.

The mainland was now steeply rising from the ocean. Clinging to its foot was a railway line, and above this a precipitous road was snaking up towards the Pass of the Ocean Clouds. I imagined pushing a bike over such a road, and sighed with relief that we were on a boat. We were passing an island that had a snug little sandy cove bounded by smooth boulders. Shrimp nets were set up in the cove, and sampans were moored next to them. On a bluff above the beach was an abandoned house that had been built by the Americans in 1968. It was a grand-looking place, and the view from it must have been spectacular. Suddenly, Dinh pulled on a green shirt and, wielding an imaginary Sten gun, mimed strafing the house with bullets.

'I, Viet Cong!' he cried.

'Was he?' I asked Hoang.

'No! Joking!' Scratching his head, he searched for more words. 'He worked for the Americans. You know, all Vietnamese people hate the Communists.'

Almost everyone we'd met said the same. But almost everyone we met had backed the losing side in the war, and were full of bitterness about how they had been treated since then. The few party members we had encountered, like Binh's uncle in the Mekong Delta, and Minh on Phu Quoc Island, had been

more than guarded in their comments about the government
and the present day events in Vietnam. Soon, we were to cross
the 17th Parallel and be in the erstwhile North Vietnam. There,
I decided, I would make a concerted effort to find someone
who was pro-government, and prepared to talk to me about it.

By ten thirty, in the distance we could see Lang Co, a strip
of dazzling white sand with a lagoon behind it.

'Luc he say, hide your map!' urged Hoang, and we folded
up the US Tactical Pilotage Charts that the crew had been poring over for the last hour, and slipped them out of sight. Hoang
lit some more joss sticks to put in the prow, and then tossed a
cigarette overboard.

'For *Ca Ong*,' he said, referring to the whale god. 'So he
help us against the police.'

Luc and Dinh were anxiously scanning the coast. There was
a fishing village on the beach, but Hoang told us we couldn't go
there because of its police post. A quarter of a mile from it was
a small hotel. Electricity pylons ran along the sand, there were
concession stands, rows of sun loungers and striped sun
umbrellas, and right behind them was a road and a railway line.

'You want to stop at this place?' asked Hoang.

'No!'

All three men looked relieved. Luc carried on until the village and the resort were out of sight, then dropped anchor in
shallow, clear, aquamarine water. Dag and I jumped in and
swam to the deserted beach. As we padded along the hot sand,
it struck me that we had no shadows: the sun was almost
directly overhead.

'What are we going to do all afternoon?' I asked.

Dag shrugged. 'Sit and fry,' he said.

When we returned to the boat, the three men were palpably
ill at ease.

'You know? The contract say we spend one night here at
Lang Co,' explained Hoang. 'But they are worried that the
police come from the village. They want to go to Hue, sleep
near there. It is safer for them.'

We promptly agreed. Without more ado the anchor was
weighed and we were off again.

*

The mountains receded and the coastline became one endless empty beach, backed by sand dunes. For miles there were no trees, no vegetation and no villages. A torpor settled over the boat. Hoang slept under the shelter, using the yellow hard hat as a pillow. Luc and Dinh took turns on the tiller, joining Hoang for a snooze when they weren't steering. We lay beneath the tarp which, with the sun at its zenith, offered us little protection. The rays finding their way through the loosely woven material joined forces with those being reflected off the water to, as Dag had predicted, slowly fry us. He fell asleep for a while with his hand on his bare torso, and woke to find a perfect outline of his fingers on his reddened skin.

Towards six o'clock we approached Thuan An Beach, a resort eight miles from Hue. It was the usual dispiriting sight: deck chairs, umbrellas, thatched concession stands. Hoang didn't even bother to ask if we wanted to go ashore, and Luc carried on for a quarter of a mile before anchoring. Again, Dag and I swam to the beach. The sky was spectacular, with orange clouds fanning out like ribbons across it. Hauled up on the sand were bamboo boats, one with sponsons filled with polystyrene chunks. We swam back in the near dark. Even before we'd clambered aboard, Luc was wieghing the anchor and Dinh was starting the engine, ready to take the boat further offshore.

All around us, the oil lamps of anchored fishing boats flickered into life, like so many fire flies. After a meal of instant noodles, fish and rice, we sat on deck chatting. Now that the journey was almost over, Luc and Dinh were relaxed, and full of questions about our life in the West. Hoang frantically paged through his dictionary in search of words to use in his translation, holding the book close to one of the oil lamps. Around 8.30, my head started nodding.

'You sleep,' said Hoang. 'We watch bags. You know, bad boys swim here and rob you.'

Unsteadily, we made our way to the foredeck. The boat, which was a pretty unstable craft at the best of times, was now pitching about wildly in the waves.

'We dancing!' cried Hoang.

This wasn't far from the truth – in our sheet sleeping bag we rocked and rolled all night, sliding about the deck, colliding with the hold cover, the sides of the boat and the edge of the cabin. Sleep was impossible, but one consolation was that a marvellous light show was being enacted over the mountains, twenty miles inland, where lightning flashed through clouds. And from the shelter on the aft deck drifted the contented sounds of snoring, as our three guards slept soundly.

Around three o'clock the sea calmed, and we, too, finally got some sleep. But not for long. By four o'clock Hoang, Luc and Dinh were awake and chatting loudly. By four fifteen Luc was stepping over us to make offerings at the forepeak.

'Dag, Maria, get up!' called Hoang.

It was patently obvious that they were anxious to be rid of us and away.

'I want to wait for the light, so I can take photographs,' muttered Dag, curling up tightly around me.

Then I heard Hoang schooling Luc.

'Get up,' he said.

'Get up,' repeated Luc.

Seconds later, someone rapped me on the head.

'Youse! Get up!' barked Luc.

'Ignore him,' muttered Dag, holding me even tighter.

At four forty-five, the engine spluttered into life and the boat began moving towards the shore.

'Youse! Go!' shouted Luc in our ears.

In a mad flurry we packed our things and pulled the bikes out of the hold. Dinh anchored the boat while we, Luc and Hoang dropped into waist-deep water and waded ashore.

The two men were hurrying to catch a bus into Hue, where they would pick up a new part for the engine. Quickly, we made our goodbyes and Dag handed Luc a hundred and ten dollars. His eyes widened with astonishment. Hoang pursed his lips disapprovingly, but said nothing. Then I gave Hoang an envelope. In it was a letter I'd scribbled the day before, expressing in writing all the thanks he and Mai had never been prepared to listen to. Slipped into the folded sheet of paper were two twenty-dollar bills. For them, over a month's wages, for us so little. Hoang gave me a suspicious look.

'What this?'

'A letter for Mai.'

He handed it back to me.

'You post it!'

It was pointless trying to remind him of all he'd done for us, what he had made possible, the employment he'd missed as a result.

'Please—'

Reluctantly, he shoved it into his back pocket.

'Tell Mai I miss her,' I called after him, as he hurried away. 'Tell her I'll send some books.'

'Nietzsche!' he cried, turning to wave one last time. 'And Jean Paul Sartre!'

10
FROM HUE TO HELL

We took a quiet back road to Hue. It ran along a narrow river channel lined with bamboo groves, banana plants and trees heavy with jack fruit. Wide stone steps, guarded at the bottom by lion statues, led down to the water where women crouched to do their laundry and wash out pots. One had left her sleeping child on the back of a tethered water buffalo, which munched on grass and flicked its ears, seemingly quite at ease in its role as baby sitter. In some areas the surface of the water was covered with hyacinths and lotuses, and people moved among them in small bamboo boats, gathering leaves and seeds. There were small shrines all along the banks; one, in the base of a banyan tree, we smelt from yards away, because already that morning hundreds of burning joss sticks had been stuck amidst its maze of roots for the spirits believed to live there.

After two nights with little sleep, I was dreading the prospect of rush-hour traffic in Hue. But I was pleasantly surprised; instead of the frenzy we'd experienced in Saigon, morning commuters were meandering to work along wide leafy streets. It was a calm, tranquil atmosphere, befitting the city's long tradition as a focus of culture and learning. In the fifteenth century, as the Viets moved south and overran the Chams, Hue became the capital of the area now covered by central Vietnam, and a centre for Buddhist study. Once the whole area now known as Vietnam had been established, local warlords began fighting with each other. Two dominant clans emerged – the Trinh lords in the north and the Nguyen lords in the south. In 1802, with the help of the French, the Nguyen lords gained control of the whole country, founded a new dynasty under Emperor Gia Long and chose Hue as Vietnam's capital, which it remained until 1954. In 1862 Emperor Tu Duc signed a treaty with the French that rendered the whole of Vietnam a French protectorate, and made himself and his successors puppets of the French government. With their real political power gone, the Emperors channelled their energies into patronizing the arts and developing Hue's scholarly reputation.

Hue is also reputed to be the home of Vietnam's most beautiful and graceful women. We had pulled up at the kerb and were checking on our map for the location of the Morin Hotel, when a group of lovely girls walked by. Identically dressed in white *ao dai*s, each had long silky hair and carried a violin case. I stared at them, wondering if this was some cunning and well-timed ruse by Hue Tourism. They smiled shyly at me and giggled, then one darted forward and asked if I needed help. The hotel, she said, was just around the corner. Did I know it was once part of the university? I did know – we were going there on the recommendation of Hoang, who before 1975 had studied mathematics in one of its rooms.

'I would like to stay and ask you questions,' she said, 'but I must go to my music lesson.'

She and her friends glided away, turning once or twice to peek coyly back at us.

The Morin Hotel was an elegant colonial building. Its cavernous rooms were made cool by thick stone walls and shuttered windows, and opened onto a quiet courtyard graced by shady trees, ornamental ponds and a tame but grumpy white egret. We had lunch in the courtyard with an English couple, Polly and Mark. Both architects, in their late twenties, they were fashionably dressed but had a reserved, rather genteel air about them. They were travelling through Vietnam by car with a driver and a suave young interpreter, Ky, who was sitting with us.

'I am student of English,' Ky told me, 'but I also work in independent travel agency, where Mark and Polly get their car. They like me very much and ask me to go with them, to help them understand the language and customs of my country.'

Mark, I noticed, was listening to our conversation and giving Ky rather dark looks. 'How old are you, Ky?' I asked him.

'Twenty-two. And I am sorry, Madam, but my name is Viet.'

'What?' interjected Mark. 'You said you were Ky!'

'No, that is the name of my manager in the travel agency.'

'Why didn't you tell us before?'

'You make mistake. I do not want to embarrass you.'

There was a prolonged and uncomfortable silence. Viet examined his perfectly manicured thumbnails, which were at least two inches long.

'Why do so many Vietnamese men have long nails?' I asked, as much to ease the tension as anything else.

'For me, it is the hobby,' said Viet, with an affected weariness. 'At home, there is nothing to do, I am very bored, so I grow my nails.'

'He's ruining our holiday,' said Mark later. 'He's moody and unpredictable and conniving. And so vain! He won't drink green tea from those tiny cups that you're offered everywhere in case he breaks a nail!'

We were on our way with Polly and Mark to see the tombs of the Nguyen Emperors, which are situated along the banks of the Perfume River. Viet had been keen to come with us, but they had insisted he take the afternoon off. To get to the river, and the boat we'd been advised to take, we'd picked our way across a building site opposite the hotel, past men doing electric welding and wearing only sun glasses and green pith helmets as protection. The boat was a sad-looking affair, with a crudely carved figurehead of a dragon on its stubby prow, and a large sign tacked onto its side announcing it as 'Tourist Boat TT14705'. On the aft deck, plastic chairs and a Formica-topped table were shaded with a fringed canopy. As we approached, its owner scrambled ashore and began desperately bidding for our business.

'Where you want? Tomb Tu Duc? Thieu Tri? Khai Dinh? Minh Mang? I take you! Very cheap! I have cold drink, beer, Coca Cola, Orange, what you want?'

Quite suddenly, Polly transformed from a reserved English rose to a ruthless bargainer. She spent a good ten minutes knocking a few thousand dong off the man's lowest price while Dag, Mark and I shuffled around on the bank, watching sampans pass by. Once she was satisfied, we climbed aboard and set off towards a range of dark green hills that lay in soft folds against a pale grey sky. We slipped past colonial mansions along the banks, and were soon away from the city and out into a lush countryside. Sandy paths led through trees and tropical bushes towards small villages set back from the shore. And another of Hue's clichés turned out to be true. The air along the river was indeed perfumed, by a blend of sweet flowers and the more earthy aromas of mud and roots.

'Coca, mama, coca, mama, coca, mama?'

The instant we climbed off the boat at the site of Ming Mang's tomb, hordes of children besieged us, pressing cold cans of Coca Cola against our arms. And they were only the advance attack: all along the path to the gates of the tomb were concession stands offering coconuts, biscuits, bottled water and pop. Each was owned by a pathetic-looking woman who beseechingly held out her wares and sent her offspring to throw themselves at our legs. By the time we reached the gates we had about thirty children clinging to us.

'Maybee later? Maybee later? Maybee later?' they chorused threateningly, as we escaped into the safety of the tomb site.

Ming Mang is remembered as being scholarly, although the history books do not clarify how he found time for serious study in between siring seventy-eight sons and sixty-four daughters. The grounds of his tomb, however, were certainly conducive to contemplation. Statues of mandarins, horses and elephants formed honour guards along red-tiled walkways leading to peaceful pavilions. Large old trees offered shade, frangipani bushes surrounded ponds covered by lotuses. Spanning the crescent-shaped 'Lake of Impeccable Clarity' was an ornamental bridge that, while Ming Mang was alive, only he could cross. On its far side, a steep stairway led to some iron gates in a high, circular wall surrounding the actual tomb. I was gazing up at this wall when an old man in a green pith helmet appeared by my side and beckoned me to follow him up the steps. As we reached the gates they opened, and two workmen appeared carrying branches over their shoulders. They made no protest as we slipped past them. I was expecting some ornate structure to mark where the body had been placed, but there was only a vast mound of earth, a steep manmade hillock overgrown with spindly trees and scrubby vegetation. The old man took my hand and we set off up its side. From the top we gazed out over the calm scene below us: peaceful gardens, a slow flowing river, a spread of fields in which cattle quietly grazed. The silence was broken only by the whirr of cicadas, the chirping of birds and the rustle of leaves. The old man nodded and smiled, and I wondered if he was thinking, like me, that somewhere beneath our feet an emperor was buried, and that he was a lucky man to have found such a resting place.

On the way back to Hue, Mark and Polly continued to grumble about Viet.

'It's been so nice, getting away from him for a few hours,' said Polly. 'When we met him we thought he was really charming, and he was obviously keen to come along with us. So we offered him a daily rate to cover his food and accommodation. Then we realized he expected wages as well. And he started taking us to expensive hotels and restaurants, where he was getting a cut of whatever we were paying. A few days ago Mark hit the roof and told him we'd pay his bus fare back to Hanoi. Viet got really upset, and admitted that he and the driver had already arranged to fill the car with tourists in Saigon and bring them up to Hanoi. The whole thing is just a scam at our expense.'

'So why didn't you get rid of him?' I asked.

'Well, he said that as his boss was behind the car business, he'd get the sack if it fell through, and that if he lost his job he couldn't continue with his studies. In the end we didn't have the heart to do it. The worst thing is that he's still so resentful of us.'

'How much are you paying him?' Dag asked.

'Two dollars fifty a day.'

Both Dag and I were silent.

'What – for wages, food and accommodation?' Dag finally asked.

'Yes. Does that seem too much?'

'No . . . it doesn't seem much at all . . .'

'It's a lot for a Vietnamese to earn,' said Polly defensively. 'And we can't afford any more!'

The sightseeing continued into the evening, when we went by cyclo with Mark and Polly to the Citadel, the old part of Hue that was built by the Nyugen Emperors and all but destroyed in the war. As usual Dag and I ordered a cyclo apiece.

'Don't do that!' cried Polly. 'Share one! We always do.'

Once again, she launched into some ferocious bargaining. Each driver wanted fifteen thousand dong, a dollar fifty. For this he would pedal two of us on one cyclo through the Citadel, wait for us while we had dinner there and then return us to the hotel. Polly thought this service was only worth ten thousand dong. How about twelve thousand dong? suggested the drivers. No, they were firmly told, still too much. The little chap who was going to pedal Dag and I around Hue didn't seem to mind the negotiations; we got fed up of them before he did.

'Come on, let's go, twelve thousand is fine,' said Dag, clambering onto the vehicle. 'Are you sure you can manage my wife as well?'

'Yeah, she skinny like Vietnamese!' he cried. 'And why she brown? What happen to her?'

As he pedalled us off through the sedate traffic, he talked incessantly about football.

'Tonight, eleven o'clock, the World Cup. Ireland and

Holland. I like Ireland. In the morning, three o'clock, Argentina and Brazil. Poor Maradona! Him I like! And at six o'clock . . .'

As he chatted away, I remembered Mai telling me of all the trouble the World Cup was causing between husbands and wives, because so many men were skipping work to watch the games, and how the economy of the country was suffering as a result.

'You'll be tired tomorrow,' I warned the cyclo driver.

'No! In morning, after World Cup, I drink coffee. Then I sleep. Afternoon, I sing karaoke. Evening, I cyclo driver for three hour, then I go see my family.'

He took us across the river on a bridge designed by Eiffel, along side streets, over a moat that was green with lotus plants and hyacinths, and through the bullet-scarred gates of the Citadel walls. Originally the area within the Citadel had been divided into three sections: the outer precincts for artisans and tradespeople, the middle area for the mandarin class and, at the centre, the Forbidden Purple City for royalty.

'You know London?' he asked, as we headed along a wide tree-lined avenue. 'I like London. I have five hundred dollar. When I have two thousand dollar, I go London one week!'

'You'll need more than two thousand dollars,' Polly called to him.

'Yeah? In television I see London. Ten million people! A queen!'

'Take your cyclo to London,' suggested Dag. 'You could make lots of money with it there.'

On either side of the avenue were fields where men in green pith helmets and women in conical hats were hoeing and weeding. Until 1968, two thirds of the population of Hue had lived within the Citadel's walls. Then came the Tet Offensive, when Communist forces simultaneously besieged every American and South Vietnamese stronghold. The battle for Hue turned into the most bitter conflagration of the American War. After routing and murdering people they believed had links with the Saigon regime, the Communists entrenched themselves in the Citadel, which they held for twenty-five days. In an attempt to dislodge them, American and South Vietnamese forces destroyed the city, razing whole neighbourhoods to the ground. At the end of it all, over six thousand civilians were dead and the city was in ruins.

As we toured around, I remembered a story Binh had told me about an aunt of his who had married a Communist in 1952 and had a son with him. When the country divided in 1954 her husband went north, took a second wife and had four more sons. During the Tet Offensive her son was outside the Citadel with the ARVN, while one of his half-brothers was inside with the Communists.

'They didn't know about each other,' Binh had said. 'But after Revolution Day, my uncle he go south to look for my aunt. They have big family reunion in Saigon. Everyone drinking and happy, and the two half-brothers they talk and find out they fight each other in Hue. But it's okay, they friends now, no problem.'

Many of the neighbourhoods were never rebuilt; in their place fields were created for agriculture. Everywhere, on the site of this dreadful battle, plants were growing and being harvested. An old man had climbed up a thirty-foot bamboo ladder into a lychee tree and was carefully covering the fruits with rush matting to stop the birds pecking at them. Close by, next to a bullet-strafed stone arch-way, another man lay sleeping on top of one of the Nine Holy Cannons, with a basket of cassava next to him. There was little traffic and the area had a pensive, melancholic atmosphere. The only excitement was outside the shell-pocked gates of the Imperial Enclosure, where Japanese tourists wearing identical white hats were marshalled by tour leaders into groups for photographs next to their incongruously sleek, modern and specially imported buses.

The restaurant was a sixteen-sided pavilion that stood on stilts in the middle of a lotus pond. Its menu was intriguing and offered, among other things, Chicken in Greases and Boiled Dick with Sauce of Fish and Ginger. We dined like kings, on a pot of eel soup that was brought to the table bubbling over a charcoal stove, on tender beef slivers wrapped in grape leaves, on enormous shrimps cooked with oodles of garlic. All this, with several large bottles of beer and glasses of freshly squeezed lemon juice, resulted in a bill that barely scraped the twenty-dollar mark.

Our cyclos headed back through the darkening and flower-scented streets of the Citadel, and across Eiffel's bridge. Along the pavement on either side of the bridge were a row of elegant, Parisian-style street lamps. And under each lamp was a sleeping figure. Young men, old men, women, teenagers and even some small children, lying on their backs with an arm over their eyes, or curled in the foetal position.

'Poor people,' said our driver. 'No family, no house.'

I asked him why they would choose to sleep in these pools of bright light rather than in the shadows between them.

'For safety,' he said.

The doors of the hotel were locked early that night, so that staff and residents could watch the World Cup undisturbed. A television was set up on a table in the courtyard, where a group of Dutch tourists had for some hours been getting steadily tanked up on beer. The shouts, hoots, whistles and roars went on until near dawn; in vain, we tried to get a good night's rest in preparation for the next day's journey by bicycle to Dong Ha, forty-six miles away.

Over breakfast, served in the courtyard by a sleepy waiter, we met a Vietnamese pharmacologist who had lived in Toronto since 1972. He specialized in research on addiction; while he talked to us, he lit one cigarette after another.

'I was a helicopter pilot. I knew we were going to lose the war and I knew what that would mean for me. So when they sent me to America for special training, I went AWOL and walked over the border into Canada.'

Three days ago he had arrived back in Vietnam and in Hue, the city of his birth, for the first time since his defection.

'At the airport, the immigration official made much trouble for me. He said, "So, you have a white wife in Canada? A big house, a car?" People here feel such emptiness. Many of the Communists are embittered, they sacrificed much in the war, and for what? Their goals were not reached, so to fill the void they turned to another war in Cambodia, and now they turn to corruption. And the poverty! In twenty-five years, no one has gone forward. I see other *Viet Kieu* come here and bargain for better prices. How can they? Look, here I eat my breakfast, coffee and eggs and bread, and it costs me cents. It is embarrassing!'

His eyes filled with tears. 'I don't know what will happen to my people. First the country is destroyed by war, then it cannot recover because of the embargoes, and now plane-loads of businessmen come who want to rape the country, who bring in more corruption and more bad influences. And Hue! Ah, it was once so lovely, you cannot imagine.'

I told him I was writing a book about our journey in Vietnam and gave him my card. He stopped talking, concentrated on eating his breakfast and did not offer a card in return.

By mid-morning we were heading into a landscape that seemed to have had its very soul ripped out. Stretching away on either side of the road was a red dirt plain, in which a few spindly trees and some rugged little cassava plants struggled to survive. Here and there were a few mud and thatch houses, desperately poor settlements with gardens scratched from the sand. It was impossible to see what the occupants of these places lived from. Nothing flourished here: it was an area of arid soil that had been finished off by defoliation. There was only dust to be had in plenty. It was in my nose, my ears, my eyes, my teeth. When I stopped to apply more sun cream on my arms, I rubbed red dust into the pores of my skin.

Worse was to come. The red dust gave way to eerily white sand. The cassava plants died out, and a few men with metal detectors moved like ghosts among the blackened stumps of trees. We were drawing close to the 17th Parallel, which runs along the Ben Hai River and was chosen at the Geneva Conference in 1954 as the border between North and South Vietnam. One of the provisions agreed on by Ho Chi Minh and the French at this conference was that a demilitarized zone, known as the DMZ, be created for three miles on either side of the Ben Hai River. Ironically, during the American War there was a concentration of fire power just south of the DMZ, and some of the worst battles of the war were waged here. Expecting the Communists to attempt a major invasion over the Seventeenth Parallel, the Americans carpet-bombed the area and sprayed massive amounts of Agent Orange to clear it of all vegetation.

I kept having to remind myself that all this happened over two decades ago, and not the week before. We passed a North Vietnamese Army war cemetery, with a huge memorial stele and thousands of tombstones crawling away into the distance. Near the turn-off to Quang Tri was an abandoned house that looked as if it had only recently been riddled with bullet holes and pounded with mortars, as if half of the roof had just been shot away. Close by were the remains of a church, equally ravaged, with the cross on its tower bent to one side. There was no point in us following the sign to Quang Tri, which was once the capital of Quang Binh Province. In 1972, after some heavy shelling, it was captured by the NVA. To win it back and to rout the Communists, the ARVN and the US Air Force bombed what was left of the city into oblivion.

We cycled on, saying little to each other, lost in our own thoughts. Figures and statistics ticked through my head, in time with the turning of the pedals. *Eleven million gallons of herbicides, ten per cent of the forests destroyed, thirteen million tons of bombs, three hundred and fifty thousand air strikes, three million dead, four million injured.* I had never believed in hell, but now I caught glimpses of it on either side of this road. The defoliated plain stretched away for miles, with nothing in sight but bomb craters and graves. These graves had no memorial steles, no well-tended grounds, only simple hummocks of earth like large sandy mole hills. Most of them were unmarked. And they were everywhere: around the pathetic houses huddled along the sides of the road, out in the few fields where farmers desperately tried to eke out a living, next to the drinks stand where we stopped to rest. We bought bottles of warm Festi Cola from a man who had lived through the holocaust that created this utter desolation. In front of his house, ducks floated on the water filling a bomb crater. When we asked him which side he'd fought for, he didn't answer. What he did say was that the unmarked graves were those of the lucky South Vietnamese Army soldiers – the remains of the unlucky ones had been dug up in 1975, and scattered.

High cirrus clouds formed; the sky became steely grey, like a vast pewter dome. Beneath it, we inched our way across this unearthly desert. The traffic died out, and we had the road to ourselves. As we pedalled on alone, only the clanking of our chains broke the ringing silence. Then the wind picked up, whistling across the plain, blowing fine sand over us. I kept thinking of all the wandering souls in this place, the ghosts of those with no one to tend their graves. I half expected to see figures materialize and come staggering towards us across the moonscape. But nothing stirred. Pain and grief seemed to hang in the air, as if all suffering here had been absorbed by the earth, which was now slowly exuding it.

It was a long, hard and depressing day. Anxious to get this area behind us, we didn't stop to eat but kept going with the help of bean cakes stuffed with peanuts and sesame seeds. By the time we were approaching Dong Ha, we were both grumpy and tired. The traffic had steadily increased, and cyclists and scooter drivers started pulling up alongside our bikes, staring at us for long periods.

'Whazzaname?' they asked. 'Whera from?'

Compared to Dag I was only of passing interest to local people. His size, his beard and his sun-bleached hair made him stick out a mile, while I grew thinner, darker-skinned and less unusual to the Vietnamese by the day. It was mostly Dag who the scooter drivers slowed down to stare at, and him that curious bicyclists pedalled next to, their eyes on stalks. Sometimes, when we passed through a village, I'd go ahead to try and deflect some of the attention. But I only served as a warm-up act, and by the time Dag appeared on the scene the audience would be raring to go with slaps and pinches, questions and shouts.

'Whazzaname? Whera from?'

'I swear they don't know what they're saying,' said Dag, as we approached Dong Ha. 'They just know that if they shout "Whazzaname" to this big red-skinned sweaty creature, he'll make a funny noise back.'

'You've got to remember that people here have only recently been allowed to speak to foreigners,' I told him sanctimoniously.

'Just try and pretend that each person you encounter is the first—'

Before I could finish the sentence, two men zipped by on a Honda. As they passed, one leaned over and slapped Dag on the arm, nearly knocking him off balance.

'Hey, Number One!' yelled the man, followed by something that sounded like, 'Go to hell!'

'—the first Vietnamese person you've ever met,' I finished weakly.

In Dong Ha, scooters flocked around us, their drivers vying for custom.

'You want cheap room?'

'I take you DMZ?'

'Mister, you want girl?'

'Hello, my name Jimmy!' cried a man in a baseball cap. 'I take you Mini Hotel!'

Ignoring them as best we could, and determined to find a hotel for ourselves, we pedalled along the main street, through a rubble-strewn market place and down a side road where two armoured tanks sat in an advanced state of rust. We found no hotels, but we did come across the only other foreigners in town, three young French people.

'We stay in Mini Hotel,' one of the men told us, 'but it is a strange place.'

Emmanuel, Jann and Stephanie were students of an elite Parisian business school, and as part of their course had opted to do four weeks of work experience in Vietnam.

'Four weeks here, in Dong Ha?' asked Dag in dismay.

'Only three. Then we go to Quang Ngai.'

'You poor buggers,' said Dag.

'You've been there? How is it?'

We were saved from having to answer this by Jimmy, the man in the baseball cap. He screeched to a halt on his scooter and went into a kind of Vietnamese rap.

'I find you nice room – Mini Hotel – very cheap – ten dollar – air condition – double bed – you sleep together – I take you DMZ – I good guide – no problem!'

The French group smiled knowingly.

'These my friends!' claimed Jimmy. 'They stay Mini Hotel!'

'We have no choice,' said the woman. 'It is the only place for foreigners.'

We followed Jimmy to a new three-storey building, painted blue and yellow like a birthday cake. Girls with faces whitened by make-up leaned over a balcony, and blew kisses at Dag and Jimmy as we went up the steps. In the foyer, several policemen sat around a low table drinking Scotch whisky. A middle-aged woman with permed hair and lots of make-up and jewellery shuffled around on plastic sandals, refilling their glasses. Madame Claude, as the French students called her, was the owner of the Phung Hoang Mini Hotel.

'The private hotels must pay police,' whispered Jimmy, as he led us up the stairs. 'Some give four per cent of all the money. Madame Claude let them drink whisky, take a girl and pay nothing.'

'How often do they come here?' I asked.

He shrugged.

'When they want.'

On the first landing, four smartly dressed men were drinking whisky in the company of some simpering girls. A gloomy corridor led off this landing, and at the end of it another couple were just stepping through a door. Our room was on the top floor. The head of the bed was up against the window, which was covered by a wrought-iron screen and opened onto a large communal balcony. I went for a shower, leaving Dag reading on the bed. I emerged to find him fast asleep with the book on his chest, and three white-faced girls stretching their hands through the bars towards him.

'Go away!' I snapped.

The hands withdrew, but the girls didn't.

'Very nice man, very big!' they called to me, giggling wildly.

One of them linked her fingers and slapped her palms together in what, judging from the other girls' reactions, was an extremely lewd gesture.

That evening we had a meal in a nearby restaurant with the three French students. Jann and Stephanie were engaged to be married. Emmanuel, twenty-one years old and with a mop of curls above an angelic face, was single, and in terror of

Madame Claude and her girls. He told us that a total of ten girls worked in shifts at the hotel.

'Yesterday, some girls got me and Jann in a corner,' he said, 'and they handled us!'

'Handled you?'

'Yes! To test our goods. To see how big we are!'

'Ah. I see.'

'They haven't been back since,' chipped in Jann. 'I think we did not pass their test!'

'And Madame Claude, she is the worst,' said Emmanuel, warming to his theme. 'Now, when she see me, she does like this –'

He got up from his chair and pawed the ground with one foot, like an angry horse. Catching sight of him, one of the waitresses in the restaurant gasped loudly and fled into the kitchen.

'What does it mean?' I asked.

'It means that with me she want to . . .' his voice trailed off. 'Well, you know how it is.'

'Does she do this as well?' I asked, linking my fingers and slapping my palms together. By now everyone in the restaurant was staring in mesmerized astonishment at us foreigners.

'Yes, she do! And the girls do that every time I see them! Is terrible! How can I tell my mother I am living in a brothel!'

With great gusto, the students were working their way through big platters of liver, squid, prawns and vegetables. Although they had been in the country only a week, they had already adopted the local habit of throwing food scraps onto the restaurant floor. As we were settling our bill, the waitress who had fled for the kitchen came out with a broom, and started sweeping up the prawn shells, lettuce leaves and rice grains around our chairs. Another woman, her face whitened with make-up like the girls in the hotel, sidled up to Emmanuel, pointed at the girl with the broom, licked her lips and wrapped one finger over another.

'My god!' he cried. 'What *have* I to tell my mother!'

By six o'clock next morning we were in the foyer, waiting for Jimmy and one of his friends. We had arranged to go with them by scooter for a tour of the DMZ and the Vinh Moc Tunnels. By six thirty we were still waiting. Jimmy arrived at seven. His eyes were bloodshot, and he told us he'd been up all night watching the World Cup.

'Bulgaria three, Mexico one!' he announced, sitting heavily in a chair and ordering black coffee from Madame Claude. 'Game still on, extra time.'

'Your friend?' we ventured.

'Tinh come soon. No worry!'

Fifteen minutes later a chubby man drove up on a rather ropey-looking bike. His face was round as a pudding and topped by a mat of thick grey hair.

'Sorry! Football extra time!' he cried. 'Bungaria wins Mexico.'

Sitting next to me on the sofa, he pulled a score card from his pocket and began filling in the latest results.

'Look,' he said, reading off the names of teams. 'Rumany, Squidgan, Holland, Brazil. Tonight, Germany and Spanish, Italia and Bungaria. I think Bungaria win.'

It was almost eight before we left. I sat on the back of Tinh's vintage 1967 motor bike, and wrapped my arms around his ample waist.

'You know, once I met President Diem,' he yelled to me, as we sped off. 'Some of his government was bad, but he was good guy, very good!'

After twenty-five minutes he swerved to a halt next to a paddy field, jumped down into the irrigation channel and returned with handfuls of mud that he slapped onto the engine.

'New pistons,' he explained. 'Very hot.'

'Ho Chi Minh a good guy too!' he yelled, as we set off again. 'Some of his government bad, but he very good. I call my cat Uncle Ho.'

Fifteen minutes later, the engine was steaming.

'Not all American soldiers good,' said Tinh, as he caked on more mud and grass. 'Some came here and steal our girls!'

Soon there were no more paddy fields in sight, only a red earth plain, with a few hardy dwarf bushes and mortar shells sticking out here and there. The only places to get water for the engine were the occasional drinks stands. We stopped at

Morning on Thu Bon River, Hoi An.

Breakfast with Hoang, as Luc's
fishing boat heads towards Hue.

Back-breaking work: harvesting t
rice in Binh Dinh Provin

aving Luc's boat at dawn, on
ʰuan An Beach, near Hue.

Winnowing the rice on Highway One.

Sunny, in Halong Bay.

Houseboats on the Red Rive

ese children expertly row their basket boat, in Halong Bay.

The 'floating village' in Halong Bay.

Xuan, Hieu and their grandson take Maria sailing on their junk in Halong Bay.

Xuan and her grandson enjoy some jackfr

c, singing and playing spoons
Bai Chay.

Vinh with a horseshoe crab
in Halong Bay.

ria and Bac.

Relaxing on the boat in Halong Bay.
From left: Vinh, Dag,
Hieu's grandson, Hieu.

On board Hieu and Xuan's junk, Halong Bay.

one near Doc Mieu. It was like an oasis in a desert, and while we waited for the bike to cool Tinh told us that once there had been villages and farms all around. That was before General McNamara attempted to build his 'wall', a barbed-wire fence strung with electronic sensors to prevent Communist infiltration to the south, and before all the settlements were bombed and napalmed into oblivion.

'Dag, take your wife's picture here,' said Tinh, guiding me towards a rather large shell sticking out of a crater.

'You'll have to get closer to it, Maria,' said Dag. 'Can you crouch down?'

It was shaped like a bullet, with the pointed end sticking out of the ground.

'Why has no one collected this for scrap metal?' I asked Tinh, who had retreated to several yards away.

'This a phosphorus cartridge!' he said, as if surprised by my stupidity. 'It can explode!'

As we carried on towards the Ben Hai River, Tinh told me that after the war he'd spent six years in a re-education camp, and had cleared mines around here, along the Ho Chi Minh Trail and around the Khe Sanh Combat Base.

'There were one hundred and twenty people in my unit in the camp,' he said. 'Twenty-two of them get blown up by mines. Three of them kill themself.'

Another spell in prison followed his son's escape by boat to Hong Kong in 1989. 'He was only sixteen year old. We want to give him a chance in life. It cost us one thousand dollar. When he escape, I write to my friend, he was an American colonel, now he retires and lives in Ohio. He sponsor my boy, he get him into America. But my boy is very lonely. In four year he will get citizenship, he will come home to see us.'

'Why were you imprisoned?' I asked.

'The government say I was a bad father, I didn't look after my boy.'

A poorly maintained bridge took us across the Ben Hai River, and the 17th Parallel, and into the old North Vietnam. After a few miles we turned off the highway and onto a rough track. Tinh's motor bike didn't like this, and began overheating with a fury. Time and time again we stopped to let it cool down, parking beneath groves of giant bamboo. At one of these, Jimmy pointed to a clump of bushes.

'See?' he said. 'Hole.'

We were on the outskirts of Vinh Moc where, in 1966, the villagers had begun tunnelling into the red clay to form a safe haven where they could escape incessant US bombing and artillery attacks. Working day and night for a year and a half, and camouflaging the excavated soil as they went, they built a complicated system of tunnels, big enough for the entire village to live underground. Before long, the tunnels were also inhabited by Viet Cong guerrillas, who had a mission to keep open supply lines to nearby Con Co Island. By night they would head out in motorized sampans to collect arms and ammunition from the trawlers waiting by the island.

A bamboo pole was placed across the track leading through Vinh Moc, and guarded by a surly woman who demanded payment before she would lift it. The houses were surrounded by high fences; as our scooters puttered by them, children ran through gates and flung stones at us.

'In the war, these people had hard time,' said Tinh apologetically.

In a one-roomed museum a collection of photos showed Vinh Moc village before 1967, and afterwards, when it had been flattened by bombs. Jimmy and Tinh wouldn't go into the tunnels with us, claiming they'd been many times before, and stayed to drink rice wine with the museum curator. We went instead with a government guide. He led us down steep, narrow steps into a dark passageway four feet high and three wide. The floor and walls were of hard-packed earth, and were dry and cool to the touch. Our guide shuffled off along the passageway, the slap of his sandals making a hollow echo. Fearful of losing him, we followed close behind, uncomfortably bent over because of the low ceilings. He kept turning corners, going along different passageways, leading us deeper into the three-level maze of tunnels.

'Woman school teacher house here,' he said, stopping so abruptly that I bumped into him. He shone his flash light into a niche in the wall measuring five feet by three.

'House?' I repeated.

'Yes. For woman school teacher.'

A little further along he stopped again. This time his beam of light was swallowed up by the darkness of a long narrow room. 'Sixty people Vietnamese sit here. For meeting room and cinema.'

'Cinema?'

In the museum, we'd been told that the tunnels had been lit by lamps fuelled with the fat of two thousand pigs.

'1972, electric,' explained the guide.

More steep steps led to the second level of tunnels. The air was completely still and so moist that my glasses steamed up. There were more small niches in the wall where whole families had lived, and a relatively large one, measuring eight feet by four, which had been the maternity hospital, and where seventeen babies had been born. At any one time, six hundred people had lived here, and some had spent months underground. Daily life had gone on, concerts and plays had been performed, children had attended school, people had got sick and recovered. A war had been waged, and partly won, from this place so far below the ground. I'd been down here half an hour, and I couldn't wait to get out. But there was still one more level to see, ninety feet below the ground. By now my skin was slick with sweat and my glasses kept slipping down my nose. We saw hooks on walls where telephone lines used to run, more niches for sleeping, for offices and for conference rooms, and toilets that were apparently fathomless holes in the ground, and that our guide advised me not to use. I longed for fresh, moving air, and I was expecting a scramble up three flights of steps before I got it, but instead we turned a corner and were hit by blinding light.

'Gate Number six,' announced our guide, as we stepped out onto a rocky ledge. A hundred feet below us, surf broke onto a curving beach dotted with wooden boats and jumbles of pink and blue nets. The air smelled of salt and of hot, dry earth, and birds wheeled and cried overhead. When the guide invited us back inside to finish the tour I shook my head, and instead set off up the cliff, back to the road.

As we cycled north from Dong Ha, I became acutely aware

that we had crossed a border, albeit an invisible one. Suddenly, there were more police posts and Communist slogans, more green shirts and pith helmets, more concrete buildings, some of them not yet finished and already crumbling into ruin. There were strange remnants of militarism, like the two armoured cars loaded with kindling that rumbled past us. And there was more poverty. Quang Binh Province, and Ha Tien Province to the north of it, make up the most impoverished part of Vietnam, suffering from frequent floods and typhoons, poor soil and everything history has thrown at it. Sometimes people begged, like the old man leading a buffalo who held out his hand to us as we passed by, and the children who raced to keep pace with our bikes, calling for dollars. But mostly they were reserved. Hollow cheeked and thin, they watched us carefully with dark eyes that quickly slid away when we tried to return the gaze. The war had reduced their land to nothing but rock, sand and gravel, and it was from this that they seemed to be making a living. Men dug sand from the plain or dived beneath the surface of a river to scoop gravel from its bed. Women sat at the side of the road, breaking rocks with mallets. They transported this raw material on baskets slung from shoulder poles, on bikes, in trucks and on buffalo carts, to God knows where. Some of it, at least, went to the road works, which stretched for mile after mile. In the middle of the highway, gravel was heaped up and black clouds of smoke billowed from tar being boiled in 45-gallon drums over open fires. The construction workers were men and women, identically dressed, their faces hidden by scarves. They tended the fires and the boiling tar, they shovelled gravel into pot holes, they worked in dirt, dust, black smoke and evil fumes, under the glaring sun, for a wage of thirty cents a day. They struggled to maintain a highway that, for me, had become a metaphor for this tragic country: first bombed to bits, and since then held together by unceasing effort and sheer willpower.

Crossing the Ngang Pass on bicycles at any time is a silly thing to do, especially on bikes with no gears; crossing it at one o'clock in the afternoon is downright ridiculous. The pass is the easternmost section of the Hoanh Son Mountains, which stretch along the 18th Parallel from the border with Laos, forty-five miles away, to the coast. Until the eleventh century this mountain range was the frontier between land ruled by the Viets and the Kingdom of Champa. Later, the French used it as the border between Tonkin and Annam. Now, it divides the poverty-stricken provinces of Quang Binh and Ha Tien. There were more beggars here. Old women, bent over and leaning on bamboo staffs, left their meagre patches of shade at the side of the road and scuttled towards us like crabs, holding out upturned conical hats. Sometimes I stopped to find a few dong for them. More often I carried on, ignoring their cackling pleas, not wanting to break the plodding rhythm I'd established. When I wiped the sweat from my eyes, I saw some wonderful views of wooded valleys falling steeply from the road down to the beach, and a glittering expanse of ocean and islands. But mostly I couldn't be bothered to look. Nor could I be bothered to stop and drink from the bottle of very warm water in the basket on my handlebars. I just knew that I had to keep going, so that eventually I could get to the top of this interminable pass, and rest. The sun was almost exactly overhead. Its rays were beating down on me, and they were bouncing up from the asphalt, getting me in vulnerable little places like the nostrils and the underside of the chin. *Just keep cycling*, I told myself, *just keep cycling*. There was a throbbing pain behind my eyes, my legs and arms ached, my hands and feet were swelling up. And suddenly I heard my mother say: *sun stroke*. During childhood holidays in Wales, she'd always lectured my brothers and me about this, insisting that we wore hats to the beach. Maybe because of her ministrations, or, more likely, because cases of sun stroke along the coast of Wales are extremely rare, I'd never experienced it. I didn't even know what its symptoms were. Now, however, I was convinced I was about to keel over and have an attack of the dreaded sun stroke, which at least gave me something to think about for the last half hour of my slog up the Ngang Pass.

On the final bend before the top of the pass, there was a drinks stand. Dag had got there before me, and his bike was propped up against a sign which read, in Vietnamese and

English, 'Restricted Area. Do Not Trespass'. After a feeble attempt to lean my bike against one of the supporting posts of the stand, I simply let it clatter to the ground. Then I staggered into the shade, and slumped at the only table.

'Drink this,' I heard Dag say, and felt him push a cold bottle against my arm.

'What's sun stroke?' I mumbled.

'Heat exhaustion,' he answered.

'What does it *do*?'

'Sends you into a coma. Why?'

Lifting my head, I took the bottle of mineral water from him, and drank. A litre of water later, I started noticing our surroundings. The drinks stand was actually the veranda of a family house, perched on the edge of a precipitous drop. The house had one room, about twelve feet wide by twenty feet long, with a mud floor and thatch walls and roof. At its far end, a woman and boy lay sleeping on a mat. Close to the door, a man tended a pot of something steaming over a charcoal burner. Hanging on the outside wall was an old beer can filled with earth and bristling with burnt-down incense sticks. On the other side of the road, a pipe stuck out of the cliff and clear, fresh water was spouting out and falling into a gully. I was sure it was a mirage; only when I stood beneath its cold, strong and invigorating rush did I believe it was true.

At the bottom of the pass there was an army base where a young man sat in a shelter next to the barrier, excavating his nose with a long fingernail. When he saw us cycling past he jumped up and yelled, 'Stop! Come in! Come in!' but we thought better of it. The highway began to climb again and to swing away from the coast. Soon we were on a scrubby plain, ringed by low hills. A few shabby villages clung to the road. Outside the houses were stalls selling wooden blocks to put under the wheels of buses and trucks, and plastic bottles of water to top up their cooling tanks. The poverty was palpable, and as we cycled by people ran along with cupped palms, calling for money and cigarettes. Soon, the houses petered out and the road, which had become more potholes than anything else, stretched ahead in a straight line. It was now almost three o'clock, we had been cycling for six hours and had covered forty-three miles. Vinh, our destination for that day, was still a good thirty-five miles away.

'Hey, there's a great bus coming,' called Dag, who was cycling behind me. 'Let's flag it down and see if they'll take us along.'

It was a Japanese bus, sleek, plush and air-conditioned, the sort we'd seen lined up outside the Imperial Enclosure in Hue. Like the beggars, we waved and held out our hands in supplication. The bus roared by, but some of the windows were pushed open, and its passengers leaned out to video us.

The next bus, however, did stop. It was bound for Hanoi. The man who climbed down from it to bargain over a price was big and burly, and looked as if his hobby was brawling in bars. A stained green muscle shirt was stretched over his voluminous belly, and decaying teeth protruded from his snarling, betel-stained lips. When we told him we wanted a ride as far as Vinh, he growled, *'Nam nghin!'* Fifty thousand dong for a thirty-five mile ride was only twice the local price, which, coming from this character, should have made us instantly suspicious.

'Nam nghin?' repeated Dag, holding up five fingers on one hand and with the other hand pointing to me, the bikes, our bags.

'Okay! Okay!' cried Muscle Shirt.

Inside the bus, he yanked a couple of passengers off the front seat and told us to sit in their place. Then he settled down directly opposite us, on the engine cover. Surrounding him was a coterie of ugly, brutish friends. One of them plunged into the aisle and returned with a young woman who could speak a little English. She wore a blue blouse with a Peter Pan collar, her hair was tied up with ribbon and she had an innocent freshness that was totally incongruous in the company of such rough-looking men. As she sat down, Muscle Shirt pulled lascivious faces and stuck his thumb between two of his fingers, a gesture that left nothing to the imagination. Ignoring this, she patiently translated the questions the men barked at her, and the answers we gave. It was all very familiar – country, ages, jobs, number of siblings, if our parents were living, the location of my father's tomb, and so on. Our answer to the inevitable question about children, however, completely threw her.

'*No* children?' she repeated, in disbelieving tones. 'Why is this?'

'We can't afford any,' said Dag jovially.

She obviously didn't get the joke. Pursing her lips, she stared with a bewildered expression into the middle distance for a minute before translating this to the men.

Equally stumped, they sat in silence. Eventually Muscle Shirt made an obviously lewd remark and then decided it was time to collect our fares. Dag handed him fifty thousand dong. He stared at the money for a second, as if he didn't know what it was, then thrust the notes back at Dag.

'*Muoi nghin!*' he demanded. 'A hundred thousand!'

'Here we go,' said Dag resignedly. He turned to the girl. 'Could you tell this gentleman that half an hour ago he agreed on a price of fifty thousand dong?'

'He say he mean fifty thousand each,' she answered, without even bothering to translate.

'No, we made it quite clear—'

'One hundred thousand for one hundred and twenty kilometre, it is the foreigner price,' she said, smiling sweetly.

'But we're not going one hundred and twenty kilometres.'

She shrugged. 'It doesn't matter.'

'*Nam nghin,*' said Dag firmly, again holding out the notes to Muscle Shirt.

Refusing to take it, he pulled a sour face and began a long discussion with his cronies. Then, after giving us an evil, side-long look, he clambered out of the door of the moving bus and up onto the roof.

'There go our bikes,' said Dag. 'He'll be stripping them down right now.'

The bikes were temporarily saved when, minutes later, the bus broke down. We were still on a straight and deserted stretch of road. There were no villages in sight, but within twenty minutes two small children had arrived bearing a kettle full of green tea and one glass, which they emptied and refilled for each customer. Meanwhile, Muscle Man and his cronies had jacked up the bus, and the driver was lying beneath it while they passed him an assortment of oily tools. Towards us, a distinct chilliness had developed. The beribboned girl stared in the opposite direction, and people sitting close by avoided our eyes.

Forty-five minutes passed before the bus juddered into life once more. Within the hour it had stopped again, this time at a cavernous restaurant. The unfriendly atmosphere followed us from the bus into the open-sided building. Our fellow passengers were automatically served with bowls of rice, egg and meat, while we were studiously ignored. A man refilling the pots of green tea on each table carefully skirted around us. Giving up the hope of ordering food, we headed back to the bus. On the way we tried to buy guavas from a fruit seller squatting outside the restaurant. The local man ahead of me bought two guavas for five hundred dong. I was charged a thousand dong for one guava. Usually I couldn't be bothered to haggle, and a thousand dong for one piece of fruit was still a very low price by Western standards. But I was in such a foul mood that I protested about being overcharged. The beribboned girl was once more called over to intervene.

'She ask you the right price,' she insisted.

I told the seller to keep her fruit, and stumped back to my seat. Muscle Shirt glowered at me; I glowered back. As we set off again, a vehicle overtook the bus at high speed, its wheels throwing up dust and grit which came flying through the window and into my eyes. I rubbed them clean just in time to see a Kim's Café minibus packed with pink bodies barrelling away into the distance. Ruefully I considered the irony of our situation, travelling like this to get to know local people, and managing to alienate ourselves from an entire busload of them.

Just before six o'clock, a police car flagged down the bus. We had left Ha Tien, and were passing through its suburbs. On one side of the road were paddy fields. On the other side, where we parked, was a channel of grey water and a line of skinny, three-storey houses surrounded by lawns that looked as if hundreds of chickens had been scratching through them. Puffing up his chest like a toad, Muscle Shirt headed down the

steps of the bus to confront the law. There were four policemen, led by a man in plainclothes whose face had a terrible
scar. Shaped like a scythe, it started at his left ear, curved
across his cheek and stopped just short of his left eye. Still red
and inflamed, with the stitch marks clearly defined, it was
obviously a fairly new addition to his looks. Scar Face and
Muscle Shirt faced up to each other, brandishing their intim-
idating attitudes like weapons. The problem, it soon
transpired, concerned the cargo on the roof of the bus.
Already, two policemen were up there, swarming over the
sacks, boxes and baskets. Like every local bus we'd seen in
Vietnam, this one was ridiculously overloaded with cargo. Just
what was in all those sacks and boxes, apart from rice or pigs
or snakes, was something that had never crossed my mind. But
whatever was on the roof of this particular bus was obviously
of great concern to the police, and to Muscle Shirt, who was
spitting out words and jabbing his finger in the air. A well-
stuffed and lumpy sack flew past my window, and crashed to
the ground next to the police chief and his suspect. Scar Face
took out a knife, ripped open a corner of the sack and reached
inside.

'It's a rock,' said Dag, peering down at what he'd pulled out.
'It can't be!'
'It is!'
And so it was. Scar Face held the rock in his upturned palm,
turning it this way and that to examine it closely. He smelt it,
then took out a cigarette lighter and tried to set fire to it.

'What the hell is he doing?' I asked.

'Maybe he thinks it's some sort of drug,' suggested Dag.
'Maybe *that*'s where the expression "getting stoned" comes
from!'

Meanwhile, three more sacks had been thrown from the
roof. Muscle Shirt was still talking, but he had pulled his
shirt up over his paunch, and was nervously scratching his
belly. Suddenly, Scar Face appeared at the front of the bus
and ordered us all to get off. We stood in groups along the
water channel, stealing surreptitious glances at the sacks,
which did indeed contain nothing but rocks. Scar Face
searched the bus, looking beneath the seats and along the

overhead racks, opening up bags and shaking bunches of bananas.

'He's just psyching up the bus crew,' said Dag, 'so he can squeeze a bigger bribe out of them.'

While we were gazing up at the roof to check on our bikes, we noticed yet more sacks of rocks. Underneath the other cargo, they were heaped three across and three deep. A quick calculation brought the total number of sacks of rocks to fifty-four. It was a wonder the ceiling above our heads hadn't buckled under the weight.

Presently, the confiscated sacks of rocks were loaded into the car, Muscle Shirt was marched away and all the policemen left. It was now six thirty, and almost dark. Except for us, none of the bus passengers seemed unduly worried by the delay. They lounged at the side of the road, washed their feet in the channel of grey water, urinated against the sides of houses and bought bowls of *pho* and glasses of green tea from the food sellers who had magically materialized. The engine had been left running, and was pumping out smelly blue smoke. The driver lit some new incense sticks and put these in the shrine on the dashboard. I found the girl with the ribbon, who was trying to keep a safe distance from us, and asked her what was going on.

'I don't understand,' she said.

Night fell, stars appeared, exhaust fumes filled the air. Then, without any warning, the bus began rolling forwards. Everyone jumped aboard and we were off – without Muscle Shirt! But it was a false alarm. We went only as far as a petrol station, where the tank was filled, before reversing back to the same spot next to the channel of grey water. This time, at least, the engine was turned off, but its noise was soon replaced by Vietnamese pop music that screeched from the driver's radio. I found everyone's complacency astonishing – for all we knew, we could have been sitting there all night. Briefly, Dag and I discussed taking our bikes off the roof and setting off towards Vinh. But we had no lights, and the chances of us getting very far before being squashed like bugs, perhaps by this very bus, were slight. So we sat, and practised being as complacent as everyone else.

*

At eight thirty, Muscle Shirt reappeared and squatted on his haunches by the water channel, scratching his belly and smoking several cigarettes in a row. The bus had begun to move away before he finally deigned to jump aboard. He was in such an ugly mood that even his cronies looked worried. He sat on the engine cover, sulking, scratching and occasionally glowering at Dag, who I could feel growing increasingly tense beside me.

'We'll soon be in Vinh!' I cheerfully commented, which was true, as the driver was trying to make up for lost time on his journey to Hanoi, and we were rattling along at a dangerous speed.

Half an hour later, as we were heading straight through a small town, a group of people ran out into the middle of the road, flagging down the bus. The driver slowed to make his way around them, and a couple of women pushed a teenage boy up the front steps. Slightly built, with a barely discernible fuzz growing on his upper lip, he was dressed in a school uniform of a bright white shirt and long black pants. He had no luggage with him, and when Muscle Shirt stood to take his fare, he said he was going to Vinh.

'*Nam nghin!*' demanded Muscle Shirt. 'Fifty thousand!'

The boy's eyes widened. It was a preposterous fare for a local, and he obviously made some sort of remark to that effect. Muscle Shirt drew back his hand and slapped him hard on the side of his head. The boy's face flooded with the sudden shock of the blow, but he had no time to recover before Muscle Shirt followed up with a punch in the stomach and a vicious volley of slaps on the neck and back. All this took only seconds, but seemed to happen in slow motion. Everyone around the boy and the vile man had frozen, taken aback by the sudden violence of the attack. But when Muscle Shirt grabbed a wooden wheel block and smashed it down on the boy's head, things speeded up. Dag was suddenly on his feet, and so were Muscle Shirt's cronies who grabbed the man's arms and wrestled the block out of his hands, possibly saving the boy's life. They restrained him for several minutes. He panted, curled back his lips and snarled at the boy, who was whimpering and holding his bleeding head.

'Don't get involved,' I hissed at Dag, tugging at him to sit down again.

When Muscle Shirt had calmed, his cronies let him go. Immediately he yelled at the driver to stop the bus. Grabbing the boy by the shirt collar, he yanked him out through the door. We were on a dark stretch of road, surrounded by paddy fields, with not a settlement for miles.

A minute later he returned alone to the bus. No one spoke to him as we carried on to Vinh; even his cronies avoided his gaze. He scrabbled around in a cooler behind the driver's seat, took out a lump of ice and stuck it between his teeth. Then, giving us a look filled with poisonous arrows, he swung out through the door and up to the roof.

'Off to dismember our bikes,' said Dag.

Considering the circumstances, it really didn't matter.

As we pulled into Vinh, I had visions of us being dropped off along an alleyway, beaten up and left bleeding with the mangled remains of our bikes on top of us. For the last ten minutes, I'd been practising saying, 'I'll call the police,' in Vietnamese and I had pulled out a handful of dollar bills, ready to offer them in return for our lives. As it turned out, none of this was necessary. The bus stopped on Vinh's wide and well-lit main street, opposite a multi-storey and rather fancy-looking hotel. Muscle Shirt appeared from the roof, relaxed and smiling. He supervised the delivery of our bikes, which were intact, and accepted fifty thousand dong from Dag without a murmur of dissent. Then the bus pulled away, leaving us standing with our mouths open. Seconds later a small pony trotted purposefully by, lacking rider or saddle but seeming to know exactly where it was going. It was surreal, like something out of a Fellini film, and a fitting end to a very long, bizarre day.

11
FREE BACTERIA

The only free room in Vinh that night was in the Hotel Kim
Lien, named after Ho Chi Minh's birthplace. As the lift swept
us to its top floor, a bell hop told us the town had been busy
like this since the Americans lifted the trade embargo. Foreign
businessmen, he said, came here every day because of the
mines. He pulled a handkerchief from his pocket and unfolded
it to reveal several pieces of red glass.

'You buy rubies?' he whispered.

From the lift he led us along a windswept walkway. Litter
blew past us, and graffiti was scrawled on the pebble-dashed
walls. I felt as if I'd been transported back to the 1970s and a
block of tenement flats in inner city Liverpool or Manchester,
the kind that drove their inhabitants to despair and have since
been torn down in disgrace. Our room was air conditioned,
but grim. The restaurant, the bell hop informed us, was closed
and there was nowhere else in Vinh to get a meal at this time.
He could, however, offer us rubies at the cheapest price in
town. We closed the door on him, squashed a few cockroaches,
then fell into bed and escaped into sleep.

*

The view from our window next morning was unremittingly bleak. Below a blanket of grey cloud lay a plain covered with four- and five-storey tenement buildings, all in various stages of decay. During Operations Rolling Thunder and Linebacker, from 1964 to 1972, the US bombed Vinh repeatedly, leaving only a few buildings standing. After the war, the East Germans arrived to rebuild the city, replacing one nightmare with another. We decided that we did not want to spend a minute longer than was necessary in this dismal town. But after the horrors of the day before, we couldn't face our bikes or a bus again so soon. The idea of a boat journey beckoned once more. We headed downstairs to the hotel tourist agent, for once intent on getting something officially arranged.

The foyer was abuzz with Malaysian businessmen and their interpreters.

'I work for the government, assisting the foreigners who want to exploit the mines,' one of these interpreters told us. 'But I am not from the North,' he added, as if this was very important to him. 'I am a Saigon person.'

His help had been enlisted by the hotel tourist agent, who spoke Russian but little English, and to whom we'd been trying unsuccessfully to convey our desire to go by boat from Vinh to Haiphong. When the interpreter translated our request, the tourist agent looked bewildered.

'He say the boats from Vinh carry things not people. And he say the police are at the port. He say he can arrange a car for you this afternoon.'

'But we want to go by boat,' I reiterated. 'We are prepared to pay extra if he can organize something for us.'

The translation of this took longer than seemed necessary. 'He ask if you want a boat with oars or engine,' said the interpreter finally.

Considering the fact we were discussing a trip of a hundred and ninety miles along exposed coastline, this seemed like an odd question.

'And he ask if you want to go straight to Haiphong by boat, or do you want to stop off for lunch?'

'Let's forget it,' Dag muttered to me. 'It's a wild goose chase.'

'An engine would be best, and we'll have lunch on board,' I told the interpreter.

'He says he can arrange it. Lunch will be included in the price.'

'And what will the price be?'

'He wants to know what you offer.'

I felt Dag's foot on mine.

'Two hundred dollars,' he said quickly.

'He must go to the port to discuss it. He will come back in some hours.

We had a late breakfast in the hotel's restaurant. It had emptied of businessmen, who were piling into the air-conditioned cars and mini buses parked in the forecourt. A mouse scurried about beneath tables, busily hoovering up crumbs, while five or six staff listlessly cleared away plates. One of them, a man in his mid-twenties, came over to us.

'You can have bread and eggs,' he said.

Minutes later he served us with omelettes, baguettes and coffee. Then he sat down at our table, introduced himself as Linh and lit a cigarette.

'The house of Ho Chi Minh is close to here,' he said, blowing smoke over me. 'You want I take you there on motor bike?'

We didn't.

'A friend of mine wishes to buy American dollar. Can you help him?'

We couldn't.

He reached into his pocket, and pulled out a knotted, rumpled handkerchief.

'You want beautiful ruby, very cheap, souvenir?' he asked.

To divert him from this sales pitch, I complimented him on his English.

'I go to Russia and study English very hard! Mr Lenin say, Study! Study!'

'And what would Mr Lenin say about black-market dollars?'

He smoked in silence for a while.

'My friend give you very good rate. Can you help him?'

A door at the far end of the restaurant opened and a man walked through it. Linh was on his feet in a second, stubbing out his cigarette in a plant pot. Suddenly, the staff were showering us with attention. Our water glasses were refilled, my half-eaten omelette was whisked away, several standing fans were dragged over to us and turned on full. The man went out of a far door, and everyone relaxed.

'New manager,' Linh confided.

We nodded understandingly, and asked for the bill.

'Six dollar,' said Linh.

'*Six?*'

'Okay, three dollar. What about my friend? You want change dollars with him?'

Instead of dealing with Linh's friend, we went to a desk in the foyer with a Vietcom Bank sign displayed above it. Next to the sign was a poster of Miss Vietnam 1993, a gorgeous girl with fluffy hair and lots of red lipstick. Standing in front of the poster was an innocent-looking bank clerk in a white *ao dai*.

'Speak Russian?' she asked.

On a piece of paper we wrote US$1 = ?

'Ah!' she cried, and wrote underneath, $100 = 1090000 VD, $50 = 525000 VD.

We handed her a hundred dollars. She looked around the foyer, and caught the eye of a man in sunglasses leaning against a wall. Hanging over his shoulder was a leather case. He walked over, unzipped the case, handed over a wad of dong, took the dollars and returned to the wall.

'Receipt?' I asked the girl.

She shook her head. I pointed to the word in the dictionary. After rummaging about in a drawer, she found a receipt book and recorded our transaction, making sure to first remove the carbon paper.

We returned to our room, where we killed a few more cockroaches and lay on the beds, feeling as listless as the restaurant staff. Within an hour there was a knock at the door, and a letter was pushed underneath it.

Dear Madam,
We are sorry to inform you that we cannot accept your price for renting a boat from Vinh to Haiphong because the price of your requirement is very low for us to prepare such boat for you. After calculating, we just accept such

price (550 USD) that we can arrange a boat for your. So if you don't accept that, we can arrange an air-conditioned 4 seat car for you without including food. If any acceptable, please contact us and sign a contract with us on this afternoon so that we can go at three pm.

Thank you.

'We'll offer three hundred dollars,' said Dag, as we went down in the lift. 'It's reasonable for a boat ride of that distance.'

The young interpreter was waiting for us by the desk. Sitting on a sofa nearby were three Malaysian businessmen, who looked as if they were being kept waiting and resented it.

'You read my letter?' asked the interpreter.

When we told him what we could offer, he shook his head.

'To Haiphong is very far.'

'We've always paid fishermen a dollar a kilometre.'

'This is not fishing boat. This is military boat.'

'Military?'

'Yes. And they insist you have a protector with a gun, a skipper and two drivers.'

'Why two drivers?'

'In case one driver is sick. It is all expensive.'

Behind us, the businessmen were coughing and shuffling and generally getting restive.

'Excuse me I must go,' said their interpreter. 'Good luck!'

Taking the businessmen's place on the sofa, we considered what to do. We could head off in a heavily armed military boat. We could get back on our bikes. We could hail a local bus. Or, of course, we could trail down to the beach, ten miles away, find a fishing village and try to communicate that we wanted to go north by boat. None of these options appealed to us. So we sat, and pondered, while businessmen got in and out of air-conditioned cars and minibuses. At his desk, the travel agent fiddled with a pen and watched us. After a while he came over and offered us a piece of paper. On it was written: Toyota car, new, go Ninh Binh, US $90.

For weeks now, I'd heard Dag swearing that he'd never end up being ferried around in an air-conditioned car, like so many other tourists. So I was taken aback by his response to the travel agent's offer.

'Sixty dollars,' he said.

'Okay,' said the travel agent.

Within half an hour our bikes were stripped of their wheels and shoved into the boot of a white, air-conditioned car, and we were making our escape from Vinh.

In our eagerness to get away, we hadn't stopped to look over the car and check the travel agent's claim that it was new. As the cheerful driver, Tran, swerved this way and that to avoid the bikes and cyclos and pony traps of Vinh's main street, I registered that he had no rear view mirror. Shortly afterwards it occurred to me that, considering the relative smoothness of this section of road, the ride was a good deal bumpier than it should have been. I had hoped to catch up on my notes during the journey, but my hand was jarred so often that any attempts at writing ended up as a spidery scrawl. Putting my notebook away, I settled for just looking out of the window. We had left the outskirts of Vinh and were heading through a steep-sided, barren valley. The monotony of the view made me intensely happy; instead of cranking a bike through this hot wasteland, I was effortlessly speeding along it in a car that, if not comfortable, was at least cool. Intense happiness, however, is usually short lived, and this was no exception.

BANG! went one of the tyres.

'*Waaah!*' yelled Tran, as the car swerved out of control.

After skidding and spinning all over a mercifully empty road, we came to a halt facing the wrong way. We got out, pushed the car to the side of the road then stood staring at the destroyed front tyre. Tran scratched his head and pulled at the crop of hairs growing from a mole on his chin.

'Yes,' he said.

'Yes,' we agreed.

A skinny farmer was heading towards us on a bike. As he passed by, Tran hopped onto the back of the bike, shouting and pointing towards an iron-roofed shack in the distance.

'He must be going to get tools,' said Dag hopefully.

'Or a spare tyre,' I added.

'He's bound to have one of those already,' said Dag, sounding far from convinced.

In Tran's absence we had ample time to wander around the car and have a good look at it. As well as having no rear view mirror, it also lacked side mirrors and its back lights were smashed in. Several bumps and scrapes had been inexpertly patched up and painted over. We were joined in our examination of the car by a woman who came clumping by in a pair of old shoes that were several sizes too big for her and had holes in the toes. She was carrying a basket filled with grass and plants that she'd gathered from the valley floor. She hunkered down a short distance away and stared intently at the underside of the vehicle. I followed her gaze and noticed that fluid was dripping from the engine, forming a puddle on the red dirt.

After half an hour a tiny figure appeared in the distance, wavering in the heat haze. As it slowly got bigger, we recognized it as Tran. His gait was jaunty, as if he was returning with good news, but he appeared to be empty-handed.

'No jack,' said Dag.

'No tyre,' I added.

Finally he arrived, sweaty and grinning. From one trouser pocket he pulled a screw driver, and from the other a wrench. Squatting down by the blown-out tyre, he whacked the screw driver against the hub cap, which obligingly fell off. Then he used the wrench to remove the bolts securing the wheel.

'Now we need a jack,' said Dag, in the tones of a man who has resigned himself to his fate.

Tran gestured to Dag that he should lift up the front of the car. To my surprise, he tried.

'Mind your back!' I protested as Dag heaved and grunted like a weight lifter, while Tran struggled to release the tyre.

Both failed. Then Tran joined Dag and they heaved together.

'Get – the – tyre!' Dag gasped at me through gritted teeth, as the chassis inched upwards.

I wasn't fast enough, and they let the car go, both glaring at me in indignation. I left them to it, and hunkered next to the woman at the side of the road, preferring to watch this pantomime rather than be drawn any further into it.

A truck went by, and then a bus. In turn, Tran chased the vehicles, yelling at the drivers to stop. Both ignored him. The next time a truck came by he leapt into its path, forcing it to slow right down, then clambered onto the running board. The strategy worked; minutes later the truck was parked up at the side of the road and Tran was hurrying towards us, wreathed in smiles and clutching a jack. A very large, truck-sized jack. Setting it down next to the tyre, he looked at it as if willing it to shrink to the right size. By now some farmers had arrived, walking across the plain to join the woman in the clumpy shoes. Thin as twigs, they were dressed in ragged shorts, shirts and frayed straw hats, and carried crudely made hoes and pick axes. With them was a little boy who was holding a bamboo cage with a tiny bird hopping around inside it. He put the cage on the ground, produced part of a wasp's nest from his pocket and began picking out pupae from it and stuffing them into the bird's beak. I was so engrossed in watching this that I almost missed the next part of Tran's performance. Quick as a flash, he'd organized the half-starved farmers to help Dag lift the car while he struggled to get the jack beneath it.

'Heave!' cried Dag, turning a peculiar shade of purple.

Brittle as the farmers looked, there was some strength in their bodies, for on the third heave they lifted the car high enough for Tran to get the jack beneath it. The wheel came off, and then we unloaded our bikes from the boot of the car to get to the spare. With a flourish, Tran pulled off a plastic cover to reveal the replacement wheel. There was a moment of shocked silence as we, the farmers and the woman in clumpy shoes stared at it.

'It's tiny . . .' I said.

'Well,' said Dag, clearing his throat, 'it's *significantly* smaller than the other three wheels.'

Undeterred, Tran cheerfully attached the significantly smaller wheel to the car, returned the jack to the truck, put the old wheel and our bikes into the boot, gave the farmers some money and asked them to return the screw driver and wrench to their owner. Then, grinning broadly, he ushered us back into the car. Soon, his grinning took on a manic quality. He began blindly overtaking, braking when he should have been accelerating, accelerating when he should have been braking, swerving to avoid bikes, scooters, horse drawn carts and people, and keeping his hand constantly on the horn. I wasn't looking at the view any more: most of the time I had my eyes shut. I consoled myself that at least we were not outside in the baking heat, at least it was cool in the car. And that was when steam started pouring out of the air-conditioning vents. Tran seemed to find this very funny.

'Yes!' he cried, winding down his window as far as it would go, letting the hot, dusty air pour into the car. 'Yes!'

As darkness fell, massive clouds moved in and we were hit by a terrific storm. First came the lightning that forked across the sky and illuminated limestone hills rising like camels' humps from the plain. Then the thunder, crashing and booming like an avalanche. Rain pounded down so forcefully that it was like being inside a waterfall. The only good thing about this was that Tran finally began driving at a sedate speed. But even at ten miles an hour, our progress was terrifying. Shapes suddenly loomed up in front of us; bikes and scooters without lights, buses and trucks with lights on full beam heading straight at us and swerving out of the way at the last second. The closest call we had was with a pedestrian, draped in a plastic cape and sloshing through puddles, whom we avoided squashing by inches. As we passed I turned around and caught a brief glimpse of an old man. His face was dignified but haunted, perhaps by everything he had seen and experienced over the years along this hellish highway.

Throughout the journey, Tran remained pathologically cheerful, even when we rolled into Ninh Binh at eight thirty, and he had to turn around and drive all the way back to Vinh in the dark and rain. As he left we gave him a five-dollar tip, and I thought his face would crack open.

'Yes!' he cried through his open window as he drove away. 'Yes, YES!'

He had dropped us off at the Thanh Binh Mini Hotel, a small and charming old building tucked away along an alley

and owned by his friends, Madame Xuyen and Mr Uy. The
'hotel' was in fact their house, and they and their three children vacated the bedrooms whenever guests arrived. With its
pastel-painted stone walls, irregular-tiled floors and windows
with carved wooden bars and shutters, it could almost have
been a French farmhouse, were it not for the photograph of
Ho Chi Minh in the hallway, and the vase of huge purple lotus
buds set beneath it. Madame Xuyen was a handsome woman
with yards of thick, greying hair. Her husband was wiry, and
his head seemed to be rather too loosely attached to his neck.
He told us that for twenty-five years he had been in the North
Vietnamese Army, and had only retired the year before. But he
wouldn't be drawn into discussing his military experiences.
What he wanted to talk about was the World Cup.

'Tonight, Fermany and Buggery!' he told us.

We asked if it was possible to have breakfast at seven o'clock.

'Too early!' he said. 'Tonight we watch World Cup.
Tomorrow tired. Breakfast nine o'clock.'

After sleeping through thunder, lightning and the World
Cup games, at six next morning we were woken by someone
crooning karaoke in a house nearby. Sitting up in bed, I looked
across red-tiled roofs with fat pumpkins growing on them, and
down into courtyards with yellow-washed walls where women
with their hair in curlers fed bowls of rice to chickens and
cats. The crooner, who was out of sight, carried on relentlessly,
churning out one schmaltzy song after another. We showered,
then read and made notes in our room, waiting for the rest of
the house to wake up. At exactly nine there was a tap on our
door, and Madame Xuyen came in bearing a large tray of
eggs, bread, butter and coffee, as well as a bottle of water
which, according to its label, offered 'Free Bacteria'.

When we'd finished breakfast we carried the trays downstairs, and found Mr Uy scratching his head over the state of
our bikes. The chains were loose, all the bolts needed greasing,
wheel spokes had parted company with wheel rims, Dag's
back fender had disappeared, my front brake pads had fallen
off . . . and so the list went on.

'*Xau*,' he pronounced. Bad.

'Tomorrow,' I told him, 'we cycle to Haiphong.'

The city was eighty miles away, and almost the end of our journey. From there we would go by ferry to Halong Bay, and then make our way to Hanoi, and a plane home. We were eager to reach Haiphong in one push, partly because we wanted this long hard haul by bike to be over and partly because we had to renew our visas, which were about to run out.

'Haiphong!' Mr Uy repeated in alarm. 'Very far. Very hard.'

His eyes drifted to the wrecked bikes, then back to the gaunt foreigners standing next to them. Now that I had finally recovered from giardia, Dag had come down with a bout of it, and the gold wedding band he'd bought in Cantho was already slipping off his finger. As well as losing weight, the anti-malarial medication we were both taking was causing us to lose hair, and in Dag's case it was coming out in handfuls. Skinny, sunburned and balding: we were not a pretty sight. Nor, in Mr Uy's opinion, did we look capable of reaching Haiphong by bike.

'Very far. Very hard. You die,' he said.

We spent the rest of the day having our bikes patched up at one of the hundreds of bicycle repair shops in Ninh Binh market, and doing a bit of sightseeing. A few miles away from Ninh Binh is Hoa Lu, which was the capital of Vietnam during the Dinh and Le dynasties, from 980 to 1009. To reach it we cycled along a winding back road through the southernmost corner of the Red River Delta. There was little left of the ancient citadel, save for a couple of gloomy pagodas. But around Hoa Lu, the landscape had a dream-like beauty. The plain glittered with the jewel colours of young, green rice plants, purple lotus flowers and yellow water hyacinths. And from it rose scores of white, limestone outcrops, dazzlingly picturesque mini mountains tufted with hardy trees, riddled with caves and sheltering ancient Buddhist shrines.

We left our bikes by the pagoda and hired a sampan to take us through the area. A woman paddled us along canals where small boys fished from wicker boats shaped like saucers. Iridescent blue beecatchers swooped and fluttered, dragonflies hovered over the water, large butterflies flapped by. The air smelled of tropical flowers and of rich, damp earth. But, as we floated along in the baking heat, there was little peace to be found. Radios blared from the balconies of houses and, on other boats, Vietnamese tourists clutched ghetto blasters that were cranked up to full volume. At the shrines, we were besieged by children who thrust packets of joss sticks in our faces, and by old ladies, their heads wrapped in black cloth, who demanded recompense for pointing to the rough carvings of winged dragons, and the wall paintings of elephants and horses.

It was good to get back to our hotel. While we ate dinner in its delightful little courtyard, Mr Uy tried hard to make us change our plans.

'Haiphong. Very far. Very hard,' he kept repeating. 'Go bus.'

But Madame Xuyen knew we were determined and had obviously decided to get us properly fuelled for the ordeal.

'Eat! Eat!' she insisted, bringing plates of fish soup, spring rolls, sautéed potatoes, rice, pork and bean sprouts, meat balls, cucumber in vinegar and finally, a bowl of glistening plums.

When we'd finished, the couple ushered us off to our room for an early night's sleep, saying we needed to rest for our journey. They also wanted us out of the way so they could settle down to watch football. They were still awake, and sitting in front of the television, when we carried our bags downstairs at four thirty.

'Germany one, Sweden one!' called Mr Uy after us, as we pushed our bikes up the alleyway.

A narrow brick road led us towards Haiphong. Our plan was to make it to Nam Dinh, twenty miles away, before stopping for breakfast. But the road, which ran between a canal and a railway line, was exceptionally bumpy. By five thirty I was convinced that some of my vertebrae had been shaken loose. By six, the sun was up and doing its business, I was sweating hard and my pace was getting slower and slower, while Dag was growing increasingly bad tempered at having to wait for me. Nam Dinh was still ten miles away, but I insisted we stop for a drink.

'It was your idea we get to Haiphong today,' grumbled Dag, as I gulped down a bottle of water with free bacteria and two bottles of Festi Cola.

The sugar did its trick, and I pedalled off at twice the speed as before. But my spurt of energy was short-lived. Three miles from Nam Dinh I practically fell off my bike in front of a *pho* stall.

'You're like a bloody humming bird, Coffey,' said Dag, as I wolfed down noodles and dubious scraps of grey meat. 'If you don't eat every half an hour, you're in danger of fluttering to the ground and expiring.'

In a shop next to the *pho* stall he stocked up with more water and bought a bagful of what looked a bit like nut brittle – sweet brown caramel mixed with nuts and something red, gritty and unidentifiable.

'I'll feed you this at regular intervals,' he said. 'That should do the trick.'

Soon we were well and truly into the Red River Delta, the cradle of Vietnamese civilization. It was here, after shaking off a thousand years of Chinese domination, that the first independent state of Vietnam was established in AD 939 by Ngo Quyen, and from here that the Viets expanded south. Now, it is the most densely populated part of the country, and it has an industrial atmosphere, with none of the lushness of the tropical Mekong Delta. Motorized ploughs worked the paddy fields and men with tanks strapped to their backs sprayed insecticide on the newly sprouting rice plants. Power lines looped between large pylons. Smoking brick works lined the banks of river channels that were the colour of ox tail soup. The boats on the water were built of iron and carried cargoes of bricks, coal, sand and lime. Several times our road met one of these channels, and we were ferried across them on rusty iron barges.

By late morning we'd done over fifty miles. My pace had improved, helped by the sweet nut brittle which I was snacking on as I cycled. But the fourth time I took a bite of the stuff, I noticed something wriggling about in the piece left in my hand. Closer investigation revealed that the red gritty stuff was larvae, from which plump wriggly little worms were hatching. I spat out what was in my mouth, and fought back the urge to retch up what I'd eaten so far.

'Couldn't you tell what these things are?' I said crossly to Dag, waving the nut brittle under his nose. 'I mean, you *are* a vet!'

The day was cloudless and very hot. For a while we were practically alone on a quiet stretch of road. Buses and trucks had stopped running for the lunch break that is religiously observed in Vietnam. Farmers were resting beneath trees, and even the water buffaloes had retreated to ponds and irrigation channels, and submerged themselves until only their ears and noses were showing. We allowed ourselves a long stop in a café where an altar to the god of business, a corpulent chap with offerings of coffee and foreign cigarettes arranged before him, was set beneath a picture of Ho Chi Minh. A friendly couple owned the place, and after lunch they invited us into their house. A television was switched on and we sat and watched Bulgaria beat Germany by two to one. I wasn't interested in the football; I was just glad to be out of the sun and sitting inside a cool room. The woman seemed anxious about my skin, which was coated in a mixture of sweat and dust. Leaving her husband to discuss the match with Dag, she took me through her back yard to a bath house. Scooping water from a large urn, she helped me to wash, rubbing hard at my arms and legs and becoming greatly disappointed as she realized that, beneath all the grime, my skin was not pink but a sun-weathered brown.

Refreshed by food and the wash, I cycled away from the café at a good pace.

'You're like a wind-up toy,' called Dag admiringly.

His words were barely out before I swerved to avoid a pink and black pig trotting across the road, and wheeled into a heap of straw which threw me off balance. It was a soft landing, but from thereon my spirits and my energy began seriously to flag. Unfortunately, at the same time the traffic became progressively worse. Perhaps because of my weariness, I was convinced that the buses and trucks passing us were throwing up bigger clouds of dust and had air horns more piercing than any we'd experienced on Highway One. But it was on the outskirts of Haiphong that the real horror began. After seventy-nine miles of cycling that day, we hit Vietnam's third largest city in the middle of evening rush hour. This was the worst traffic I'd ever seen, never mind been part of. Rumbling trucks, merciless buses, frail ponies and carts, scooters, bikes,

cars and pedestrians were concentrated into a heaving, honking, trilling anarchic mass, and I was somewhere in the middle
of it. The light, blurred by dust and fumes, lent a softened,
unreal quality to the harsh scenes around me. An untethered,
emaciated pony stood at the side of the road, its head hanging
down, looking utterly beaten, and I knew exactly how the poor
animal felt. Two men on bikes held between them a long bamboo pole and a hanging mat with a pair of bare, human feet
sticking out of it. Grimly, I cycled on, narrowly avoiding
countless collisions and probably causing many that I never
noticed. Once I wobbled uncertainly onto a crossroad, giving
the impression I was about to turn right and then carrying on
straight and creating mayhem on all sides.

'Take care! Take care!' yelled one man from a scooter.

By now I was dizzy, nauseous, afraid and close to tears.
Further along the street I could see Dag, head and shoulders
above the crowds. He had become expert at weaving through
traffic, and was easily pulling ahead, but stopped often to wait,
turning back to check worriedly on my progress.

'Almost there!' he called encouragingly when I caught up
with him, and it crossed my mind how stupid it would be, after
cycling hundreds of miles on this bloody bike along a dreadful
highway, to get nailed by a truck during the last few hundred
yards.

The Hotel de Commerce looked like heaven incarnate: an
old colonial building with yellow-washed stone walls, wide
balconies, gracious colonnades and a cool and airy foyer. I
booked into a room without enquiring about the price or
checking with Dag if he'd mind air conditioning. Suddenly
my legs seemed barely capable of movement and my arms had
lost all strength. Walking up the two flights of stairs with my
bag was the hardest thing I'd done all day. And no one helped;
this was, after all, a government-run hotel, so the bell hop
could not be detached from the paper he was reading, and the
receptionists floated about in their blue *ao dais* looking too
bored to intervene. Our bathroom had white-tiled walls and a
real shower, which we stood under for so long that the water
seeped beneath the door and formed a large puddle on the
wooden floor of the bedroom. Then we collapsed onto the

beds and fell asleep with the air conditioning and the ceiling fan both full on.

In the government-run tourist office, where we went next day to enquire about having our visas renewed, the girl behind the desk had her hair in curlers and was plucking her eyebrows into wedge shapes. Her face was made up like a China doll, she wore a halter-neck blouse tucked into bell-bottomed pants and her tiny feet were slipped into high-heeled platform-soled sandals.

'Go Hanoi,' she coldly told us, glancing around the mirror.

Aloofness seemed to be one of the legacies of the French, who had controlled Haiphong for eighty years and built it from a small market town into a major port and industrial centre. Their influence was also evident in the elegant, if now decaying colonial buildings lining the city's wide streets, and in its inhabitants' preoccupation with style and sophistication. Anyone in Haiphong with enough money was impeccably dressed in fashions redolent of the 1960s, unaware perhaps that time had caught up with them and the same designs were once again all the rage in the West. And they seemed to spend an excessive amount of time and money on their hair. To every square mile there were an inordinate number of hairdressing salons, places that had no running water but offered satellite televisions tuned into MTV. From these salons, women emerged so well curled, backcombed and sprayed that even a typhoon wouldn't have dislodged their new look. But the height of sophistication, it appeared, was to be seen with a book by Danielle Steel, whose works had been pirated and translated into Vietnamese, and were for sale on newsstands all over Haiphong.

The girl in the tourist office had been right – after numerous enquiries we discovered it was impossible to extend our visa in Haiphong. Our only option was to make a quick trip to Hanoi then retrace our steps and carry on with the journey to Halong Bay.

'Let's cycle to Hanoi,' suggested Dag.

While I was glad that he'd regained his enthusiasm for the trip, this was going too far. Feeling wretched at the thought of cranking one more pedal along a Vietnamese highway, I insisted we went straight to the railway station.

'You want hard seat or soft seat?' asked a young girl with grey teeth and a blue and white uniform.

Weeks on a Forever bike had given me all the experience of a hard seat that I could ever wish for: I opted for soft.

'Travelling like the locals are we?' Dag commented wryly.

When we boarded the train, I was glad I hadn't been shamed into changing my mind. The hard seats were straight-backed wooden benches. Our soft seats looked rather like garden chairs, with strips of plastic crisscrossed over the back, but at least they offered a modicum of comfort. Ten minutes before departure time, the first-class compartment was full and being besieged by people who had tickets for seats that were already taken. Our fellow passengers were all well-to-do Vietnamese, men in suits and girls with beautifully cut hair, tailored dresses, high heels and golden anklets. They all managed to look cool and collected, despite temperatures near melting point inside the train. I kept thinking we were moving, but this was an illusion created by the smoke-blackened steam engines, jovially hooting and whistling, that were shunting cargo trains about on the other tracks. Finally, and without any warning, we did pull out, and the small fans on the ceiling of the compartment whirred into life. As the train left the station, someone on the tracks alerted the guards that a couple of stowaways were hanging onto it. Two men in blue uniforms hurried to the back door of our carriage, and hauled in the offenders. They were an old man and a young boy, both barefoot and skinny, wearing grey rags and frayed conical hats. The old man carried a staff and had a cloth bundle slung over his back. As they were marched along the aisle, past us foreigners and the well-to-do Vietnamese, the old man proudly held up his head, and met no one's gaze.

The train crawled through Haiphong, along a track that passed so close to the tightly packed houses I could easily have reached out of the window and snatched washing from the lines strung across balconies. I saw men sleeping on cots, women hunched over woks, babies being rocked in hammocks. It seemed that for weeks now I'd been constantly getting such intimate glimpses into people's lives. Several times the track crossed roads where hordes of bikes, scooters and cyclos were pressed up against the barrier, their drivers' faces only a yard away from the train windows. They looked impatient, waiting for the train to pass so they could carry on into the scrum of rush hour. I sat back, utterly grateful that I wasn't out there with them.

The sixty-mile journey across the delta to Hanoi took five hours. Two girls wheeled a trolley up and down the train, offering drinks and snacks. Each time they came past we tried something new: a neon-green bean cake coated with sesame seeds, that tasted like toothpaste and had in it the same red grit that we'd found in the peanut brittle; a box of what we thought were nuts but turned out to be dried prunes coated with salt; some drinks so sweet they made us wince.

Mountains appeared to the north and big clouds built up over them, promising rain. Popping up from the paddy fields were square, concrete family tombs. Around them, the same scenes we'd witnessed all along the coast were being endlessly enacted: people bent over, working in the mud, planting and transplanting, weeding and harvesting. Year in, year out, their lives followed the cycles of rice growing. And, according to Dag, they would still be part of it after death.

'There must be lots of seepage from those tombs when the rains come,' he commented. 'Excellent fertilizer.'

Towards evening the paddy fields were bathed in an amber light and farmers began heading home along red dirt dykes. We passed a small airstrip, and a field full of anti-aircraft guns, then began crossing across one of the two long bridges that span the Song Hong, or Red River. A quarter of a mile away was the bridge for buses, cars, trucks and scooters. Ours was for trains and bicycles, and our progress over it was so slow that all the bikes were easily overtaking us. Leaning out of the window, I could see holes in the asphalt of the road alongside the train track. Halfway across the bridge, some steps led down to a small, skinny island. Almost every inch of its soil had been planted with cassava and at its centre was a thatch hut and some washing laid on the dirt outside it to dry. So much effort had been put into this little settlement, yet soon the monsoon would arrive, the river would rise and flood, and the island would disappear.

It was dark by the time we arrived in Hanoi. While Dag went to claim our bikes, I stood guard over our bags, and watched people boarding the night train to Saigon. I felt sorry for them, facing such a long journey. Then it struck me that we'd spent almost two months battling along a route they would cover, in relative comfort, and in only forty-two hours.

12
EVOLUTION OF PEACE

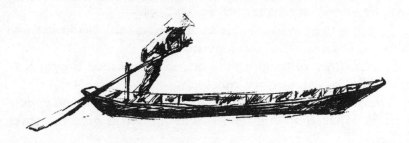

We cycled around a lake gleaming with reflected lights, then plunged into Hanoi's Old Quarter. Along narrow, crowded streets were the smells of *pho*, barbecued meat, smoke and incense. Old trees grew between tightly packed houses and shrines peeped from niches in their gnarled trunks. Children played shuttlecock in the middle of the road, men stood in the gutter cleaning their teeth, women slapped wet laundry against the uneven stones of the pavement. The streets were named after the wares sold along them: Silk Street, Carpenter Street, Paint Street, Tailor Street. There was a Ghost Street, where all the paraphernalia for ancestor worship could be bought, and another whose sign we never found but which must have been Tombstone Street. Just inside the doorways of shops along these streets, men sat around television sets watching the latest World Cup game and mothers spread mats on the ground and lay down with their children to get them off to sleep for the night.

For us, finding a place to sleep was not so straightforward, as all the hotels and guest houses in the Old Quarter appeared to be full. We got plenty of help in our search – cheerful cyclo drivers paused from pushing their large, upholstered vehicles to point us in the right direction, and the owners of hotels which couldn't take us led us to places that possibly could. Finally we ended up in the newly built Van Xuan Hotel, where a receptionist showed me a comfortable room with a large double bed, a bathroom, a telephone, a fridge, air conditioning and a balcony looking straight into the second floor of a house just a few yards across the street.

'Room is twenty-five dollar a night,' she said. 'But please sit down so I can speak some sentences.'

Sinking gracefully onto the bed, she smoothed the tunic of her yellow *ao dai* over her knees.

'You say to my director that twenty-five dollar is too expensive. You pay only eighteen dollar, and you give me three dollar.'

Taken aback by this, I simply blinked at her.

'You want the room?' she asked brusquely.

'Well . . . yes . . .'

'Okay. You tell her only fifteen dollar, you give me five dollar. You remember the sentences for my director? Only fifteen dollar!'

Next morning, I stayed in the room to make some telephone calls while Dag went to sort out our visas. All the numbers I called turned out to be wrong, or they were busy, or I got through to a secretary who could understand neither my English nor my feeble attempts at a few words of Vietnamese. I was interrupted by three chambermaids who spent an hour cleaning our already spotless room. On the landing outside the room, a fourth girl was languidly dusting potted plants. It was close to midday before Dag returned. After being sent from one tourist office to the next, he'd finally been informed that he could only renew our visas directly through the Immigration Police.

'When I found the police they said I had to get the visa through a tourist office, and that the chief of police's brother just happened to own a special tourist agency which could help me and which, by chance, had an office very close by. Then they gave me this.'

He handed me a business card. In red and blue letters on a white background it said:

> **BS COMPANY LTD**
> Company's Function
> *Visa Extension
> *Tourist Service
> *Business

'BS?' I asked incredulously.

'Apparently,' said Dag wryly, 'it stands for Better Service.'

Despite being so well connected to the Immigration Police, the soonest the BS Company could deliver our renewed visas was four days. At first I was annoyed by this, as we had less than two weeks left in Vietnam, and hanging around for a visa meant curtailing the time we had planned to spend in Halong Bay.

'Don't worry,' said Dag. 'The city looks great. Let's go for a stroll around it.'

Soon, Hanoi's charm had completely won me over, and four days didn't seem long enough.

Along the frenetic streets of Saigon, the concept of taking a stroll was alien, and probably dangerous; in the centre of Hanoi, however, it seemed the thing to do. People were ambling around Ho Kiem Lake, which we'd cycled by the night before. They paused to rest beneath a shady tree, bought an ice cream from a seller on a bike, or got weighed by one of the old ladies who had set up scales on the pavement. Boys kicked footballs about – a trend that had begun with the World Cup – and couples courted on stone benches. In the middle of the lake was a tiny pagoda which could be reached by a bridge that arched across the dark green waters. According to legend, those waters are the home of the Turtle God, which emerges during times of national crisis to give the leader of the day the necessary weapons to fight off his aggressors. Its last appearance was in the fifteenth century, when it gave Le Loi a magic sword with the power to throw off Chinese colonial rule and regain independence for the country. After Le Loi's victory, the Turtle God emerged from the lake and claimed back the sword. The legend doesn't explain why the god hasn't bothered to appear again, during all the wars Vietnam has been involved in these past few decades.

Another difference to Saigon was that the people here seemed generally reserved and private. No one rushed up to us, wanting English conversation and offering their story. Most of our encounters were with the expatriates who I finally managed to reach by phone and make arrangements to meet. A few streets away from our hotel in the Old Quarter, we were greeted by Valerie Mackenzie, a pretty, fashionably dressed French woman. She led us through a traditional 'tube' house which, like all the houses in the area, was a hundred feet long, ten feet wide and had two inner courtyards. A tiny puppy dashed about Valerie's feet, and in the kitchen her nineteen-month-old twins were being fed by a maid. Valerie called to John, her English husband, who appeared from upstairs. Red haired, freckled and serious, John was in the second year of his contract with the E.E.C Programme for Repatriated Vietnamese. Because of my links with refugees in Britain and Canada, I was eager to talk to him about his work, but he was reticent in his replies and chose his words carefully.

'Most of the returnees are from the Hong Kong camps, and ninety per cent come voluntarily. In 1985 a policy was instigated to pay refugees $360 each on their return, but this became a bit of a scam. Some people were returning, scooping up the cash and then escaping again – when big families did this it was a lucrative business. But once the government introduced *doi moi*, surrounding countries started closing their doors to refugees, and pressure has built to clear the camps.'

'How do people feel about returning?' I asked.

'Some would rather stay where they are. Most of the camps aren't pleasant places, and the worst ones are like prisons, but even there people get to eat every day, and live in better conditions than they do in the coal mining areas north of here, where many refugees come from. Those are dreadfully bleak places – it's hard to blame anyone wanting to escape from them.'

He was more relaxed when the subject changed to what life in Hanoi had been like for him and Valerie over the last two years.

'We were among the first foreigners to be allowed to rent a house. Before then expatriates had to live in one of the compounds. The maids there were employed by the Ministry of Foreign Affairs, and acted as their spies. We still get our phone tapped from time to time, and of course our faxes are copied.'

'How do you know?'

'Because I've stayed on the line while the fax goes through, and sometimes it takes up to ten minutes to appear at the other end. It's diverted through the police station first. We don't worry about it though – the authorities must be swamped with so much information going out of the country, they can never get around to reading it all.'

Valerie was laying the table for lunch, and setting down platters of French cheeses, baguettes, steak, spring onions and a mango and carrot salad.

'When we first came there was so little available to buy,' she said. 'Sometimes, I wonder what it must be like for the old people, after all these years to suddenly have such a choice of things in the market.'

She told us that their expatriate friends could not understand why they had chosen to live in the Old Quarter rather than in the compounds for foreign workers.

'But the Vietnamese do not understand, either. They are puzzled that only four people take up a house usually occupied by nine families.'

I mentioned how much more reserved I'd found the people north of the 17th Parallel, and how, unlike the southerners, they were so reticent to talk about the war.

'So many new changes are happening now, people want to close that chapter,' said John. He paused. 'But when they do talk about the war, everyone has a terrible story to tell.'

Through the expatriates I was contacting in Hanoi, I had hoped to meet some Communists who would be willing to talk freely to me. This turned out to be a naive hope. John and Valerie told me about an artist friend of theirs who had been at the battle of Dien Bien Phu, recording events there with his sketches and paintings. And they knew Bao Ninh, who wrote the acclaimed *Sorrow of War*. But when I hinted at the possibility of being introduced to these people, they clammed up.

'It takes time to win their trust. They are very cautious about who they talk to. Bao Ninh is especially introverted. All the angst in his book is something he's still dealing with.'

An American film-maker we met next day was equally guarded about his contacts. Melvin was tall and loose limbed, wore his long dark curls in a ponytail and had a habit of pressing his fingers and thumbs together as he spoke. Since 1991 he had been visiting Vietnam to collect material on *Phu Nu Cong Hoa*, the 'women warriors' who fought with the Viet Cong. Officials from Viet My, his sponsoring agency, accompanied him whenever he was filming, and had advised him never to leave the city without informing them.

'I do, of course, but they always seem to find out. On a Monday morning I'll go into the office and one of them will say, "So, Melvin, you went to Sapa for the weekend. How was it?"'

When I told him I wanted to talk to someone who supported the present government, he smiled wryly.

'That might be difficult. Many Communists are bitter about this government, and wonder what it was they fought for.'

He leaned forward, pressing his fingers together. 'Recently I interviewed a woman warrior who is still a party member, and she told me that Vietnam has been through three economic stages: feudalism, colonialism and the market economy. When I asked her about Communism she laughed and said, "Oh, we've never had that – we missed it."'

'Could you put me in touch with her?' I asked.

'You're here without official permission, and I have to be very careful not to upset anyone at the agency,' he said, leaning back, and gazing around the café we were sitting in. 'How about ordering some lunch? I can recommend the ham waffles. When they're warmed up and covered with ketchup you can pretend you're eating Egg Macmuffins.'

During the night there was a harbinger of the monsoon that was soon to arrive. For hours rain hammered down, and by morning Hanoi was awash. Whole streets were blocked by knee-deep puddles, and people wearing brightly coloured plastic rain capes waded through them, holding umbrellas aloft. The sky was heavy and grey, and seemed to hang about three feet above the city's rooftops, threatening more rain. We took a taxi to our appointment with the one person Melvin had agreed to put us in contact with. Although not a party member she would, he assured us, have positive things to say about the government. And, ironically enough, she was an American.

The taxi pulled up in the forecourt of the La Thanh Hotel. We followed signs that led us along a row of colonnades and round to the back of the building, to the offices of the American Friends Service Committee, part of Quaker Service Vietnam. We were met at the door by Lady Borton. 'Lady' was not a title, but a first name bestowed on her at birth some fifty-odd years before. Dressed in a loose shirt and baggy trousers, with wire-rimmed glasses and greying hair pulled back from a lined face, she was a woman who obviously made no room in her life for vanity. Nor was she concerned with niceties; she began our meeting by sternly lecturing us about our lack of official permission.

'What you are doing is essentially illegal. And you must remember that Vietnam is open to Canadians, while Vietnamese people cannot enter Canada as tourists. If you run into trouble with the authorities here, please bear that in mind.'

Lady Borton had been connected with Vietnam since 1969. During the war she trained people to make artificial limbs for civilian amputees. Later she worked with Vietnamese refugees in Malaysia. Now, as field director of the American Services Committee, she was involved in grass roots development projects. And, on an unofficial level, she was informing government agencies of the possible deleterious effects of large scale foreign investments and joint ventures.

'In one of the coastal villages where I work, the provincial head is proposing to let foreign companies fish the offshore waters with large factory ships. There have been no stock assessments or impact studies done, and the Japanese and

Taiwanese are already vying for contracts. If they go ahead as planned, local fishermen will be put out of work and within a few years there could be no fish left. This provincial head is an intelligent man, but he hasn't had the experience we have had, he hasn't seen the effects of over-exploitation of resources, he hasn't read and skimmed through all the literature we've had access to for years. Economic liberalization has lifted the lid on people held down for a long time, and they're racing ahead with blinkers on. And foreign companies know there are no safety regulations here, and that the environment controls that exist can easily be bribed around. That's why they are coming, as much as for the resources and the cheap labour.'

She, more than any of the other expatriates we'd talked to, had seen tremendous changes in the country.

'It took me years to get permission to ride a bicycle! Even by 1989 there was nothing in the shops, hardly any motorized traffic, no televisions, no proper telephone system. Few people in Hanoi had seen a computer unless they'd been outside the country, and now look –'

She waved her hand around her office, where two of her staff tapped away on the keyboards of their IBMs.

'It's all happened so fast. Some of the changes are good, especially in the rural areas. Before *doi moi*, most of the rice crop was handed over to the government and farmers were sometimes lackadaisical about planting and harvesting. Now they pick every stalk of rice, they go back and retrieve what fell in the mud and feed it to the pigs, then they let their ducks into the fields to find whatever is left over. In the last few years, Vietnam has gone from importing rice to exporting it. But fundamental values have changed. Vietnamese people used to have a long-term vision. During the wars they strove for independence, if not this year then next, if not for this generation then for the next one. But now many people are on the look out just for their own family. They're striving for the present, making money now, not thinking about future consequences.'

'And what do the old Communists think?' I asked.

'Some people who fought the war of independence grieve for this, but most people applaud it.'

I told her of some of the impressions I'd gained during our journey. Of the compulsion of people in the south to share their stories. Of the reticence of people in the north. Of widespread corruption and a general dissatisfaction with the government. Of the misplaced power wielded by the police. When I had finished, Lady turned on me, like a mother who is prepared to speak of her child's mistakes and shortcomings but is fiercely defensive if anyone else mentions them.

'Of course there is corruption here. Do you think it doesn't exist in our countries? Don't you realize it's simply more covert there? And of course people in the south seek you out. More of them speak English, and many of them have a need to off-load some of their bitterness about backing the losing side and being dumped by the Americans. Sure, some of them went to re-education camps, and sure, some of them nearly starved there. But what they won't tell you is that everyone in this country went hungry, because of the American embargo, and because of the war in Cambodia.'

'My sympathies have always been with the nationalists,' I said, 'but it seems to me that people in the south have been punished enough by now.'

'Remember the American War of Independence?' she countered. 'Remember what we did to the people who backed the Tories? We tarred and feathered them and sent them to Canada! So who are we to judge?'

What she hadn't addressed were my comments about the police and the general air of disillusionment with the government. When I raised these again she carefully chose her words.

'Since 1987 some people have been dismayed by the rapid changes and by the loss of ideals. They fought for independence but now, instead of land colonization they see economic colonization looming. The government is concerned about the speed of change. It allows liberalization in one area, then sees bad influences coming in and tightens up again. Things keep opening and closing. It varies from area to area. And provincial police can be like warlords, because no one is in touch with what the central government is doing.'

She sighed. 'The Vietnamese have endured so much, and not just in the wars. You've seen how tough their lives are.

How they cycle with hundreds of pounds of weight on their bikes, how they work in the fields – backbreaking work, believe me, I've done it with them. And they have no security. If there's a typhoon, if their harvest is lost, they have nothing to fall back on and no choice but to start again – and that is what they do, time and time again.'

As we were leaving the office, one of her assistants arrived with a bundle of paper.

'Here's another example of the speed of change in the country,' she said. 'Two years ago the only photocopier in Hanoi was in the French embassy. Now there's one on every street corner. I sent three books off to be photocopied this morning, and they're done already.'

Her gaze turned to me, and her eyes widened. 'Oh! I shouldn't be telling you that!' she cried, gently mocking herself. 'What was I saying about illegalities?'

When we walked into our hotel room, we were both hit by the same, strong sensation. Something had changed. Things had been moved. My eyes flickered over the furniture. The waterproof bag containing my notebooks, tape recorder and tapes was no longer on the table where I'd left it. With panic rising in my chest I rushed across the room, and found it on the floor, under the bed. Everything was inside it, but jumbled up.

'We're just getting paranoid,' I told Dag, as he checked through his film box. 'The chambermaids must have come in again and cleaned up.'

But that night, when we went out for dinner, all my notebooks and tapes came with me.

Curiosity led us to the Sunset Pub, renowned as a hangout for expatriates, and owned by a Finn and his Vietnamese wife. It was on the top floor of a hotel, up a total of ninety-seven steps. As we pushed open its double doors we were met by a hubbub of voices, clinking glasses and loud, hearty laughter. It was a busy night, a build up to the last game of the World Cup due to be televised at two the next morning. And it was a scene that could have been straight from a golf club house in Surrey. On stools around high tables sat tanned men in open-necked shirts and tense-looking women wearing too much jewellery, swigging back gin and tonics that cost the same as they would in Britain.

'When people want cigarettes,' said Anna, the Australian barmaid, 'I tell them to buy them on the street. They cost four times as much up here.'

Anna had been in Hanoi for several months, and was studying Vietnamese at the university. 'My teacher has experienced much,' she said. 'Today he was talking about being taken by his father to watch the Japanese ships coming in to invade, and seeing the tracer bullets across the sky.'

I asked her how she liked working in this pub.

'It's very strange. The other day I had an accident on my scooter on the way to work, and I was taken to the hospital. There were families there with sick kids who had probably saved for months to afford the three dollars for the hospital bill. I just had a few bruises so I came to work. It was a Saturday night and people were throwing *hundreds* of dollars across the bar. Sometimes I think half of these people don't even know what country they are in. And they certainly don't care.'

'Economic colonization,' I said.

She leaned over the bar and lowered her voice.

'Some Communists call it "the evolution of peace." It means that America has not forgotten, that it still intends to conquer Vietnam by means other than military. And that Vietnam is in danger of ending up with a rich élite while the masses get poorer and poorer. I'll write it for you in Vietnamese.'

She scribbled *dien bien hoa binh* on the back of a receipt which she furtively slid across the bar.

'Don't let my boss see it – it's a very revolutionary term and she'd be annoyed about me talking to customers like this.'

'It's double speak!' said Dag, as we descended the ninety-seven stairs. 'The government is so desperate for dollars it allows in foreign companies to exploit the country's resources, and at the same time it rails against the corrupting influences of Western capitalism!'

Outside the hotel, seven cyclo drivers haggled with each

other over who should take us back to the Old Quarter. Then they charged us three times the local price for the ride. Several times, I tried saying '*dien bien hoa binh*' to my driver, then showed him the piece of paper. He nodded and shrugged, as if to say, 'So what?'

We couldn't leave Hanoi without going to pay our respects to Ho Chi Minh, and set off for his Mausoleum early one morning. Dag insisted on cycling there; I couldn't face the thought of climbing on my bike and went instead by cyclo. The morning was grey and muggy, and despite there being only a sprinkling of rain, my driver insisted on entombing me in a canopy of thick plastic. He dropped me off on the perimeter of a large square. At the far end of a wide empty boulevard was an imposing building, cuboid in design, surrounded by oblong stone columns and without a single window. Guards in crisp white uniforms with red epaulettes stood stiffly to attention around it. Others patrolled its grounds, peering into bushes and tall stands of bamboo, shouting 'Halt!' at tourists who stepped off the designated paths.

One of these guards directed me to a small building where I found Dag checking in his cameras. We were told to report to the guards who would escort us to the Mausoleum. Before we could do so, a crocodile of Vietnamese tourists appeared, led by a guide holding a rolled umbrella. Almost seventy people silently marched past us to the boulevard, where they all turned left at the same spot, then sharp left again to be swallowed up by the Mausoleum. When it was our turn, a guard marched slowly ahead of us, and I found myself mesmerized by glimpses of his socks – one brown, one green – as he swung forward each of his white-clad legs. He led us up the steps of the Mausoleum and through a portico flanked by baby-faced guards clutching rifles with bayonets. The grandeur of the place was muted by a bad leak in the ceiling of the entrance hall, which had made the red carpet sopping wet. We squelched across this, then along a corridor that sloped down and turned several corners.

Steadily the number of guards increased, the air got cooler and drier and the atmosphere became more hushed and

solemn. I've never been good at dealing with enforced rever-
ence, and soon I could feel the approach of a giggling fit. In an
attempt to fend it off, I concentrated on the entrance ticket in
my hand. On the back was a list of rules: No talking, touching
the walls, putting hands in pockets, smoking, wearing sunglasses or wearing underclothes in the Mausoleum.

No underclothes? The thought of hundreds of tourists
solemnly checking in their knickers along with their cameras
pushed me over the edge; laughter bubbled up, and I vainly
tried to disguise it by coughing.

'Sssh!' said the guards, their hands tensing around their rifles.

By the time we reached the doorway to the inner sanctum, I
was suitably composed. In the middle of a huge, shadowy room
was a large square pit, surrounded by a viewing gallery. Rising
from the pit was a glass case where Ho Chi Minh lay, bathed in
a pool of golden light. Rather than dead, he appeared to be
deep in a long and dreamless sleep. *Snow White!* I thought,
struck by the fact that whoever designed this place must have
been a Walt Disney fan. I flashed a look at the guards posted at
each corner of the room, hoping they hadn't been trained as
mind readers. But their job was to keep us walking at a steady
pace along the gallery, and to stop any lingering or pauses for
awestruck reflection. As I was already halfway round, I concentrated on getting a good look at the body. It was dressed in
a simple black suit with a mandarin collar. The face was
pinched and drawn, the skin waxen and the white goatee beard
looked soft and newly combed. Unlike Snow White, attempting
to awaken Uncle Ho with a kiss wouldn't have been a pleasant
prospect, or a hopeful one. Until recent years his body had
been regularly attended to by Russian embalmers. But, since
doi moi, relations with Russia and its embalmers had cooled off.
According to rumour, the great man's body was steadily
decomposing. John Mackenzie had told us that when he first
visited the Mausoleum, there was no blanket over Uncle Ho.
The next time he went, there was one covering his feet. As
months passed it crept further up his body. Now it was at chest
level, with Ho's hands lying on top of it. Disconcertingly, there
was no outline of limbs or feet beneath the blanket.

★

The tour was quickly over, and we were winding our way back along corridors, out through a doorway and into the grounds.

'Poor bugger,' said Dag. 'Pumped full of formaldehyde and put on display like a stuffed animal.'

Indeed – particularly in the light of the explicit instructions Ho Chi Minh had left about the disposal of his body. He had asked to be cremated, and his ashes to be divided among three ceramic pots. One pot was to be buried in the north of the county, one in the central part and one in the south. Above each grave a house was to be built where people could rest, and trees planted around it. Ho Chi Minh had been a man of high ideals and simple tastes and, although I had to admit to a certain ghoulish fascination in being able to see what was left of him, I felt sad that after such a life he should end up as an expensively kept relic, surrounded by foolish pomp and grandeur.

The path from the back of the Mausoleum took us to the Dien Huu Pagoda. It had a pretty courtyard, with rock and water gardens and plants growing from large ceramic pots. Along one wall, beneath trees still dripping with rain, eighteen people sat in a row on low stools. They ranged in age from a man in his early twenties to an old woman as wizened as a tortoise. All of them were bristling with acupuncture needles. Long needles, stuck in their scalps, all over their faces, their necks, their shoulders, their hands. An elderly brown-robed monk had worked his way along the line and was now heading back, checking the needles, removing some here, adding more there. The needles lay on a tray. He picked one up, wiped it with a rag and stuck it through a young man's trousers and into his upper thigh. The man winced, then glanced up at me. He had needles in his eyebrows and hanging from his cheeks. He looked resentful, as if I was intruding on his privacy and his dignity. Next to me, Dag was putting away his camera.

'Come on,' he said, 'let's leave these people in peace.'

13

UNEXPECTED
ATTACHMENTS

We took an early train back to Haiphong, and by noon we were
boarding the ferry to Halong Bay. Scores of children clustered
around us, selling chewing gum and cigarettes.

'I go school one o'clock,' one girl told me. 'In the morning
I work.'

She helped me carry my bag and bike onto the small, rusty
ferry. There were two compartments for passengers. One had
a couple of wide, table-sized benches, where families sprawled
out. The girl advised me to go into the other compartment,
which had several rows of hard upright seats and a floor strewn
with lychee and banana skins, chewed-up sugar cane and
empty cigarette packets.

'Be careful!' she warned. 'Many thieves!'

As the ferry pulled away, Dag went up on deck to take photos.
I stayed by our bags, peering out of the window at women sitting in small sampans, rowing them with their feet through
water the same rust colour as the ferry. From the corner of my
eye I registered a movement next to me, and turned my head
to see an unkempt boy sitting on our bags. He was holding a

wooden crutch, and one of his legs was missing from below the knee. Black hair fell in a straight fringe above a sweet face. He gave me a sidelong smile, but I noticed his hand was resting on the bulge in my bag made by one of our remaining stashes of money. I checked to see if any zips on the bags had been opened. Dag came back, and sat down next to the boy.

'Keep an eye on him,' I said. 'I think he's waiting to pinch something.'

Dag gave me a bemused look.

'Since when have you been so suspicious?'

Far from being concerned with our belongings, the boy was busy with his own. From a plastic bag he took out a soft straw hat, which he donned, and a pair of aluminium spoons. Then handed me the plastic bag.

'Madam?'

'He wants you to look after it,' said Dag. He turned to the boy. 'Be careful, kid, she might pinch something.'

Putting the crutch under one armpit, the boy hopped off into the other compartment. I peered into the bag. It held a few thousand dong and about ten identical sets of postcards, the type we'd seen street children peddling all over Hanoi. Each set sold for a dollar, and getting rid of one or two a day meant good business for the children. I felt wretched. This little boy, who I had taken as a thief, had entrusted me with his money, and the means of his livelihood for at least a couple of weeks.

'Listen!' said Dag.

From the other compartment came a clear lilting voice, soaring easily up and down the scales. Accompanying it was a rhythmic metallic tapping. The sound drew closer, and then the boy reappeared, leaning on his crutch. He closed his eyes as he sang, lifted his chin and expertly ran the spoons across his fingers. The compartment fell silent; everyone was listening. Across from me, an old man wiped tears from his eyes. At the end of the aisle the boy turned and made his way back through both compartments, collecting money in his hat. Presently he returned, sat next to Dag and nonchalantly counted his earnings.

'What's your name?' I asked him.

'Vinh,' he said, without looking up.

'How old are you?'

'Twelve.'

'Where are you going?'

It occurred to me that I was subjecting him to the sort of cross examination that had driven me crazy these past two and a half months. He looked up, puzzled by the question.

'Hong Gai, Madam.'

Of course he was going to Hong Gai. The boat didn't stop anywhere else.

'Your family Hong Gai?' asked Dag.

Vinh shook his head.

'Father Haiphong.' He held his hands over his eyes. 'Father no see.'

Retrieving the plastic bag, he carefully placed his newly earned money, the satchel, hat and spoons back inside it.

'Thank you, madam,' he said, and was gone.

We found him a little later, when we moved our bags up to the top deck of the ferry. He was sleeping in a corner, curled up in the arms of another boy. Vinh's head rested on his plastic bag, and his crutch lay beside him. The stump of his leg was hooked over his friend's thigh. We put down our gear close to them, and sat in silence, wrapped in our own thoughts. The sky was low, and threatened rain. Marshy islands with electricity pylons on them slid pass. Barges went by, heaped with coal slurry. It seemed that we would never leave behind the industrial Red River Delta, but gradually the river mouth widened and flowed into the sea. The water turned from milky red to a deep green and was as calm and as flat as a lake. Ahead of us, behind a bank of clouds, lay Halong Bay.

'Over there,' said Dag, sitting up. 'Junk sails.'

They were a faded grey, with bamboo battens, and they were pushing a two-masted sampan. During our entire journey up the coast we'd seen only a handful of boats with sails, and these were the first with this traditional design. Dag was on his feet, fitting his zoom lens onto his camera.

'Holy *smokes*!' he cried, peering through it. 'Maria, come and look!'

Ahead, through the mist, strange shapes had begun to materialize. Limestone rocks rose sheer from the water up to several hundred feet. They were strangely humped and angled, patterned with fissures, caves and arches and improbably covered with trees. As we moved past them, more and more appeared, in serried ranks stretching back into the fog, as if some clever trick with mirrors was creating the illusion of hundreds of these surreal islets. But there *were* hundreds of them. It was a mysterious scene, straight from some ancient painting, and it lent credence to the legends of this enormous bay: that the flailing of a great dragon's tail created its islets, and that sea monsters still lurk in its waters.

Our cries of delight woke the two boys. They stretched and rubbed their eyes, then Vinh began looking through his friend's hair for lice. After squashing a few, he set to work on his blackheads. Next it was time for a massage. He slapped his friend's head and shoulders with the side of his hands, pummelled his back, rubbed his scalp and pinched the skin on the bridge of his nose. Meanwhile, the mist was lifting, revealing the jagged peaks of Cat Ba Island. Another junk appeared, but its sails were bright red and orange, and it was moving upwind at an impossible speed.

As it drew closer we saw that it was newly built, and was being propelled by an engine rather than the sails. All over its decks were tourists, with video cameras stuck to their faces. They videotaped us going by; then they caught sight of the real junk in the distance and signalled to the skipper, who turned his boat and headed towards it.

Hong Gai was a small, pretty harbour, bounded by sheer islets. Fishing boats and sampans crowded together, and houses painted in pastel colours clung to the foot of a steep cliff. As soon as the ferry docked, women with shoulder poles hurried along the jetty and pushed through the disembarking passengers, vying for the work of unloading cargo. We had barely stepped ashore before a well-dressed man with mirrored sunglasses offered to take us by boat to Bai Chay, the main town of Halong Bay, for two dollars. We accepted, and looked around for Vinh and his friend to see if they wanted a ride. But they were already at the far end of the jetty. Vinh was hurrying along, easily overtaking the two-legged people in his way.

During the short ride our driver, Hung, managed to persuade us that he knew the perfect mini hotel for us. We had already agreed to let him take us there before we arrived in Bai Chay and discovered that it was a boom town, and that mini hotels were popping up everywhere. Hung led us along a dirt road that had been recently chewed by earth movers. It was lined with construction sites and with brand new hotels, tall and skinny like the one we checked into. The owners gave us a rapturous welcome. As well as being the only guests in the hotel, we were the first. The place smelt of wet plaster. Our room had a blue and pink Formica dressing-table-cum-wardrobe, with handles cleverly positioned to make the glass-fronted cupboard resemble a television set. The white, fake satin bedspread had big rosettes sewn onto it, and the pillows were embroidered with silver lamé hearts. The pink and blue padded headboard of the bed was inset with heart-shaped mirrors. Our tiny balcony looked directly across to another hotel, five storeys high and three-quarters built, where two men stood on the roof, hoisting up by hand baskets of sand that two more men were filling with shovels on the road beneath.

All along Bai Chay's sea front, the doorways of shops were hung with bathing suits, rubber rings, plastic sandals, buckets and spades and shell souvenirs. Vietnamese tourists sat on deck chairs along the gravelly beach, and splashed about in the murky water. Beyond them, spectacular islets ringed the bay. But there were no boats in sight, save for the ones moored by the bus station and offering short tours of the area. These were crudely built and designed to squash in as many people as possible. They set off in droves at ten o'clock in the morning and again at two, heading out towards a few grottoes that had been sanctioned by the government for visitors.

'The authorities have moved the fishing boats away from the eyes of the tourists,' said Mr Sang, a friendly café owner who spoke English with a strong French accent.

'Where have they taken them to?' we asked.

'You go a mile south of here. You see some houses and

shops by the road, and then the boats. Ask for my friend
Denny. He is French. He will help you.'

We found the fishing boats. They were rafted together a hundred yards from the shore, and a couple of them had masts
and sails. But before we could get a closer look, we were
stopped in our tracks by an unexpected sight. Lying on the
sand outside a squat concrete building were two rather battered ultra light planes. A man was bending over one, tinkering
with the engine.

'Denny?' called Dag.

The man looked up. He was dressed in old, stained clothes,
his skin had an unhealthy pallor and his fine sandy hair was
mussed up, as if he'd just rolled out of bed.

He squinted at us through thick, greasy glasses, and it
seemed to take him several seconds to focus.

'Ah, the Canadians,' he said. 'Mr Sang, he telephone me
you are coming.'

Denny owned the planes, and part of the fledgling tourist
company run from the concrete building. But he looked more
like a mad chemist than a business man. And his sales pitch
was far from convincing.

'We have a new junk, forty-five feet long, to take out the
tourist. But I don't think you will like it. My partner design it.
Inside the cabin he put plastic and, how do you call it – instead
of wood –?'

'Formica?' I guessed.

'Yes! Everywhere. And plastic flowers. The Vietnamese they
love this.'

His partner was a dapper little man in his fifties called Mr
Duong. He shook our hands, handed over business cards and
invited us into the concrete building for green tea.

'He say you should hire our junk and go to Cat Ba Island,'
said Denny, who had been brought along to translate. 'But you
will like the old fishing boat more. It have no engine, only sail.
I will take you to see it.'

Mr Duong continued to chat away to us, unaware that
Denny wasn't translating a word of what he was saying.

'I begin a company with this man and some other

Vietnamese,' said Denny. 'I bring the planes from France, and also a catamaran and some row boats. Our company buy this land, make this house and the junk. But now there is no money left in the company and all is falling down.'

Mr Duong was looking expectantly from Denny to us, as if waiting for an answer to something he'd asked. Denny's face took on a strained expression.

'I have to get back to my planes. Shall we go to see the fisherman?'

He rowed us over to a thirty-foot, two-masted, weather-beaten junk. Hunkered on the prow, squinting at us beneath a green pith helmet, was Mr Hoi, a wiry little man with a wispy beard. He greeted Denny enthusiastically and welcomed us aboard.

'Last night we drank rice wine together and he say he like to do business with the tourist,' Denny told us. 'So he think I am very clever, arranging it so quick.'

Dag was examining the boat in detail. It had a shallow draught, a centre board that dropped through a well in the hull, and a rudder that could be hauled up. There were two long oars for rowing and the bamboo masts were rigged with mottled grey sails. Dag was entranced.

'This is a *real* boat,' he kept repeating.

We sat beneath the low woven canopy, and Mr Hoi lifted a plank in the deck to get at a bottle of rice wine. While this was passed around he produced a length of bamboo with a pipe inside it. He stuffed tobacco into the pipe and lit it, inhaling deeply.

'Mr Hoi is a strong man,' said Denny. 'Five year ago he escape in a boat just like this one, with no engine. After he get far, a gale come and the boat sink.'

He paused in the story to explain to Mr Hoi what he was talking about. The man's eyes lit up, and he made undulating motions with his hands to show us how big the waves had been. 'The Chinese pick him up. They bring him back here and he spend ten months in prison.'

Mr Hoi pointed to the numbers and letters that had been tattooed on his leg by the prison authorities. The rice wine went round once more before we got down to business.

'Mr Hoi want three dollar an hour for this boat,' said Denny, 'and he ask when you want to go.'

'Whenever he's ready,' Dag replied.

'I think he is ready now.'

Dag gave me a beseeching look.

'Any problems with the police?' I asked.

When this was translated, Mr Hoi laughed in derision.

'No,' said Denny. 'I think he is not so worried about police.'

After rowing his boat a short distance out into the bay, Mr Hoi raised the sails. And we were off, moving nicely despite only a light breeze. Through Denny, Dag had made it clear to Mr Hoi that we didn't want to go anywhere in particular, just to sail about and look at the rock formations and the other boats. And that, for several hours, is exactly what we did. We sailed past rock islets shaped like fighting cocks and cats. We sailed close to huge rock arches which perfectly framed the myriad of islets beyond them. We sailed this way and that, letting the wind take us. Mr Hoi was in his element, steering the tiller with his foot, drinking his way through a bottle and a half of rice wine and smoking one pipe after another. He chortled to see Dag fiddling with the rigging and getting such delight from his simple boat. From time to time he pulled up a plank in the deck and baled out the boat, which was steadily taking on water.

Around one o'clock he dropped the sails and sculled the boat into a cove, where a long jetty led to a rock stairway cut into a steep cliff. We tied up, and followed Mr Hoi along the jetty to a house that was dwarfed by the sheer rock wall above it. A young man greeted us there. There were caves in the cliff, he told us, and he was the official guide. We handed over the dollar he asked for, then set off behind him up a steep staircase. Both Dag and I were a bit disgruntled. We hadn't wanted to get off the boat, and we felt we'd already seen more than enough caves and grottoes in Vietnam. But then we stepped inside the yawning entrance. Ahead of us was a scene straight from Solomon's Mines, a series of vast caverns bristling with stalactites and sta- lagmites. There were rocks in the shapes of lions, a Buddha, a reclining woman, and covered with lichen that turned them startlingly bright shades of blue, green and brown. Following the guide and his flashlight, we waded through pools, scrambled up and down rocks, slithered over mud, ducked under narrow arches, squeezed through tight passageways. Our route took us back to where we'd started and we emerged, blinking, into the bright light. From the top of the steps, I saw another strange sight, a convoy of fifteen tourist boats heading into the cove. Mr Hoi let out a yelp, and took off down the steps to save his boat from being squashed by one of these monsters. As the first boat docked, it disgorged about thirty passengers who headed in an undulating line towards the narrow staircase.

'Quick!' said Dag. 'Or we'll never get down!'

We reached the junk just in time to help Mr Hoi fend off the bow of a tourist boat driven by a man who seemed most put out that a lowly fisherman had taken his spot on the jetty. As we left the cove, the rain set in. Taking shelter beneath the canopy, we shared more rice wine and watched the mist swirl around the islets and finally envelop them. We sailed back slowly and contentedly through the fog.

By the time we reached Denny's beach, a deal was struck: we would return tomorrow, set off with Mr Hoi and spend a couple of nights on his boat. He took the money we paid him, and staggered off to replenish his supply of rice wine.

Back in Bai Chay, stalwart Vietnamese tourists were out strolling along the sea front, protected by large umbrellas. Foreign tourists, like us, gazed out at the rain from inside cafés. We were at Mr Sang's again, for dinner. From time to time, street children came by, trying to sell us identical sets of postcards of Halong Bay. I asked Mr Sang if he knew the one-legged boy who sang so well.

'Everybody know this boy. They call him *Vinh mot chan*, it mean Vinh with one leg. When he was seven year old a train run over him and he lose the leg.'

I thought about the train tracks in Haiphong, running so close to the houses, and I shuddered. Mr Sang told us that most of these children had families, who sent them to Bai Chay for two weeks at a time to beg and sell to the tourists.

'Where do they live when they are here?'

Mr Sang shrugged.

'Where they can. These kids, you know, they look after each other.'

We were walking away from the café when we spotted a familiar figure on the other side of the road.

'Hey, Vinh!' called Dag.

The boy swung around, and broke into a hopping run.

'Sir, Madam!' he greeted us.

'You have postcards?' I asked, eager to give him business.

'Yes,' he answered, making no move to produce any. He was gazing at Dag. 'Sir, you play billiard?'

We wandered up and down the sea front with him, stopping to play billiards at a couple of the tables set up under thatch shelters next to the beach, then sitting down at a food stand for a snack. He took out his spoons, and absentmindedly tapped out a tune. I remembered a man being moved to tears by Vinh's song on the ferry, and how I'd wished I could understand the words. A thought struck me.

'Will you sing for us now?' I asked Vinh.

He nodded; no problem. Leaving him and Dag to play another round of billiards, I hurried back to our hotel to get our tape recorder.

The rain had eased off, so we sat on a bench beneath a tree in a quiet park, away from the karaoke bars along the waterfront. Vinh seemed perfectly at ease with the microphone, which I held a few inches from his face. He sang without stopping for ten minutes. My arm began to ache but I didn't dare to move in case I broke the spell he wove with his voice. Ants began crawling over my feet. Some of them ventured up my legs and onto my knees. Solicitously, Vinh squashed them with the spoons he was playing without ever missing a beat. When the song finally ended, Dag and I were both silent for a while.

'Brilliant, buddy,' said Dag finally.

'I go,' said Vinh. 'See you tomorrow.'

We gave him some money to pay him for his time and the trouble he'd gone to. In return, he insisted on giving us some packs of postcards. When he wasn't looking, I slipped them back into his bag.

★

In the morning we stocked up on food in the market then cycled out of town along streets slick with rain. Both of us were greatly looking forward to getting away from hotels and restaurants for a while. But our anticipation quickly turned to disappointment when we arrived at Denny's beach. The ultralight planes, the catamaran and the tourist junk were there, but the fishing boats had gone.

'They go squid fishing,' explained Denny.

Mr Huong was hovering around us excitedly.

'My partner want to invite you to breakfast,' said Denny wearily.

Close to the beach was a little shack where a woman was preparing *banh cuon*, a breakfast traditional to this area. She steamed thin rice pancakes on a muslin screen over a large pot of boiling water. When they were cooked she sprinkled them with fried meat, onions and garlic, rolled them up and chopped them into small pieces, which she served with a dip of *nuoc mam*. Mr Huong kept the woman busy, ordering plate after plate of *banh cuon* for us, along with bottles of Coca Cola.

'He say Mr Hoi won't come back for some days,' said Denny. 'So he suggest you go in our junk to Cat Ba Island, where you can meet many fishermen. On our junk you can sleep, the driver make the food and you have cold drinks. It will be fifty-four dollar a day.'

The junk lay at anchor not far from the beach. It was newly painted in red and blue and had a large square wheel house and some brand new sails.

'It's not bad as tourist boats go,' said Dag.

Still rattled by Mr Hoi's desertion, I sniped, 'It's not a *real* boat.'

'I think the fishermen will not come back soon,' said Denny. 'So perhaps it is better if—'

The rest of his sentence was drowned out by a scooter which drove past the shack, did a sharp U turn and screeched to a halt right outside it. Its driver was a chubby man, barely five feet tall, with curls tumbling into his eyes and an assortment of camera and video equipment strung around his neck.

'My god, the planes!' he cried, rushing into the shack. 'Who owns the planes?'

I soon learned that wherever Son Nhu Hoang went, a whirl-wind of energy followed him. Within minutes he'd forgotten about the planes and was sketching us an outline of his life story – how he had left Vietnam in 1975 and gone to live in California, where he became an artist then went into busi-ness. Seven months ago he had returned to Vietnam for the first time in nineteen years, and was now dividing his time between Haiphong and the States, trying to set up various businesses: importing heavy equipment from Japan, exporting meat from Vietnam to the world market, setting up cheap loan systems for farmers – the list went on.

'But the government here is always napping,' he said. 'I call up some department at two o'clock and they say, "Sunny, we take a nap, please call back at four."'

Sunny, a nickname bestowed on him in California, suited him perfectly. His round face was constantly wreathed in smiles, and he had an infectious laugh.

'I'm so lucky!' he cried. 'Yesterday in Haiphong I wake up in the middle of the night and I think – I need a holiday! So I get on my bike and I drive to Halong Bay. And straight away I meet you guys. Hey, Denny, how much you charge for a ride on one of those planes?'

Denny winced.

'I still have to work on them a little, and—'

'They have karaoke here!' Sunny interrupted him, his atten-tion caught by the unit in the corner of the shack. 'Come on, let's sing!'

The video he sang along with showed a sad-faced girl strolling in the grounds of a pagoda and gazing wistfully at flowers.

'This is a good song, very popular in the South,' he said. 'Listen, I translate.'

> *'Where are you now?*
> *Are you in the training camp?*
> *Are you in the Officer Academy?*
> *Where are you now?*
> *Are you in Laos destroying the enemy?*
> *It doesn't matter where you are, I'll love you forever.'*

As soon as the song finished, he leapt to his feet.

'Hey, Denny, can I videotape your planes?'

'Why don't we hire the junk for a few days, and invite Sunny along?' Dag suggested, when the two men had left the shack. 'He could interpret for us.'

'I can't see him agreeing,' I said. 'He seems to be into high tech toys, not basic boats.'

Minutes later, he came racing back, the cameras around his neck banging against each other.

'Denny just tell me about your trip on the junk to Cat Ba Island. It sounds fantastic!'

'You want to come with us?' asked Dag.

'Yeah. Why not? Let's go!'

Mr Hoang was thrilled when we struck a deal, and came out in a row boat to personally usher us aboard his brand new junk. The large wheelhouse was, as Denny had promised, lined with Formica and strung with plastic flowers. But it was certainly a more comfortable boat than Mr Hoi's to spend a few days on. It had a roomy foredeck and, best of all, two large plywood outhouses on the back of the aft deck. As we motored away from the beach, Sunny ran from one end of the boat to the other with his video camera glued to his face.

'My God! I don't believe this! So beautiful!'

When Luong and Kiem, the two crew members, pulled up the sails, Sunny became nearly apoplectic with delight, frantically switching between cameras and video.

'Fantastic! Maria, stand there by the sail so I can get a shot! God, I wish I had my Polaroid with me! Next time I bring it!'

'He's like Vietnam's answer to Danny Devito,' mused Dag.

'So what you do for a living, Maria?' asked Sunny, when he'd calmed down.

I told him I was a writer, and that our trip would be the subject of a book.

'Really? Hey, I tell Kiem this, I bet he has a story!'

Luong took the wheel, while Kiem sat and talked to Sunny. After a while he took a wallet from his pocket and pulled out a passport photograph of himself. On the back was written his name, and a serial number.

'He says you are lucky to meet him,' Sunny translated, 'because he is a survivor from the war, and now the government allows the people to speak. He wants you to have this picture, so the government can know him and it can be proved he says the truth.'

I started jotting in my notebook, but it was hard to keep up with the story that tumbled out. Kiem joined the North Vietnamese army at the end of 1966, when he was seventeen. In 1972, he was sent to the Quang Tri area, in South Vietnam. I interrupted him to say that we had cycled through that area, and been deeply shocked by the devastation there.

'He says they called Quang Tri the "meat grinder",' said Sunny.

Kiem described the biggest battle he was in, around the cathedral in Quang Tri. The South Vietnamese troops were hidden inside the cathedral and the NVA were advancing on it with tanks. When all the tanks and some of the men were inside the cathedral grounds, the South Vietnamese Army closed the gates. Two thousand North Vietnamese soldiers were killed. Kiem was outside the gates, with a heavy machine gun. Out of his battalion of 540 men, he was one of only ten survivors.

Sunny paused in his translation. 'Kiem gave everything to the army. That is why he is poor now.'

When the war with Cambodia ended, Kiem was demobbed and, like thousands of other soldiers, found himself struggling to find work.

'It's not fair,' said Sunny, 'because he is a good man and he loves our country.'

Kiem stopped telling stories to check where we were. Seeing that we were leaving the protection of the islands and heading towards open water, he hurried into the wheelhouse and returned with several burning joss sticks. Holding them between his palms, he bowed towards the north, south, east and west.

'He says we are coming through the Gate of the South Sea,' Sunny told us. 'So he must pray to the four spirits in the four corners of the sea.' He paused. 'I think it is like us paying a toll fee on a highway in the States.'

*

Close to Cat Ba Island, we motored slowly through a maze of islets before choosing a spot to anchor for the night. Limestone walls towered above us. Long vines trailed down from gnarled trees that had somehow taken root in fissures in the rock. The water was still, and the deepest, darkest green. There was silence, save for the echoing calls of unseen birds, the squeaking of bats, the steady whirr of insects – and Sunny's cheerful whistling, as he sat on deck, chopping up potatoes and preparing heaps of French fries.

'I feel like a billionaire! This is why I came back to Vietnam, for the simple life. In the States I worked and played too hard!'

He told us about his car collection in the States: a 300 Diplomat 1959, a 1957 Mercedes, two 1960s Mercedes Coups, two Sunbeams, two French convertible Caravelles and two Jaguars. From a leather bag he pulled out some photographs of these vehicles. In each one, the car was graced by a gorgeous dusky girl in a swimsuit, striking pin-up poses against the bonnet.

'Look at her!' he said, passing the snapshots around. 'She wants to be a model. She's hot! She works at Kentucky Fried Chicken in San Francisco. But my real girlfriend is in Saigon. Her name is Bich Hoa. I lost her for fifteen years.'

As Sunny's story unfolded, the night crept over us. Kiem placed candles on the deck, and their flames flickered in the soft, warm breeze.

'I met her when she was twelve, at Catholic high school in Dalat. And I loved her the first minute. But she was training to be a nun, so I thought I had no chance. When she was sixteen, she left the convent and went with her family to Saigon. She wrote me a long letter to tell me that she cared about me. I could hardly believe it. So straight away I replied, to tell her I loved her. But her family hid my letter. She wrote three more times, saying, why didn't you reply? Each time I wrote back, but she never got the letters. What could I do? She stopped writing, she didn't visit Dalat. I grew up, I got popular with girls, but I never forgot her. Three years later she came back to Dalat and I saw her in the market place. But she was changed! Last time I'd seen her, she was only sixteen, and innocent. But now, she was like a princess! She wore silk, had painted fingernails, a little lipstick and her body – wow! It was like a movie star's. She was on a motor scooter with a tall man, he wore an Italian suit. When she saw me she yelled to him to stop, she ran over to me. I was shaking, I couldn't breathe, I couldn't say a thing to make sense. Then she cried and said, "Too late, too late," and she ran back to the bike. And I didn't see her again. But I always think of her. In 1975, when I got to the States, I put ads in the Vietnamese papers, asking for news of her. I never heard anything, and I was scared she had died in the bombing. But in 1989, my sister was in Dalat and she found out my girl-friend was alive, she had a beauty shop in Saigon. When my sister phoned me I told her to go there, I sent a letter and pre-sents for her. The letter was careful, I thought maybe she had a husband who would be angry, so I just asked after her fam-ily, things like that. But when my sister saw her she told her that I was still single and looked for her fifteen years. And my girlfriend told her that the day she saw me in the market, she broke off her engagement with the man in the Italian suit. Because of me! But her parents got angry, and they forced her to marry another man. So she had a wedding, and children, but she and the husband were unhappy, and now they are divorced. When I found this out I wrote to her, non stop, for forty pages. Like a whole book! I said everything in my heart. When she read my letter she cried so much she had to cover it in plastic, in case her tears washed the words away. For three years we wrote to each other. Then last Christmas I came home. I didn't tell her, I just came to her beauty shop and knocked on the door. And she opened it.' He took a long drink of beer.

'And then what happened?' I asked impatiently. I should have known.

'I took pictures,' he said. 'Lots of pictures! She was so happy. I stayed with her one week. Then I went back to the States and called her all the time. Since then we stayed together only twenty days, but it is like forever. Next week I will see her again. Our story is so beautiful, you could make a movie out of it. Maybe you write about it, Maria, and someone in Hollywood is interested!'

*

Kiem laid out straw mats for us on the deck, and he and Luong went off to the wheelhouse to sleep. We were stretched out and staring at the stars when I remembered the recording I'd made of Vinh's song. I asked Sunny if he'd mind translating it for me sometime.

'Sure,' he said. 'Hey, you got it there? I'd like to listen now.'

He put on the headphones, and I settled down next to him with a flashlight and my notebook. Moths flapped around my face, and a bat flickered by. From the Walkman, I could hear a faint tinny sound, as Vinh's song began.

'My God!' yelled Sunny. 'I don't believe it!'

He ripped off the headphones.

'Play it back! This boy is fantastic! And his song – it is like my story! I don't believe it!'

The peace of the night was broken as Sunny, with the head-phones on, shouted out a translation of what Vinh had sung for us in the park.

'In the suburbs I had a hut, small and simple.
A girl lived close by, but in the wealthy area
Where she was driven around by a chauffeur.
I don't sing well, I'm not a good musician
But my lovely next-door neighbour used to listen to my songs
And she always applauded and made my heart tremble.
I knew I had no chance of a future with her
So one day I went far away, and I tried to forget her.
But I thought about her beauty all the time.
One day I received awful news, that she had married a rich
*   man.'*

'Stop the tape,' said Sunny. 'This is breaking my heart.'

Tears were pouring down his cheeks, and it took a bottle of beer to compose him sufficiently to carry on with the translation.

'And now I wonder if she remembers the poor musician.
Just the other day, I had a good life, like everybody.
But today I have to go out on the street and sing for a
*   living.*

*Thanks to all of you, giving me a few pennies here and
    there,
I can survive, in the rain and under the sun.
For the rest of my life I'll remember your help.
Maybe in the next life I can pay you back.
I wish you always to have happiness and wealth.
I wish you luck in your travels, near and far.'*

By now we were all in tears. We told Sunny about Vinh, his
missing leg, his blind father.

'We'd like to help him in some way,' said Dag. 'Get him off
the streets, pay his way through school.'

'How long you stay in Vietnam?' asked Sunny.

'Only a few more days.'

'So why don't we go and find him tomorrow, take him out
on this boat, talk to him about what you can do?'

'Is this possible?'

'Sure! Why not?'

We were all too charged with excitement to sleep much.
When the sky began to lighten, we roused Kiem and Luong,
and instructed them to take us back to Bai Chay.

After reassuring Mr Huong that all was well with his boat, we
collected the bikes and motor scooter from his office and set
off towards Bai Chay. Along its sea front, Sunny called out to
people, asking about *Vinh mot chan*. We found him in the bus
station, at the far end of town. He came hopping towards us
with a delighted grin on his face. As soon as we sat down with
him at a food stall, about fifteen other street children gathered
around us, laughing excitedly and teasing Vinh. He handed the
boy nearest to him his can of Festi Cola, and the children
passed it around, each taking a tiny sip.

'Vinh sleeps here with the other kids,' said Sunny, pointing
to the space between the row of food stalls and the brick wall
enclosing the bus station. 'In the summer it is okay, but in the
winter they have to find cardboard and paper to keep warm.'

He talked quietly and kindly to the boy.

'He says he has a brother and a little sister here. The sister
sings too. He wants you to meet her.'

Vinh led us to one of the buses parked close by. It was packed with passengers, and cargo was being loaded onto its roof. He clambered up the steps, squirming his way through the crowd, and I followed as best I could. From inside a bus came a childish, lilting voice, and a tapping of spoons. Determinedly making her way along the aisle was a tiny girl with tousled hair and a heart-shaped face. She wore dusty brown pants and a flower-patterned blouse. Around her neck hung a pink cloth bag, roughly stitched with brown thread. Like her brother, she sang with her chin uplifted and her eyes half closed, holding out a hat for money. Vinh reached forward to grab her hand, interrupting her mid-song, and the three of us got off the bus and stood on the gravel.

'Name, Bac,' Vinh told me, hugging the bewildered little girl.

I hunkered down so I was eye to eye with Bac.

'Name,' I said, pointing to myself, 'Maria.'

'Ma-ri-AH,' she repeated shyly. 'Ma-ri-AH.'

Then she fished around in the pink bag, pulled out a plastic comb and dragged it through her hair.

The two children sat between us at the food stall. Bac hungrily slurped her soup, but her brother was more restrained, carefully chewing on a baguette and breaking off pieces to share with his friends, who were still crowding around us.

'I haven't asked Vinh about the boat yet,' said Sunny. 'I don't want to frighten him with too many things, so I just say that you like him very much and want to make friends.'

Twenty minutes later, he broached the subject of coming with us on the junk. As he spoke, Bac's face brightened, but Vinh looked serious, and answered with downcast eyes.

'He says they have to work to earn money for their dad. Their dad is sixty year old, he is blind and has no teeth.'

'We'll make up their earnings,' said Dag. 'And a bit more.'

At this news, Vinh smiled shyly.

'He says he has to ask their big brother,' translated Sunny.

Their brother was sent for, and arrived within minutes. Seventeen-year-old Hung was small and skinny, and could easily have passed for thirteen. But he was more savvy than his siblings. He could read and write a little, and he organized the street children in Bai Chay, making sure they had a place to sleep, deciding which sections of the town they worked and sorting out any problems or arguments.

'A middle man,' said Sunny. 'He would do well in the States.'

We gave him a cash advance on his siblings' earnings, and he seemed genuinely pleased with the arrangement.

'You know what he told them?' said Sunny as we left. 'Have fun!'

We must have been a strange sight, heading through Bai Chay: little Bac sitting in front of Sunny on the motor scooter, Vinh perched behind Dag, and our bikes loaded with all the food we'd stocked up with in the market: eggs, bananas, bread, cheese, a whole jack fruit, a bag of papayas and yet more potatoes, oil and coffee. Our departure on the boat was delayed by the battery of Sunny's video machine, which he had left charging up in Denny's office.

'It will take an hour more,' Sunny told me. Before I could get annoyed, he added, 'see that hairdresser's across the road? Let's take the kids there, get their hair washed.'

The hairdresser's was in an open-fronted and rather scruffy shack. Vinh seemed unfazed by the place, but Bac stood in the doorway, gazing wide eyed at the photos of models, the gilt-edged mirrors and the glass-fronted counter filled with bottles of bright nail polish. One of the hairdressers led her to a reclining chair, where she lay with her head hanging over a steel wash stand. At first, she gripped the pink bag around her neck and stared fearfully at the ceiling. But as the woman began massaging her scalp and gently washing her face and neck, Bac relaxed, closed her eyes and smiled. Meanwhile, Vinh and I sat side by side in front of the mirrors. Two girls, both with spotty cheeks, took greasy combs from jars of grey water and yanked them through our wind-tangled hair. They poured a little water on our heads, added some shampoo and began working it into lathers, vigorously scratching with their long red nails. Vinh took it stoically; I winced and whimpered. When Bac went into the yard behind the shack to have her feet and hands scrubbed, we took turns in the reclining chair. By now my scalp felt as if someone had run a garden rake across it, and I feared worse was to come. But the soap was gently rinsed out of my hair with cool water, and then I too got a soothing face and neck wash.

'Ma-ri-AH,' said a voice in my ear, and I turned my head to see Bac. Her hair was clean and combed, and the skin on her cheeks was buffed to a shine.

'*Dep lam*,' I said approvingly. 'Beautiful,' and her face broke into a wide, delighted smile.

She held my hand as we crossed the road, then excitedly helped to load the bags of food onto the junk. But as we headed out into the bay, she became wary. She stored away her spoons and her pink cloth bag in the front compartment of my large shoulder bag, and carefully zipped it shut. Then she sat next to Vinh, looking out at the islets in the distance, frowning a little and constantly pushing back the hair that fell into her eyes.

By mid-morning we had arrived at the caves Dag and I had visited the day before.

Sunny was keen to see them, and the men and Vinh all went ashore. I decided to stay aboard. At first Bac made to follow her brother, then changed her mind and returned to sit with me on the deck. We watched Vinh lead the way up the steps, climbing them more nimbly and speedily than anyone else. When he disappeared into the mouth of the cave, Bac gave a little cry of alarm, and pressed herself against me. To divert her attention, I took out a bottle of nail polish I'd bought in the hairdresser's. Looking at me expectantly, Bac hesitantly placed one of her hands on my knee. She sat very still while I painted each of her tiny nails. When they were dry, she insisted on painting mine, and smeared polish all over the tops of my fingers. To wipe it off she ripped a scrap of paper from a makeshift dressing on her leg. I tried to look beneath the dressing, which was a wad of toilet paper tied on with string, but she winced and drew back. After I'd combed her hair, and clipped it with a slide, we looked through my guide book. Bac pointed to every photo and sketch, solemnly telling me the Vietnamese name. Like her brother, she could neither read nor write.

We were playing a game of noughts and crosses when the men returned. Vinh was triumphant, glowing with everyone's admiration at how well he got around on his crutch.

'You should have seen this little guy climbing up and down rock walls,' said Dag. 'He went places I wouldn't go. He's totally fearless. And he got really cross when the guide tried to help him over a particularly tricky section.'

For the rest of the morning, the two were inseparable. They sat together on the deck, with Vinh resting his leg stump on Dag's knee. When Dag treated the burn on Bac's leg, Vinh was his helper, holding bandages and tubes and ointment. Bac clung to me, quivering and mewing as Dag carefully removed the toilet paper, cleaned the wound and dressed it.

'I'm sure I'm not hurting her,' said Dag.

'She got this burn from the exhaust pipe of a scooter,' said Sunny. 'She remember the pain and she is scared.'

Bac was seven, but looked five. For half of her life, she had been without a mother. And, now that her initial shyness was gone, she seemed intent on making up for all the nurturing she'd missed over the past few years. She wasn't in the least bit interested in the islets, grottoes, arches and sea caves we were cruising past that morning. She wanted to be cuddled and fussed over, and she wanted to examine my breasts. Sitting on my lap, she'd look down my shirt, then feel for my nipples through the cotton and pinch them. Sometimes she was content just to rest her head against my chest, and for her sake I wished I was far more generously endowed.

'Did you see what happened in the market?' said Sunny, from behind his video camera. 'When Vinh and Bac got off the bus, an official tried to shoo them away from you. These kids get treated like rats. Even when the tourists buy post cards from them, they are afraid to touch them in case they catch something. They are tough kids, they can survive on their own, but look how they open up with a little love.'

There was no shortage of love between brother and sister. While Vinh was singing for us, Bac disappeared into one of the outhouses for ten minutes. In mid-refrain, Vinh stopped and swung his head about, his eyes searching for Bac. Sunny's reassurances that she was safe were not enough; without his crutch he hopped over to the outhouse and clambered up its wall to peer inside.

As the day got hotter, Kiem anchored the boat between several towering islets. Vinh clambered onto the gunwale, balanced there on his one leg then dived in. Dag followed him and together they swam over to some water-level caves and disappeared from sight. This time Bac wasn't worried, and she helped me and Sunny to lay out the food for a picnic lunch. When Dag and Vinh returned, we all sat around a mat with the food spread over it. The idea was that everyone help themselves, but the children insisted on serving us adults. Vinh gave everyone drinks, and Bac solemnly handed out baguettes, triangles of cheese, lychees, slices of fruit. Then they asked each of us in turn, starting with Kiem who was the oldest, if they could begin to eat: '*Moi ong, an com? Moi ba, an com?* Sir, may I eat, madam, may I eat?'

And even when they had permission, Vinh served his sister first.

While we were eating, a two-masted sampan appeared from behind one of the islands. Its faded grey sails had been patched up and brightened with scraps of orange, purple, red and black cloth. The couple aboard were as weathered and rustic as their boat. At the prow, an old lady sat on a coil of thick ropes. Her long-sleeved shirt was patched up like the sails, and her head was wrapped in cloth. At the helm was a wiry old man, who dropped the sails just as Sunny was scrabbling for his video, and rowed over to us with two long oars. Only then did I notice the little boy, peeking out from beneath the canopy. Barely was their boat tied up to ours before Vinh and Bac were passing food down to the child – some of the sweets and gum we'd given them earlier, bread and oranges from the picnic and then, after they'd asked Sunny's permission, a can of Coca Cola from the cooler box.

Vu Van Lieu and his wife Nguyen Thi Xuan were sixty-eight and sixty-four, and the boy with them was one of their thirty grandchildren. At first, they were too shy to accept our invitation to come aboard, and talked to us from their sampan while chewing on the quarter of a jack fruit we gave them. They were out on a fishing trip, and on their way to spend the night in a floating village. Despite the jumble of blue-grey and orange nets on deck, there was a distinct lack of fish in their boat. The family's only catch that day had been several horse-shoe crabs, strange creatures resembling green army helmets with long pointed tails. We bought a couple, then Xuan asked shyly if Sunny could take a photograph of her next to Dag.

'Maria, she wants to know if you will be jealous,' said Sunny.

'A little,' I parried. 'She's a fine-looking woman.'

Xuan cackled delightedly at this, and put her arm round Dag's shoulder as he hunkered next to her on deck.

Kiem arranged to follow the couple to the floating village, and Xuan insisted I should come aboard for the journey. Lieu hoisted the moth-like sails, and we drifted off through the green water, dwarfed by the surrounding islets.

'Vietnam – *dep lam*,' I told Xuan, waving my arm to indicate the stunning scenery. Beautiful.

She shook her head, suddenly serious.

'Vietnam – *doi*,' she replied. Hungry.

As we sailed along she boiled water over a charcoal stove and made a pot of green tea. It was the best I'd had in Vietnam, without a hint of bitterness. While I was sipping it, she suddenly grabbed my knee with a rough, calloused hand.

'Knee!' she said firmly, surprising me with her perfect pronunciation. As it transpired, it was the only English word she knew.

'Knee!' she repeated several times. Then she rolled up her trousers and compared our legs. Hers were wiry and firmly muscled, and put my spindly pair to shame.

In the floating village, scores of sampans were rafted together, and the sounds of radios playing, children laughing and out-board engines puttering bounced off the cathedral-like islets towering above them. Some sampans had moved away from the main village, and were slipping into caves and arches at the base of one of the cliffs. Intrigued, we lowered our boat's ten-der into the water, and followed them. The arch we found was a hundred feet long and so low in places we had to duck as we paddled. Hanging from its ceiling were fat stalactites, drip-ping with water. At its far end we emerged into a lagoon, completely encircled by sheer, high limestone walls. We sat in the boat, staring up at the rock all around us. Stone faces, long and angular, and fashioned by water and wind, stared back at us. Trees sprouted from cracks, and twisted themselves around to grow skywards.

'It's a perfect place to shelter from a storm,' said Dag.

It was, I mused, as we paddled back along the arch, simply a perfect place.

We persuaded Xuan, Lieu and their grandson to join us for dinner, and three generations sat down to share food. We ate fish we'd bought in the village, rice that Xuan had cooked, and fruit, bread and cheese. It had been a long time since the old couple had tasted papayas or the large lychees called *chum chum* and it was Xuan's first experience of beer. Sunny made sure they were kept well supplied with all three new delights, as well as everything else we had to offer.

'Eat these bananas, they have lots of vitamin A,' he'd say, passing them around. 'Lieu! Eat more papaya! Here's another beer!'

Helped by the alcohol, the old couple were in fine form.

'What is it like in an aeroplane?' Xuan asked Sunny. 'In the war, I never understood how the planes could fly so high with all the heavy bombs inside.'

Lieu told ribald jokes, all based on the difference between accents in the north and south of Vietnam.

'After 1975, a man from the north went south to work for the government. At the weekend, he suggested to one of his female colleagues they should go out and enjoy themselves in her boat. Because of his dialect, however, instead of boat she thought he'd said vagina. "Comrade!" she protested. "How can you be so forward? We've only just met."'

As Sunny translated his jokes, Lieu chuckled happily, and his eyes disappeared into the creases of his face.

Around us, lights twinkled on other boats, and the village grew quiet. No one wanted our party to end, but tiredness crept up on us all. I was the first to give into it. At ten o'clock I eased back from the circle of people and stretched out on the deck. Bac soon joined me, snuggling up and laying her arm across my breasts. She began to sing in a high, breathy voice, pausing every now and then, as if she was thinking of the words.

Sunny leaned back to listen. 'Maria, she makes a song for you,' he said quietly. 'She says, "Tomorrow I will pick purple flowers to hang in your hair."'

I dozed, only half aware of Lieu, Xuan and their grandson leaving. At some point, with Bac still attached to me, I shuffled over onto the mat Dag had spread on the deck. A sheet was gently laid over us. Then I was conscious of nothing more until the dawn, when bird song woke me.

For a few minutes I gazed upwards at a majestic rock wall towering above me.

'My god, I don't believe it,' I heard Sunny mutter. 'So beautiful, I feel like a billionaire.' Then I registered that while Dag was in his usual sleeping position, lying on his side with his arms around me, Bac was gone. Propping myself on an elbow, I squinted around the deck. Something stirred behind Dag, then a little hand appeared above his shoulder.

'Ma-ri-AH,' said a sleepy voice.

She was cuddled up to his back. Next to her lay Vinh, still fast asleep. A camera flash dazzled me; Sunny was taking photos.

'Don't move, I have to catch this,' he said.

He was in such a hurry that he'd forgotten to put on his trousers. His shirt tails hung down almost to his knees and beneath them his legs were skinny, and startlingly pale.

'I didn't talk to the kids yesterday about their education,' said Sunny a little later. 'I wanted to wait and see if some kind of bond developed.'

Bac was sitting in my lap while I gently combed the tangles out of her hair. As Sunny continued talking, I felt tears pricking at my eyes.

'But now they really trust you, they know you won't just go away and forget all about them.'

'What would happen,' I asked, 'if they didn't go to school?'

'Now, they are okay. They are cute, they can sing and beg and people will give them money. But soon Vinh will grow up, it will be hard for him to get a job. And Bac –' he paused, and sighed. 'Maria, men come across the border from China and Taiwan, they pay a lot of money for a pretty young virgin, maybe two or three hundred dollars. For a poor family it is a big temptation, but for the girl it is the end, afterwards she can only be a prostitute.'

Dag and Vinh came over to join us, and we sat close together while Sunny talked to the children. They told him they had never been to school. When he explained that Dag and I would like to help them get an education, Bac's face lit up with a wide, amazed smile. But Vinh reacted more soberly.

'He says it is not possible because of their father,' Sunny translated. 'If they go to school they can't work and he won't have food to eat.'

'We could support their father,' suggested Dag, 'and leave the kids free for school.'

'I won't tell them this,' said Sunny. 'I think we have to go to Haiphong and talk to their dad.'

'Ma-ri-AH,' cooed Bac, reaching up to pat my cheek. Despite my successful efforts to fight back the tears, she had sensed that something was wrong.

'Dag, do you realize that we're flying out on Saturday?' I said in a choked voice.

Our original plan had been to travel by road from Halong Bay straight to the airport, for our afternoon flight.

'Holy smokes,' he replied, looking alarmed. 'So we are.'

'And today is Thursday. So if we're going to do something, we'd better be quick.'

Sunny quickly came up with a solution. 'We'll go to Haiphong right away, take the kids and see the father. I invite you to stay in the house of my cousin, and from there you can go to Hanoi, to the airport.' Picking up his camera, he took what must have been the hundredth photo of me and Bac.

'Maria, I think you fall in love,' he said tenderly.

I kissed Bac, lifted her off my lap and fled to the outhouse, where I locked myself in for a good, long weep.

We left the floating village, and headed back in tandem with Xuan and Lieu to the place where we had swum the day before. On the way, we decided to spend one more night on the boat, return to Bai Chay very early next day and leave immediately for Haiphong. The last day of our little holiday stretched ahead – until the police arrived. Dag and I were sitting with Vinh and Bac, teaching them to write their names, when a large black motor launch with a red flag came zooming towards us. Vinh pushed his crutch under the bench, and slipped the stump of his leg inside the cover of the Therm-A-Rest mat we were sitting on. Lieu untied his sampan from our boat, and rowed away without a word. A policeman boarded our junk, and instructed Sunny, Kiem and Luong to report to the cabin of the launch. When they'd gone, he began questioning the children. Bac cringed against me, but Vinh was obviously used to being interviewed. He sat up straight, and quietly gave his answers in a cool, collected manner. Meanwhile Sunny's raised voice drifted from the cabin of the motor launch.

'They'll take the kids off the boat over my dead body,' I muttered to Dag, and I could tell from the way his fists were clenched that he felt the same.

Suddenly, the policeman switched his attention to us. 'Canada?' he asked, pointing to the children and then to us.

The thought had crossed our minds. But we shook our heads, and said, 'Haiphong.'

He gave us a long, steady look. I glared back, but then it occurred to me that this man might be genuinely worried about the welfare of these children, and concerned about the motives of the foreigners who had whisked them away in a chartered boat. I'd heard stories of European and American tourists, as well as Taiwanese and Chinese businessmen, coming to Vietnam for the child sex trade, and also that the government was taking steps to protect the vulnerable street kids. My expression softened and I smiled at the policeman; he gave a ghost of a smile in return. The voices drifting from the launch had grown quiet, and suddenly Sunny came bouncing back to the junk.

'You know, the problem is this boat is so new it has no registration for the tourists, and not the proper safety equipment and no permission for the foreigners to sleep overnight. And they are worried for the children. So they say we must go straight back.'

Without any arguments, we agreed.

★

For the last stretch of the journey, Vinh and Dag lay on the deck, practising writing. I caught up on my notes while Bac sat next to me, singing and playing her spoons. When Denny's concrete office was in sight, both children carefully collected up their new belongings – note books, pencils, nail polish, sweets, chewing gum – and put them into the zip lock bags I'd given them. Then Bac gathered all the left-over food, stale bread, triangles of cheese, some oranges and a few lychees, and squirrelled that away too.

'The kids should stay in their usual place tonight,' said Sunny, as we wheeled our bikes to the road. 'Otherwise the police might think we have bad intentions.'

While he went ahead on his motor scooter to talk to their older brother, Bac and Vinh climbed onto our bikes. Sitting on my luggage rack, Bac clung to me like a limpet with her frail arms and tiny hands. I cried all the way into town, pedalling fast to keep ahead of Dag and Vinh, so they wouldn't see. Sunny had been right, I was in love with this little urchin. She had drawn out mothering instincts I never knew I was capable of, and the thought of leaving Vietnam without her was unbearable. But what could I do? Spirit her away from her family and the world she was familiar with? Even if it was possible, I asked myself, would it be unfair, would I be pandering more to my needs than hers? By the time we reached the bus station, I'd composed myself. Bac and Vinh climbed off the bikes, and were instantly surrounded by the other street children. Pulling out their zip lock bags, they began sharing their booty. Sunny was sitting with Hung, and they had already made arrangements for us all to travel together to Haiphong the next morning. We gave Hung some money, then went to say goodbye to Vinh and Bac. We had to interrupt them – they were sitting surrounded by friends, excitedly telling tales of their trip.

Next morning, I heard Bac before I saw her.

'Ma-ri-AH! Ma-ri-AH!'

She raced across the bus station towards me, and flung herself into my arms.

Vinh came hopping up behind her, clutching a small plastic bag he'd packed for the trip to Haiphong. They both wore clean clothes, and had combed their hair and washed their faces. We went with them and Hung for breakfast in a café across the road. *Pho* was ordered all round, and Vinh wiped everyone's spoon and chopsticks with a paper napkin, and made sure the grown ups were served first. I noticed Bac whispering to Sunny.

'You know what?' he told me. 'She says she would like an egg with a baby inside it.'

I watched her chomp determinedly through the incubated duck egg, and its fully developed embryo. When she finished she wiped her mouth with the back of her hand, and looked up at me with a wide smile.

'Go papa?' she asked.

Vinh took total control of the travel arrangements, organizing the tickets for the small public boat to Hong Gai and the big ferry to Haiphong, showing us where to wait and telling us when it was time to embark. As it was a rainy morning, he led us inside the ferry, to the compartment with the two wide benches. We spread ourselves over half of one bench, which we shared with a wealthy Vietnamese family. They were expensively dressed, and were playing cards for money. One young woman had a baby girl, who was constantly passed around the group for kisses and cuddles. On the opposite bench were several work-weathered old peasant women, dressed in black pyjamas. They watched the baby avidly, clapping their hands to attract her attention. Finally one of them plucked up courage to go across the aisle for a closer look. The baby was promptly deposited in her arms. Back on her own bench, she and the other old women clustered around the child, fanning her with their hats, smacking their betel-stained lips at her, marvelling over her pretty clothes. Her mother carried on playing cards, glancing over from time to time to check on the baby, who seemed perfectly content, but generously leaving the old ladies to enjoy themselves with her.

We lolled around on the bench, watching Halong Bay slip by through the portholes. Vinh and Bac leaned against us, squabbling a little over whose turn it was to pull Dag's beard. Then

Bac curled up and fell asleep against Dag, who was lying on his side with his head propped up on one hand. Vinh and I both leaned on him. I was making notes and Vinh was drawing, with his stump crooked companionably over my knee.

'Hey, you guys, you look just like a family!' called Sunny, who was standing on deck with Hung, letting him videotape us through a porthole.

'When I was younger I always used to think I'd like a big family,' said Dag nonchalantly. 'Then I sort of went off the idea.'

The statement hung in the air between us for a while.

'Don't get your hopes up, Maria,' he said. 'The important thing is to somehow find a school for the kids, a place where they'll stay off the streets and get an education. That way they could at least be safe for now, and then maybe later—'

Vinh pulled Dag's nose, eager to regain his attention.

'Dag! Go Haiphong, see papa!'

In Haiphong, Hung hired a motor scooter to go ahead and warn his father of our imminent arrival. We took Vinh and Bac to choose some new clothes at a store owned by Sunny's cousin. It was the usual open-fronted place, with the clothes displayed on the walls. For a good five minutes, the children gazed up at what was on offer. Then they made their choice, firmly and without equivocation. For Vinh, a pair of long grey pants, a T-shirt and a belt. For Bac, a yellow dress with gold buttons and red braiding. And for both of them, new underwear. Sunny's cousin let them use her bathroom and bedroom for half an hour. After showering, the children dressed up in their new outfits. Vinh sat on the bed, combing his hair, while his sister twirled in front of a mirror, enchanted by her own image. Then Dag changed the bandage on her burn. This time she was braver about it, and sang quietly to comfort herself until the operation was over.

We had a quick meal at a street stall. Vinh and Bac chose pork and incubated eggs, and Dag tried broiled silk worm pupae.

'Be careful,' Sunny teasingly warned me. 'These worms are a big aphrodisiac. In Vietnam the teenage boys are not allowed to eat them.'

We didn't linger over the food. Now that Hung had gone, the children were growing increasingly anxious about getting to their father. Before Hung left, he had written down the address of their village: *Ben Binh Haiphong, Xom bui bo de –* Binh ferry station, near the police station, opposite side of Haiphong.

'Can we send letters to this address?' I asked.

Sunny gave me a sad smile.

'I don't think so. The people are squatters.'

A barge took us over the Red River. We stood crammed in among bicycles and scooters with their engines still running. Bac patted my leg, telling me to keep it away from the hot exhaust pipes – it was on this ferry, it turned out, that she got her burn. From the ferry we cycled along a short stretch of road, then turned onto a narrow sandy path on top of a dyke. The children dismounted from our bikes. Bac skipped along ahead of us, and Vinh broke into a lopsided run. A village came into view: two score of wattle and daub houses with thatch roofs, built below the level of the dyke, in the fields. Vinh and Bac pointed, and jiggled with excitement. And we'd been spotted: people ran up from the village and along the dyke towards us.

'Hey, I feel like a film star!' called Sunny.

'What happens to this village in the monsoon?' I asked him, as helpful hands carried our bikes down the steep bank to the path through the houses.

'It floods,' he answered, with a shrug. 'Like I said, it is only a temporary place.'

A washing line hung outside Bac and Vinh's house, and some bright flowers bloomed in pots. We ducked under a low doorway into one of the two rooms. Mr Le sat on a low wooden stool, wearing a shirt open to the waist and patched trousers. On the mud floor before him were set a tea pot and tiny cups. The room was empty, save for a wooden bed base. A few odds and ends – a comb, a pen, a pack of cigarettes – were stuck into the thatch ceiling. More stools were brought for us. We shook hands with Mr Le, and he poured tea for us, feeling for each cup before carefully and expertly filling it. Vinh and Bac stood behind him, their hands on his shoulders. As Sunny began quietly speaking to him he listened with his chin upturned, like his children when they sang. On the bed base behind him sat another son, a year younger than Vinh.

'It is traditional for the blind man to sing and get money, but he got too sick so he taught his children to do this,' said Sunny. 'Three years ago his wife got influenza in the monsoon and died. So now one kid stays and helps him, and the others go out and work.'

Vinh and his brother went outside, to where lots of curious villagers were hanging about, peeking in through the doorway and the window. I told Mr Le how impressed I was by his children, by their kindness and talents and good manners, and how proud he deserved to be of them.

'You know, he is overwhelmed,' Sunny told me. 'They are the poorest family in the village. They have nothing. I told him you want to help his children, to send them to school. He says this was always his dream. I warned him it might take some time to organize. He says it doesn't matter, because someone thinks of him and loves his children.'

That, of course, was me gone. I hunkered on the stool, sniffling into a wet tissue, while Sunny and Dag continued to discuss things with Mr Le.

'I won't say too much about money,' I heard Sunny tell Dag, 'because the other villagers listen and it could be a problem.'

Bac had run out to join her brothers. Through the doorway I saw her twirling to show off her new dress. It was time to go. Mr Le stood to shake our hands, and we left him some dollars. Then we headed back to the dyke. Our bikes were pushed and carried up the bank for us, and a crowd of people followed us halfway to the road. Somewhere among them were Vinh and Bac, busily answering questions and buzzing with excitement.

'Let's say goodbye here, Maria,' said Dag. 'It will be easier.' In turn, we hugged both children.

'I told them I will bring messages from you,' said Sunny.

'And that we'll come back,' I reminded him.

'Yeah,' he smiled. 'I already said this.'

'Ma-ri-AH,' whispered Bac, when I lifted her up. She was puzzled by my tears.

'Bac,' I whispered back. 'Go papa.'

I cycled away as fast as I could. Some of the other children of the village ran alongside my bike, waving and shouting. Then, from behind, I heard another voice ringing out.

'MA-RI-AH!'

I stopped, and turned to wave at the tiny figure in a yellow party dress, standing on a dyke with the vast expanse of the Red River Delta spread out behind her.

14

BETWEEN TWO WORLDS

We followed Sunny through Haiphong's darkening streets, to the house of his cousin.

'Goodbye, bike,' I said, leaning mine against the wall.

'What will you do with them?' asked Sunny.

'We'll give them away,' I told him.

'Really? No! When my cousin comes home, I'll ask him, maybe he buy them.'

The house was part of an old colonial building. In the living room, two of Sunny's old aunts were watching the Test Card on a colour television. They wore their long hair plaited and wrapped around their heads, and placidly chewed on betel as they stared at the screen. We sat in the kitchen with Sunny, drinking beer and eating the pile of French fries he prepared. Presently his cousin arrived. He was a brisk, well-turned-out man.

'He works for the government department,' said Sunny. 'He says it's okay if you stay the night, but don't go outside.'

'Why not?'

'The people in this street aren't used to foreigners, they'll crowd around, make things uncomfortable for you.'

As the real reason was probably that the cousin didn't have permission for foreigners to stay in his house overnight, we decided to concur. The cousin's wife had gone straight upstairs. I met her a little later, when I walked past her bedroom door on my way to the toilet. She was sitting on the bed, counting money. In greeting, she waved a wad of dollars at me.

'She hide her money under the bed,' Sunny confided later. 'Don't tell anyone.'

To our surprise, Sunny's cousin was keen on our bikes and suggested we trade them for a car ride to the airport in Hanoi.

'It's a new air-conditioned car,' Sunny assured us. 'Very comfortable. And I'll come with you, I have business in Hanoi.'

Next morning, Sunny insisted that, instead of us going out for breakfast, he should order in eggs and bread from a food stand close by.

'When the car comes we must leave quickly,' he said.

The driver with his car was over an hour late. Eventually Sunny's cousin arrived on a scooter, and they had a brief conference.

'He says the car is here but the air conditioning has just broken down. Is that all right for you guys?'

'No problem.'

'Okay, let's go.'

After saying goodbye to the aunts, who were again sitting in front of the television watching the Test Card, we followed Sunny outside. He darted across the road, to a battered Lada parked beneath a tree. As the boot was already filled with luggage, one of our bags had to go in the back seat with us. The upholstery was ripped, and held together by packing tape. And it was obvious that the car had never had any air conditioning to start with.

'Okay? You comfortable?' asked Sunny, squashing into the back seat with us.

'Sunny, why don't you go in the front?' suggested Dag. 'Then we'd all have more room.'

'Didn't I tell you? My cousin's coming with us to Hanoi.'

★

Soon we were back on the highway. Over the last few magical days, the memory of how bad it had been had faded away. But now, it seemed worse than ever. The bus and truck drivers were more aggressive, the fumes were more noxious, the horns were louder. And the road works went on forever. All the car windows were open, and clouds of smoke from drums of boiling tar billowed in. I wrestled with a handle on the door next to me, trying to wind up the window. No matter how much I turned the handle, however, no glass appeared.

'I'd give up if I was you,' said Dag after a few minutes. 'There isn't a window in there.' Because of the late start and the road works, we were anxious about being on time for our plane, and told Sunny that we'd like to carry on straight to the airport instead of stopping anywhere for lunch.

'Okay, we'll just pick up some food,' he assured us.

But lunch, as we'd learned, is religiously observed in Vietnam. In the middle of a small town, the driver swung the car down a side street and parked outside a café.

'We'll just have soup, no rice, only ten minutes!' insisted Sunny.

'Bloody tenacious Vietnamese,' grumbled Dag, as we clambered out.

A bit of an altercation followed, when it appeared the driver was about to leave unattended a car which didn't lock and had no glass in its side windows. Worried for our bags, I volunteered to stay with the vehicle, but Sunny wouldn't hear of it. He instructed the driver to sit in the doorway of the café, from where he could see the car. He sat with his back to the door, and once wandered off down the road to buy cigarettes.

It was an hour before we managed to winkle our contingent out of the restaurant, and by then we were most definitely in danger of missing the plane. The rest of the journey was nightmarish. We sped along the highway as if we were being chased. The driver jerkily braked and accelerated, and whenever he changed gear there was a sharp cracking sound, as if the car was about to fall apart.

'I'd rather miss my plane than die,' I pointedly told Sunny, but he didn't bother to translate this to the driver.

By the time we were approaching Hanoi I was caked with dirt and grit, as if I'd been on my bike all day. A solid bank of clouds had built up in the sky and was steadily moving towards us. Within minutes, we were being lashed by rain and sprayed with mud through the windows of the car, and rivulets of grimy water were running down my face and arms.

We reached the airport with minutes to spare, and after a brief flurry of goodbyes rushed through passport control.

'Maria, don't feel sad,' Sunny called after me.

'Run! Run!' urged the officials at the departure gate. Panting and sweating, we dashed across the tarmac and up the steps.

The doors of the plane were closed behind us as soon as we boarded. Suddenly, we were in a cool, quiet, sanitized world. Stewardesses were handing out plastic-wrapped headphones and blankets. Soothing music piped from the intercom. Everything was in order, and under control. We had barely settled into our seats before the engines whined and the plane began taxiing along the runway. Numbly, I gazed out of the window. I hadn't yet really registered the fact that our long journey was over, that we were finally leaving. Next to me, Dag was silent. The plane took off, flying low over a highway snarled up with traffic. Gaining height, it banked sharply to turn. I could see for miles across the delta: its patchwork of rice fields, its waterways that were spread out like veins and the colour of blood. I peered down, wondering if we'd pass over Haiphong. Mist swirled by the glass, and we were suddenly engulfed in cloud. A lump formed in my throat. Swallowing hard, I turned away from the window and met the eyes of a man across the aisle. He was staring disparagingly at me over his newspaper, and I remembered how grimy and dishevelled I looked after the car ride. Reaching into my shoulder bag, I felt around for a comb to repair my appearance. In the corner of the front compartment, my fingers closed over something unexpected. Even before I pulled it out, I knew exactly what it was: Bac's pink cloth bag, childishly stitched up with brown thread, wrapped around two aluminium spoons. I laid it on my lap and sat staring at it for a long time, as Vietnam dropped away beneath me, tugging at my heart.

POSTSCRIPT

As Sunny predicted, the process of trying to organize an education for Vinh and Bac has been long and frustrating. After months of letters, phone calls and faxes, and the kind persistence of the SOS Children's Village Society in British Columbia, word came that both Vinh and Bac could be accepted at the SOS Children's Village, Hanoi. This is a highly regarded, non-denominational facility, where children taken in from the streets live in 'family' groups, are looked after by house mothers and attend the on-site school.

Staff members from the SOS Children's Village made several trips to Haiphong to visit Vinh and Bac's father and new stepmother. The couple said they could not let the children go to school in Hanoi, as they needed their income. In response to our suggestion that we could replace what Vinh and Bac earned, the SOS staff strongly advised us against offering money directly to the family in connection with the children's education. This is against the ethics of the SOS organization, and in their experience it is a situation which usually leads to future problems. They also believe the family could get by without the income of at least Bac, who is most eligible for, and in most need of, the services offered by the SOS Children's Village. Some of the SOS staff members are shortly to visit the family again, hoping to convince them to change their minds and provide Bac, and possibly Vinh, with the chance of a promising future.

All of this has been a hard lesson for us. We had hoped it would be easier to help the children. We have learned that there are neither any quick and easy ways to alleviate grinding poverty, nor that we can breeze into a foreign community, offer money to a few individuals and thereby magically transform their lives.

For several months in 1996, Dag and I will be working in northern Vietnam. This will give us the opportunity to spend some time with Vinh and Bac, and to continue with our efforts to improve the situation. Meanwhile, we are planning to help promote the SOS Children's Village Society, which has impressed us immeasurably.

Last year, we set off on what we presumed was to be our one and only visit to Vietnam. But life never turns out as expected: Vietnam now has a very special place in our hearts, and we foresee our connection with it lasting for many moons to come.

Protection Island, British Columbia
November, 1995

HISTORICAL NOTES

Chinese Rule
In the second century BC China annexed the area covered by
the northern part of present-day Vietnam. After many upris-
ings, Chinese rule was finally overthrown in AD 939.

Early Independence
The Viet people began expanding southwards, displacing the
Cham culture. Independent Vietnam was ruled by a long
series of dynasties. Between 1224 and 1789, invasions by the
Mongols, the Chinese and the Thais were repelled.

French Colonization and Resistance to the French
In 1858 the French colonized Vietnam, Laos and Cambodia,
renaming it Indochina. Resistance against the French grew in
Vietnam, and in 1930 Ho Chi Minh founded the Vietnamese
Communist party.

In 1940 Japan seized Indochina, ruling jointly with the
Vichy French. In 1941, with Chinese and American aid, Ho
Chi Minh formed the Viet Minh. Throughout the Second
World War, the Viet Minh carried out guerrilla activities

against the Japanese and the French. In early September 1945, the Viet Minh took over Hanoi and Ho Chi Minh declared the independence of the Democratic Republic of Vietnam.

Franco-Viet Minh War
In 1946 French forces attacked the Viet Minh in the north. China assisted the Viet Minh and the United States backed the French. The war continued until 1954, when France was defeated at the battle of Dien Bien Phu.

The Geneva Conference
The 1954 Geneva agreement stated that: Vietnam be temporarily divided along the 17th Parallel; Ho Chi Minh's government be recognized in the north and the French remain temporarily in the south; nationwide elections be held in 1956 to decide the future government of a united Vietnam. The agreement was signed by France, Britain, China, the Soviet Union and the Viet Minh. The United States refused to sign.

With US backing, in 1954 Ngo Dinh Diem took control of the south and established the Republic of Vietnam. He cancelled the impending elections and began a campaign against political dissidents and Buddhists. The National Liberation Front, dubbed the Viet Cong by Diem, was formed in the South.

The American War
By 1964 there were over 20,000 US advisors in Vietnam. After a US destroyer was attacked in the Gulf of Tonkin, the war escalated and intensive bombing of North Vietnam began. The air war spread to South Vietnam and a five-year defoliation campaign was started.

By 1967 the number of troops in Vietnam had risen to half a million. The Tet Offensive and the My Lai massacre of 1968 caused anti-war feelings in the United States to soar. President Nixon began withdrawal of ground troops in 1969.

In 1972 the North Vietnamese Army struck across the 17th Parallel and took Quang Tri. US bombing missions against the north were intensified.

Paris Peace Accords

The Saigon government, North Vietnam and the United States agreed on a cease fire, the withdrawal of US troops and an exchange of prisoners. Vietnamese troops from both sides were allowed to stay in place.

With the Soviet Union backing North Vietnam and the United States backing the south, the war continued until April 1975, when Saigon fell and Vietnam was unified.

More Wars, and an Embargo

In 1979 Vietnam invaded Cambodia to oust Pol Pot and the murderous Khmer Rouge. A decade-long war ensued. Also in 1979, China invaded northern Vietnam and was repelled, and the United States enforced a trade and lending embargo to isolate Vietnam from the global economy.

Doi Moi

By 1985 inflation had risen to 700 per cent, and unemployment had reached 3 million. Doi moi, a programme of economic and social change to move the country towards a more market-orientated economy, was instigated in 1986. The American embargo was lifted in 1994, and a year later America had re-established diplomatic ties with Vietnam.

ACKNOWLEDGEMENTS

In Vietnam, Dag and I were frequently shown great kindness and offered friendship and hospitality by local people. Many of these people are mentioned in the text; in some cases I have changed their names to spare them worry or embarrassment. We are greatly indebted to them all, especially Le Thai Binh and Son Nhu Hoang, for making our journey possible, for enriching our experiences and for allowing us an intimate, unforgettable view of their country.

We are also grateful to the expatriates and foreign workers we met, in particular Lady Borton, for their insights on life in Vietnam.

Our thanks to Tom Myers of Cascade Designs, who generously provided us with waterproof bags and Therm-A-Rest'R mats, bringing some much appreciated comfort to an arduous trip.

While we were planning our journey, we sought advice from several quarters. Rob Hind, author Tim Severin, journalist Paul Harris and broadcasters Judy Stowe and Liz Mardall kindly shared their experiences of dealing with officialdom in Vietnam. Margaret Horsfield sent tips on research and led me to the School of Oriental and African Studies in London, where Dr Dana Healy provided me with useful reading material and pointed me in the direction of much more. Sheila Swanson of Malaspina University College, Nanaimo, gave us contacts in Cantho and Hanoi. To all these people, and to others I may have overlooked, we extend our gratitude.

For their part in the creation of this book, my thanks go to my literary agent Vivienne Schuster, to Hilary Foakes, who so enthusiastically responded to the initial concept, and to Andrew Wille of Little, Brown, who has steered *Three Moons in Vietnam* to completion. I am also grateful to Carol and Mike Matthews for their appraisal of the first chapters, to Jurgen Goering for providing a hideaway where I could complete the manuscript, and to Dag for his editing and good humour.

Finally, many thanks to Hanh Ha and her husband Tuyen, for a friendship that has survived many years and many miles, and for inspiring us, albeit unwittingly, to travel along the coast of their homeland.